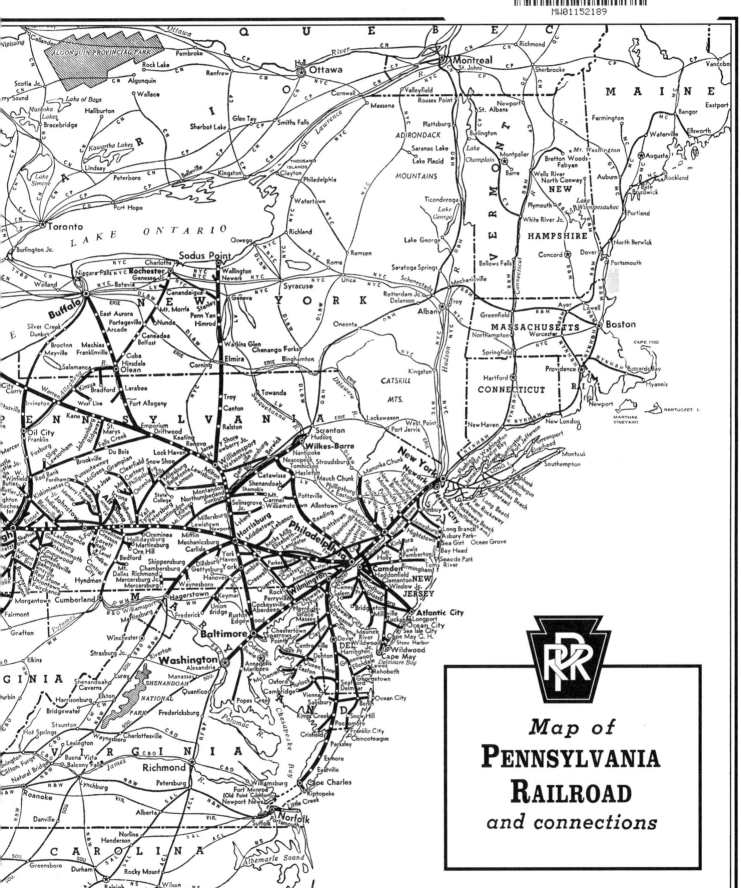

Map of
PENNSYLVANIA
RAILROAD
and connections

Pennsylvania Railroad Passenger Trains

Consists and Cars -1952
Volume 1, East-West Trains

by Harry Stegmaier, Jr.

Published 2003

TLC Publishing Inc. • 1387 Winding Creek Lane • Lynchburg, VA 24503-3776

Pennsylvania Railroad Passenger Trains

Consists and Cars -1952
Volume 1, East-West Trains

Title Page: In 1950, two Pennsylvania Railroad passenger Baldwin shark-nose diesel locomotives lead train No. 22, *The Manhattan Limited*, out of Chicago, Illinois. It is the morning train out of Chicago on Pennsylvania Railroad's main Chicago to New York run and is departing right at the noon hour, being the earliest that one could catch a through train to New York on the Pennsylvania Railroad. On this day, two passenger shark-nose diesels are being used to pull the train. These units proved to be unreliable for through mainline trains and were eventually relegated to New Jersey commuter service between Perth Amboy and Bay Head Junction.

Dedication Page: On a morning in 1952, an A-B-A set of passenger Alco's lead Pennsylvania Railroad's No. 66, *The American*, out of St. Louis Union Depot. This was Pennsylvania Railroad's early departure from St. Louis for the east coast with a 9:00 a.m. leaving time, about an hour and fifteen minutes ahead of *The Penn Texas*. *The American* was still a good looking train in 1952, but within a few years, to be precise in April of 1956, it would pass from the pages of the Pennsylvania Railroad timetables as service was cut. *The Penn Texas* and *Spirit of St. Louis* could handle the traffic by then.

Both: Thomas W. Dixon, Jr. Collection

Library of Congress Control Number: 2002109644
ISBN 1-883089-81-6

*Layout and Design by Kenneth L. Miller
Miller Design & Photography, Salem, Va.*

*Printed by
Walsworth Publishing Co. Marceline, Mo. 64658*

Dedication

For Joe, close friend and trusted companion, whose help, support and presence
through a difficult year encouraged me to complete this book.

Introduction

The Pennsylvania Railroad ran an extensive passenger service in the years following World War II. Its East-West passenger train consist book of September 28, 1952 is a thick document and gives the reader an idea of the complexity of the mainline operations. This book is an attempt to take the raw data from the Pennsylvania Railroad East-West consist book of September, 1952 and attempt to put a face on the contents. Besides the trains in this book, the railroad also operated other non-mainline passenger trains and a large commuter operation. Because of the scope of the Pennsylvania Railroad passenger service, it is impossible to cover all of the other trains which the railroad fielded, for example, the Washington to Buffalo service, the Pittsburgh to Cleveland service and trains like *The Northern Arrow*, a summer only resort train to Mackinaw City, Michigan, as well as the almost hourly daytime service between New York and Washington. In fact, the Pennsylvania Railroad itself did not attempt to put all of its passenger trains in one consist book but issued separate books for the trains on the New York-Washington corridor, the Delmarva Peninsula, *The Northern Arrow*, and what it called the Ohio River Trains operating out of Chicago to Cincinnati, Louisville, and Columbus.

1952 is a good year to study the through passenger services between New York-Pittsburgh, and Chicago, Cleveland and Detroit, as well as the New York-Pittsburgh-St. Louis through trains, including the Cincinnati service. While some services had already been eliminated by 1952, the Pennsylvania Railroad was still operating an unbelievable number of passenger trains, plus mail and express trains on its mainline routes. It is these trains on which the book concentrates and, in fact, in the interest of continuity, some of the trains in this 1952 consist book, such as the Washington-Buffalo service and the connections between Harrisburg and Washington will have to be treated separately in a later book. Many of the trains which the Pennsylvania was still operating in 1952 would soon disappear.

Gone by the middle of the decade, for example, would be *The Gotham Limited*, which actually continued to run but received *The Pennsylvania Limited* name. *The American* and *The Iron City Express* would be eliminated. Other trains would be combined, such as *The Golden Triangle* with *The Manhattan Limited* westbound and *The Pennsylvania Limited*, formerly *The Gotham Limited*, eastbound, between Pittsburgh and Chicago. By the late 1950s, many trains were completely gone. By 1960, on the Chicago route, one could forget about an independently operated *Golden Triangle*, *The Trailblazer*, *The Liberty Limited*, *The Pennsylvania Limited*, and the westbound *Admiral*. *The Clevelander* had been combined with other trains east of Pittsburgh on the St. Louis route and trains like *The Jeffersonian* and *The American*, *The Metropolitan* and westbound, *The St. Louisan* were history. *The Red Arrow* was also dead by 1960 as well as runs like *The Iron City Express* and *The Akronite*. Therefore, 1952 is a good year to take a final look at the Pennsylvania Railroad's passenger

Scheduled for Convenience
Styled for Comfort

The West-East Fleet!

CHICAGO • NEW YORK
BROADWAY LIMITED
All-Private-Room Fleet Leader
THE GENERAL • THE TRAIL BLAZER
Pullman and Reserved-Seat-Coach Streamliner
PENNSYLVANIA LIMITED
Pullman and Coach Train
MANHATTAN LIMITED
Pullman and Coach Train
THE ADMIRAL
Pullman and Coach Train
GOTHAM LIMITED
Pullman and Coach Train
CHICAGO • WASHINGTON
LIBERTY LIMITED
Pullman and Reserved-Seat-Coach Streamliner
DETROIT • NEW YORK
DETROIT • WASHINGTON
THE RED ARROW
Pullman and Coach Train
PITTSBURGH • NEW YORK
THE PITTSBURGHER
All-Private-Room Streamliner
ST. LOUIS • NEW YORK
ST. LOUIS • WASHINGTON
"SPIRIT OF ST. LOUIS"
All-Pullman Fleet Leader
THE JEFFERSONIAN
All-Coach Reserved-Seat Streamliner
THE PENN TEXAS
Pullman and Coach Streamliner
THE ST. LOUISAN
Pullman and Coach Train
THE AMERICAN
Pullman and Coach Train
CINCINNATI • NEW YORK
CINCINNATI LIMITED
Pullman and Coach Streamliner
CLEVELAND • NEW YORK
CLEVELAND • WASHINGTON
THE CLEVELANDER
Pullman and Coach Train
CHICAGO • PITTSBURGH
THE GOLDEN TRIANGLE
Pullman and Coach Train

Whatever your requirements for convenient schedules and modern travel comforts . . : you are sure of the finest on this great fleet: The choice of accommodations is comprehensive . . . from private rooms in newest-type all-room cars, restful berths in section-type cars to reclining coach seats in latest overnight coaches. Inviting Pullman Lounge facilities. Delicious meals, expert service in attractive dining car surroundings. For your next trip, choose one of the fine trains listed here. You'll enjoy travel at its comfortable best with smooth electric power all the way over the world's finest roadbed.

Form 1 (1st Edition)   1-13-53

service when it was still in its heyday, before the cut-backs started with the end of the Korean War.

The Pennsylvania Railroad, of course, was not alone in cutting back its service through the 1950s, but few other railroads, except the New York Central, out-did the Pennsylvania in getting rid of its money-losing trains and attempting, at least, to cut passenger losses. One should remember that the railroad was suffering massive passenger deficits by the 1950s and should not be blamed for attempting to stop the bleeding. As freight traffic revenues also declined, the passenger revenue losses became more and more of a burdensome on the corporation.

In this book, one also tries to put a face on the trains themselves with the photographs and other illustrations. It might be pointed out here that every attempt has been made, drawing upon what was available, to place specific cars on specific trains. The February 1954, *Pullman Company Car Assignment* list for lightweight equipment on the Pennsylvania Railroad gives a good indication of the actual cars that were probably running in late 1952 on certain trains. When one sees that a particular car is assigned to a particular train, they should note that this information is culled from the Pullman Company, February, 1954, assignment list. which is a little over a year later than the consist book. However, most car assignments were probably still valid for the train in 1952. An earlier assignment list from 1952 does not seem to have survived or be available.

The author would like to thank many people who helped make this book possible. First, however, there is an excellent book by Joe Welsh, *Pennsy Streamliners: The Blue Ribbon Fleet*, provided the author with a great deal of information, especially about the later discontinuance or combination of trains that took place in the 1950s and 1960s. William F. Howes, Jr. also helped research Pullman car lines on the Pennsylvania Railroad and provided a great deal of information on the dates that certain cars were discontinued, especially the through car lines that went from Pittsburgh and New York to various points on the Louisville and Nashville railroad. The car illustrations were drawn from many sources, including the author's collection, Bob's Photos, and from others who have been generous in loaning their photographs for the book. Most of the menus come from the author's collection while a great deal of the illustrative material was shared by TLC Publishing from its archives. All of these sources, Pullman list, *Official Guides* and public and employee timetables, plus the consist book, helped provide the

author with a great deal of expertise on the subject as did two fine books by Robert A. Liljestrand and David R. Sweetland on the passenger equipment of the Pennsylvania Railroad. Without these sources, books, and people, it would have been impossible to complete this volume. The author would also like to thank, especially, David E. Staplin, an old friend for over 35 years, who went around the country photographing many passenger cars that were still operating in the late 1960s and into 1970. Dave is very knowledgeable about passenger equipment, and its use and assignments. He certainly helped answer many questions about Pennsylvania Railroad service in the 1950s.

Much gratitude is to Ken Miller for the layout and additions from his collection, Dana Cayton for the arduous job of typing the manuscript, and Tom Dixon of TLC Publishing for his suggestions and encouragement. Particular thanks should also go to my special friend Joe for his close friendship and presence throughout this undertaking, and also to Frank B. Fowler, a long-time friend, who carefully checked the manuscript. Frank, although recently retired from CSX, as a Director of Train Operations, is the son of the former Assistant Manager of Special Passenger Movements for the Pennsylvania Railroad.

The author would like to express his gratitude to those who made a difficult year bearable. Don Oker, CSX Special Agent, and his wife Melissa were always there to talk with during the completion of this project. The author was always welcome at the home of Vagel Keller, a historian and walking encyclopedia about the Pennsylvania Railroad, and his wife Debbie who offered me encouragement and care during work on the book. Last, but not least, Dan and Annie Whetzel, virtually adopted me into their family over the last 18 months. Their friendship and hospitality will never be forgotten, especially the love present and warmth of their home and family, and my welcome there, particularly at special holiday gatherings. Let no one forget that this manuscript was carefully inspected by my housecats, Puddy Tat and Terrible Ted, especially in the final stages of preparation.

Without the help of all these people, this book could not have been completed. However, all opinions and conclusions are the authors alone and any errors, therefore, are his responsibility.

Harry Stegmaier
Frostburg, Maryland
October 1, 2003

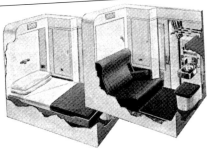

ROOMETTE — For 1 Person

Complete with every facility for privacy including individual toilet and lavatory. Comfortable pre-made bed lowers from wall to replace wide, daytime sofa-seat. Enclosed wardrobe, overhead luggage rack, full-length mirror, extra-wide window, among other features, afford convenience and comfort.

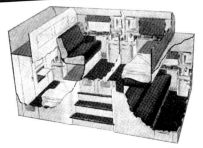

DUPLEX ROOM — For 1 Person

"Duplex" rooms are located on either one of two levels and afford spacious privacy with modern conveniences. Illustration shows group of four rooms prepared for both day and night service. Roomy lounge sofa becomes a comfortable bed at night. Complete toilet and lavatory facilities. Large luggage compartment.

DOUBLE BEDROOM — Parallel Type
For 1 or 2 Persons

Two adjoining rooms are shown—one in day, the other in night service. Complete toilet facilities are enclosed in a separate annex within each room. Two folding lounge chairs afford daytime relaxation. Lower bed is drawn out of the wall. Upper bed moves down from ceiling. Other features include wardrobe, full-length mirror, panorama window.

DOUBLE BEDROOM — "B" Type
For 1 or 2 Persons

Adjoining rooms are again pictured in day-night use. Rooms differ in furniture and location of beds. One has long, comfortable sofa—the other a folding lounge chair and sofa-seat. In one, beds are placed crosswise of car—lengthwise in the other. Each room has its own enclosed toilet annex with complete lavatory facilities. Wardrobe, full-length mirror and other modern refinements.

K.L. Miller Collection

The Pennsylvania offered a wide variety of sleeping car accommodations on it's Blue Ribbon fleet. Many are depicted here on these two pages from Timetable Form 1, January 25, 1953.

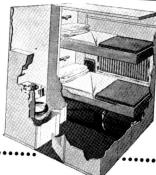

COMPARTMENT
For 1 or 2 Persons

By day, a little sitting room with restful sofa-seat and folding lounge chair. Toilet and lavatory facilities have been enclosed in an annex. Full-length wardrobe is also enclosed. At night, roominess is retained. Lower bed takes the place of the sofa-seat with the upper berth positioning directly above it.

DRAWING ROOM
For 1, 2 or 3 Persons

Complete with every personal need, the spacious Drawing Room with its long sofa and two folding easy chairs affords a living-room atmosphere in day service. Folding lower bed is let down at night. Sofa also becomes a lower bed. Easily accessible upper berth is located directly above it. Toilet facilities enclosed in an annex.

MASTER ROOM
For 1 or 2 Persons

Offers the ultimate in refined comfort. Three folding arm chairs for daytime use. Commodious wardrobe for clothing, full-length mirrors, radio. At night, two folding lower beds are let down from the walls. Private bathroom includes shower.

INTRODUCTION

In 1952, the Pennsylvania Railroad was operating quite an extensive New York to Chicago passenger train service on its main route to the west. The leader of the fleet, of course, was the all Pullman, exclusive *Broadway Limited*, which was in competition with New York Central's *Twentieth Century Limited* for the premier traffic on this route. Eventually, *The Broadway Limited*, by the 1960s, would emerge the clear winner in the New York-Chicago race. Other fine trains were *The General* which preceded *The Broadway Limited* by about an hour in both directions and had been, by 1952, except during the holiday season, combined with the all coach *Trailblazer*. Surrounding the departure of these trains was the early train westbound out of New York, *The Manhattan Limited* and following them were *The Pennsylvania Limited* and *The Admiral*, with the late night departure of *The Gotham Limited* rounding out the day. This meant a total of seven regular passenger trains westbound between New York and Chicago in 1952, if one

considers *The Trailblazer* as a separate train. Eastbound, the day led off with the noontime departure from Chicago of No. 22, *The Manhattan Limited*, followed by the premier trains, the combined *General* and *Trailblazer* in midafternoon, except during the holiday season when *The Trailblazer* ran most days as a separate train, and followed by the leader of the fleet, *The Broadway Limited*. *The Admiral* and *The Pennsylvania Limited* departed an hour and two hours, respectively, after *The Broadway Limited* with *The Gotham Limited* being the late night train from Chicago, again a total of seven trains if one considers *The Trailblazer* as a separate train.

On the mainline, as well, there was also the Pennsylvania Railroad's entry in the Washington and Baltimore to Chicago market, where it was in direct head-to-head competition with the Baltimore & Ohio. This was the overnight *Liberty Limited* between the nation's capital and Chicago in both directions. *The Liberty Limited*, however, could not compete with the Baltimore & Ohio in either service, courtesy or the unbelievable meals which it served in its dining car. Actually, by 1952, the train was being discussed as a candidate for discontinuance or consolidation. In addition to these through trains, one must not forget the overnight New York to Cleveland train, *The Clevelander* or the overnight New York-Detroit *Red Arrow* and there was still, although it had been combined east of Pittsburgh, *The Akronite* which had through cars from New York to Akron, Ohio and was still a substantial train in 1952 with coaches, a dining-lounge car and through sleeping cars from New York.

The Pennsylvania Railroad's service then, on the New York-Chicago main line, was not only extensive but well timed to give the traveling public various options for departure in either direction. Pennsylvania Railroad's New York-Chicago-Cleveland-Detroit passenger service, as well as *The Liberty Limited* from Washington, provided the

NOTES				
Unless otherwise indicated, all passenger carrying cars are Air Conditioned.				
Railroad Passenger Equipment Designations				
Reclining Seats				
PDB-70R	Dormitory-Lounge	Chairs	23	--
PB-70ER	Lounge Car - No dormitory	Chairs	23	--
PLB-85-R	Baggage-Lounge	Chairs	27	--
PLC-85-R	Recreation Car	Reading Room		
		Seats	12	--
		Bar-Lounge	24	
P-70GR	Scheme 4 Coach	Seats	68	60
P-70-GSR	Scheme 4 Coach, Streamlined	Seats	68	60
P-70-KR	Scheme 4 Coach, Streamlined	Seats		
	Men's and Women's Rooms	Seats	56	52
P-82	Light-Weight Coach	Seats	66	60
P-85-BR	Light-Weight Coach	Seats	44	44
POC-70	Observation-Lounge-Buffet	Lounge Seats	31	
		Tables	4	
		Seats	16	
POC-85-AR	Observation-Lounge-Buffet	Lounge Seats	37	
		Tables	4	
		Seats	16	
LW	Light-Weight Cars			
SW	Standard-Weight Cars			
%	Reclining Seats with Headrest Covers			
¢	High Speed Betterment			
#	Parallel Beds in Double Bed Rooms			
	Unless otherwise noted all MS-60 cars are SOLID			

traveling public in late 1952 with plenty of choices and, because of the extra traffic generated by the Korean War, most of the through trains were still carrying large numbers of passengers in 1952, although even a full train often was a loser because of the cost of operations. In a sense, 1952 may be considered one of the premier postwar years for Pennsylvania Railroad passenger service. A look at a timetable from the late 1950s or early 1960s shows how much disappeared in less than a decade from the Pennsylvania Railroad's main line.

No. 1 and No. 2
THE PENNSYLVANIA LIMITED

The Pennsylvania Limited's primary purpose in the scheme of the road's New York-Chicago service was to handle overflow traffic and passengers who had not secured space on *The General, Trailblazer* or *Broadway Limited*. Just like *The Admiral*, which departed after it for Chicago westbound, and preceded it out of Chicago eastbound, *The Pennsylvania Limited* handled both coach and sleeping car passengers. Westbound, No. 1 handled some New York-Chicago headend cars and a dormitory car for the crew, plus a combine and two

reclining seat coaches of the P85BR type, along with a reclining seat P70GSR. In addition, the train carried a dining car and a 6 double bedroom-sleeper-bar-lounge and one postwar 21 roomette car. Most of the rest of the sleepers were heavyweights with the exception of the through New York to San Francisco sleeping car which No. 1 handled. This 10 roomette, 6 double bedroom transcontinental sleeper was handled every day for the western roads. Every other day, the New York-San Francisco sleeper was handed over in Chicago to *The California Zephyr* and on alternate days to No. 27, the C&NW-Union Pacific-Southern Pacific *San Francisco Overland*. In addition to these cars, at Harrisburg, the train picked up a heavyweight sleeper from Washington and carried two heavyweight sleepers to Harrisburg from New York for forwarding to Erie and Emporium, respectively, on Pennsylvania's No. 581, *The Northern Express*. In addition, on Fridays and on Sundays, the train carried P70 coaches on the rear for local New York-Harrisburg traffic.

No. 2, the eastbound *Pennsylvania Limited*, was very much like the westbound train except for the addition of an additional lightweight prewar

Train No. 1
Blue Ribbon
THE PENNSYLVANIA LIMITED

Car Type	Description	From	To	Details	Car Des
1 MS-60	(X)	Harrisburg	Chicago		
1 Express	R50 or X29 D.E. Sun., Mon., Holidays and days after Holidays	New York	Chicago		
1 MS-60	(X)	New York	Chicago		
1 MS-60	Semi-Open D.E. Saturday, Sunday and Holidays	New York	Chicago		
1	Dormitory	New York	Chicago		
1 PB-70	Scheme 6	New York	Chicago		
1 P-70GSR	Reclining Seats	%New York	Chicago		
2 P-85SR	Reclining Seats	%New York	Chicago		
1	Diner	New York	Chicago	LW	
1 SL-Lounge	6 DBR Bar	#New York	Chicago	LW	12
1 SL	21 Roomette	New York	Chicago	LW	14
1 SL	6 Section 6 DBR	New York	Chicago		15
1 SL	12-1	New York	Chicago		16
1 SL	12-1 DE Sat. and Nov. 27, 28 Dec. 24, 25, 26, 31, Jan. 1, 2	New York	Chicago		17
1 SL	10 Roomette, 6 DBR	*New York	San Francisco	LW	CZ11
1 SL	10 Roomette, 6 DBR	%New York	San Francisco	LW	PA-1
1 SL	8 Section, 1 DR, 2 Cpt	Washington	Chicago	From 531 Harrisburg	19
1 SL	8 Section, 5 DBR	New York	Erie	To 581 Harrisburg	110
1 SL	12-1, Mon. and Thur., Will NOT run Nov. 27, Dec. 25, Jan. 1	New York	Emporium	To 581 Harrisburg	111
3 P-70	Sunday	New York	Harrisburg		
1 P-70	Friday	New York	Harrisburg		

*	Alternate Dates	Even - September, October, January, April — To CB&Q 17 leaving Chicago 3:30 p.m.
		Odd-November, December, February, March — To CB&Q 17 leaving Chicago 3:30 p.m.
*	Alternate Dates	Even - Odd-November, December, February, March — To C&NW 27 leaving Chicago 3:30 p.m.
		Odd-September, October, January, April — To C&NW 27 leaving Chicago 3:30 p.m.

Both: Harry Stegmaier
Denver & Rio Grande Western Pullman sleeper *Silver Glacier* is seen here in Denver, Colorado in early 1970, just before it was sold to the National Railways of Mexico. *Silver Glacier* was one of the 10 roomette, 6 double bedroom sleepers that pooled with the Pennsylvania Railroad in the through New York to Oakland, California service and was carried by *The Pennsylvania Limited* westbound. *Silver Glacier* was built by the Budd Company in 1948 and delivered to the Denver & Rio Grande Western which used the car until 1970.

Like *Silver Glacier*, Western Pacific owned sleeping car *Silver Surf*, seen here in July, 1968 in Oakland, California, was in the through Pennsylvania Railroad pool that carried the transcontinental sleeper connecting in Chicago with *The California Zephyr*. Containing 10 roomettes and 6 double bedrooms, *Silver Surf* was finally retired after the Western Pacific had pulled out of *The California Zephyr* service in 1970 and it too, like *Silver Glacier*, was sold to the National Railways of Mexico shortly thereafter.

12 duplex single room, 5 double bedroom sleeper from Chicago to New York. Instead of the San Francisco cars, *The Pennsylvania Limited* eastbound handled a through Los Angeles to New York sleeping car which the Union Pacific-Chicago & Northwestern *Los Angeles Limited* delivered to Chicago. However, in the fall of 1952, shortly after the publication of the September consist list, the railroad also switched the through San Francisco to New York sleeper received from *The San Francisco Overland* to *The Pennsylvania Limited* on its alternate day operational schedule but not *The California Zephyr* car. As mentioned previously, No. 1 departed New York after the pre-

	Train No. 2				
	Blue Ribbon				
	Pennsylvania Limited				
Car Type	**Description**	**From**	**To**	**Details**	**Car Des**
	Milk and Perishable (X)	Chicago	Philadelphia	To 526 (602 Sunday) Harrisburg	
	Perishable (X)	Chicago	Hudson Cut Off	To 14 Harrisburg	
	Perishable (X)	Chicago	New England	To 96 Harrisburg	
	Milk (X)	Chicago	New York		
	MS-60 (X)	Chicago	Long Island City	PCC	
1 PB-70	Scheme 4	Chicago	New York		
2 P-85BR	Reclining Seats	%Chicago	New York		
1 Diner		Chicago	New York		
1 SL-Lounge	3 DBR, 1 DR, Bar	#Chicago	New York	LW	26
1 SL	21 Roomette	Chicago	New York	LW	25
1 SL	12 Duplex SR, 5 DBR	Chicago	New York	LW	24
1 SL	12-1	Chicago	New York	LW	23
1 SL	12-1 DE Sat. & Nov. 27, 28, Dec, 24, 25, 26, 31, Jan. 1, 2	Chicago	New York		21
1 SL	10 Roomette, 6 DBR	*Los Angeles	New York		22
1 SL	8 Section, 1 DR, 2 Cpt	Chicago	Washington	To 502 Harrisburg	20
1 MS-60	B-60 DE Sunday	Chicago	Fort Wayne		

* From C&NW 2, due Chicago 2:00 p.m

Harry Stegmaier

Union Pacific 10 roomette, 6 double bedroom sleeper *Pacific Waters*, seen here in Denver, Colorado on July 19, 1966, was one of the Union Pacific cars in the New York to Oakland pool which was operated on alternate days with *The California Zephyr* sleepers. *The Pennsylvania Limited* carried *Pacific Waters*, along with two other *Pacific* series assigned sleepers, *Pacific Lodge* and *Pacific Union*, in the New York to Oakland sleeping car service, handled by the Pennsylvania from New York to Chicago and on the C&NW-Union Pacific-Southern Pacific *San Francisco Overland*, between Chicago and Oakland, California. This 10 roomette, 6 double bedroom sleeper was built by the Budd Company and delivered to the Union Pacific early in 1950. After service with the Union Pacific, *Pacific Waters* was purchased by Amtrak and served that company until the 1990s.

Harry Stegmaier Collection

Built by Pullman Standard, and delivered to the Southern Pacific in the spring and summer of 1950, were a whole series of 10 roomette, 6 double bedroom sleeping cars which carried numbers only, without names. Sleeping car No. 9037 was assigned, like *Pacific Waters*, to the through service between New York and Oakland, operated via *The Pennsylvania Limited* and *The San Francisco Overland*. No. 9037, seen here at Denver, Colorado in 1963 was, as can be seen, a smooth side car compared to *Pacific Waters*. No. 9037 was painted in Union Pacific yellow for overland route service and served the Southern Pacific until 1969 when that company scrapped the car.

Harry Stegmaier Collection

Pennsylvania Railroad 12 duplex single room, 5 double bedroom prewar sleeping car, *Mar Brook*, was in Chicago to New York service on *The Pennsylvania Limited* in the 1950s. Pullman Standard built the *Mar Brook* for the Pennsylvania Railroad's *Spirit of St. Louis* in the spring of 1938 and the car served the Pennsylvania Railroad for almost three decades in various types of service. This car handled local sleeping car traffic between Chicago and New York and was not retired by the Pennsylvania Railroad until 1967 when it was sold to Railco Corporation. It is seen here on a Shriners Special at Kansas City, Missouri in October, 1962 in a 22 car train bound from that city to New Orleans for a convention.

mier trains at 6:45 p.m. with an arrival in Chicago the next day, midmorning, at 10:35. Eastbound, the train departed Chicago at 6:30 p.m. with a noontime arrival in New York's Penn Station. No. 1 and 2 made additional stops that the premier trains did not make, especially in Ohio, for example, Van Wert and in Indiana. The eastbound train skipped some of these stops but made more stops the following morning on its eastbound trek. Thus, it served to provide blue ribbon train service for a few of the intermediate stops on Pennsylvania's New York-Chicago main line.

The Pennsylvania Limited lasted until April, 1956 when it was discontinued. Passenger traffic had fallen off and other trains could handle the cars which *The Pennsylvania Limited* still carried. For a short time, a New York to Harrisburg section of *The Liberty Limited* was established to handle some of the former *Pennsylvania Limited* cars. The name, however, did not die with the train. The railroad decided to rename *The Gotham Limited*, *The Pennsylvania Limited*, although in reality it was *The Gotham Limited* that survived, not *The Pennsylvania Limited*, No. 1 and 2. Nevertheless, carrying the name of *The Pennsylvania Limited*,

but running on its old schedule and with its old numbers, *The Gotham Limited*, now *The Pennsylvania Limited*, soldiered on from 1956 until Amtrak in May of 1971.

No. 9 and No. 10
THE AKRONITE

Pennsylvania Railroad's No. 9 and No. 10, *The Akronite*, was a New York to Akron overnight train in both directions but, by 1952, this train had been cut back to a Pittsburgh-Akron operation. East of Pittsburgh, the New York to Akron cars, two prewar lightweight sleepers as well as a prewar 3 double bedroom, 1 drawing room *Colonial* series lounge car, a heavyweight sleeper and a reclining seat coach were carried on *The Admiral* as far as Pittsburgh. Eastbound, these cars were carried as far as Pittsburgh on *The Akronite* where the cars were combined into *The Clevelander* for the trek to New York. At Pittsburgh, *The Akronite* picked up and dropped, respectively, a dining-lounge car which served breakfast westbound and an evening supper eastbound, as well as a combine car and, on Sundays, an extra coach, plus some headend equipment which was carried to and from

Car Type	Description	From	To	Details	Car Des
1	Diner-Lounge	Pittsburgh	Akron		
1 SL	12 Duplex SR, 5 DBR DE Sunday and November 28, 29, December 26, 27, January 1, 2, 3	New York	Akron	LW From 71 Pittsburgh	97
1 SL-Lounge	3 DBR, 1 DR, Bar Will NOT operate Nov. 28, 29, Dec. 26, 27, January 1, 2, 3	New York	Akron	LW From 71 Pittsburgh	96
1 SL	10 Roomette, 5 DBR	New York	Akron	LW From 71 Pittsburgh	95
1 SL	12-1	New York	Akron	From 71 Pittsburgh	94
1 P-85BR	Reclining Seat	%New York	Akron	From 71 Pittsburgh	
1 P-70	Sunday	Pittsburgh	Akron		
1 PB-70		Pittsburgh	Akron		
1 B-60	Mail and Express, DE Sunday	Pittsburgh	Akron		
1 B-60	Mail and Express DE Sunday	Pittsburgh	Youngstown		

Train No. 9

Car Type	Description	From	To	Details	Car Des
1 Express	B-60 DE Saturday, Sunday and Holidays	Akron	Pittsburgh		
1 PB-70		Pittsburgh	Akron		
1 P-70	Sunday	Pittsburgh	Akron		
1 SL	12 Duplex SR, 5 DBR DE Sunday and November 28, 29, December 26, 27, January 1, 2, 3	Akron	New York	LW to 71 Pittsburgh	110
1 SL-Lounge	3 DBR, 1 DR, Bar Will NOT operate November 28, 29, December 26, 27, January 1, 2, 3	Akron	New York	LW to 38 Pittsburgh	112
1 P-85BR	Reclining Seat	%Akron	New York	To 38 Pittsburgh	
1 B-60	Mail and Express, DE Sunday	Pittsburgh	Akron		
1 SL	10 Roomette, 5 DBR	Akron	New York	LW to 38 Pittsburgh	113
1 SL	12-1	Akron	New York	To 38 Pittsburgh	114
1	Diner-Lounge	Akron	Pittsburgh		
1 B-60	Mail and Express DE Sunday	Youngstown	Pittsburgh		

Train No. 10

Harry Stegmaier Collection

Regularly assigned to *The Akronite* between New York and Akron was a 12 duplex single room, 5 double bedroom prewar lightweight sleeper, *Moor Brook*. This car was built by Pullman Standard for the Pennsylvania Railroad and delivered to the company in June, 1939 and thus stands as a classic example of a prewar, lightweight duplex single room sleeper. The car is seen here on May 15, 1965 in Denver, Colorado. By then, it carries the name *James Hay Reed*, having been the only prewar 12 duplex single room, 5 double bedroom sleeper renamed for *The Pittsburgher* in 1956. The *Moor Brook*, like most of the duplex single room, 5 double bedroom prewar lightweight sleepers, served the Pennsylvania Railroad in special service, after regular assignments were finished, well into the 1960s. The railroad did not dispose of the *James Hay Reed*, ex-*Moor Brook*, until its service finally came to an end in 1966. It was retired and sold to a private individual.

Youngstown and Akron. *The Akronite* was an important train to serve the rubber capital of the United States and, thus, it remained fairly well patronized by businessmen until the mid 1950s after which, as passengers deserted the train, Nos. 9 and 10 eventually became nothing more than a Hudson, Ohio to Akron connection for *The Clevelander*, at the end, simply a combine coach and a through sleeper from New York. On April 26, 1958, what was left of 9 and 10, *The Akronite*, made its last run between Hudson and Akron, thus bringing to an end through Pennsylvania railroad service between New York City and Akron.

Harry Stegmaier Collection

Another prewar lightweight sleeper assigned to *The Akronite* on a regular basis in the 1950s was 10 roomette, 5 double bedroom prewar lightweight sleeper, *Cascade Timber*, seen here on a Shriner's Special bound from Kansas City to New Orleans in October, 1962. *Cascade Timber* contained 10 roomettes and 5 double bedrooms, the 5 double bedrooms being noticeable for having the smaller windows, while the roomettes had larger windows. The Pennsylvania Railroad took delivery of *Cascade Timber* in the summer of 1940 from Pullman Standard and the car continued on the Pennsylvania Railroad, although by the 1960s it was primarily in special and charter service, until 1967 when the car was sold to a scrap dealer.

Merry Christmas
and a Happy New Year

PENNSYLVANIA RAILROAD

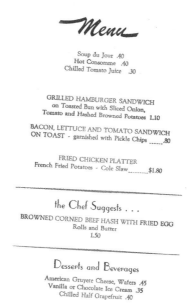

Menu

Soup du Jour .40
Hot Consomme .40
Chilled Tomato Juice .30

GRILLED HAMBURGER SANDWICH
on Toasted Bun with Sliced Onion,
Tomato and Hashed Browned Potatoes 1.10

BACON, LETTUCE AND TOMATO SANDWICH
ON TOAST - garnished with Pickle Chips _____ .80

FRIED CHICKEN PLATTER
French Fried Potatoes - Cole Slaw_____$1.80

the Chef Suggests . . .
BROWNED CORNED BEEF HASH WITH FRIED EGG
Rolls and Butter
1.50

Desserts and Beverages
American Gruyere Cheese, Wafers .45
Vanilla or Chocolate Ice Cream .35
Chilled Half Grapefruit .40

Pot of Coffee .30   Hot Chocolate .30
Pot of Tea .30   Milk .25

As your host, the steward will welcome your suggestions about our food and service.
If you prefer, your comments may be addressed to:
Sidney N. Phelps, Manager, Dining Car Service, Pennsylvania Railroad, Long Island City 1, N. Y.

Harry Stegmaier Collection

This menu from the holiday season of 1952, has a very colorful Christmas cover and was used on, from the coding (not shown), on both *The Clevelander* and the eastbound *Akronite*. One should note that, because of its late evening departure from Akron, No. 10 did not serve an extensive menu but pretty much confined itself to sandwiches, beverages and a fried chicken platter, plus corn beef hash with a fried egg. No large meals were served, as was the case on other Pennsylvania Railroad trains which catered more to the dinner crowd.

No. 22 and No. 23
THE MANHATTAN LIMITED

Both westbound and eastbound, Pennsylvania Railroad's *Manhattan Limited* had long been, and

would remain until Amtrak, Pennsylvania Railroad's early through train between New York and Chicago in both directions with a 2:50 p.m. departure from Penn Station westbound and a 12:01 p.m. departure from Chicago Union Station eastbound and an early morning arrival in its respective terminal cities of Chicago and New York. As a daylight run east of Pittsburgh westbound, and a daylight run eastbound between Chicago and Pittsburgh, No. 22 and No. 23, *The Manhattan Limited*, made many of the stops that were passed over by other trains and, thus, it was one of the Pennsylvania Railroad's slower schedules on the New York-Chicago main line. For example, westbound, *The Manhattan Limited* called at such towns as Mt. Union and Huntingdon, Pennsylvania. Eastbound, the train made many stops simply ignored by faster luxury trains such as Warsaw, Indiana, Van Wert, Ohio and Wooster, Ohio. *The Manhattan Limited's* main purpose, besides hitting the intermediate stops for the railroad, was to provide an alternative to the later departures and an earlier arrival in its terminal city.

	Train No. 22					
	Blue Ribbon					
	Manhattan Limited					
Car Type	Description	From	To	Details		Car Des
Express	Perishable (X)	Chicago	Eastern points			
I MS-60	B-60 Wednesday LIFE	Chicago	Harrisburg			
I MS-60		Chicago	Pittsburgh			
I BM70M	Letter End East	Chicago	Pittsburgh			
I MS-60	(X)	Cincinnati	New York	From 204 Pittsburgh		
I MS-60	X-29 DE Sunday and Monday	Cincinnati	New York	From 204 Pittsburgh		
I MS-60	Semi-Open Saturday and Sunday	Pittsburgh	New York			
I M-70	DE Sunday	Pittsburgh	New York	Letter End West		
I BM70M		Pittsburgh	New York	Letter End 70East		
I BM-70	30 foot apt., DE Saturday and Sunday	Pittsburgh	New York	Letter End East		
I B-60		Chicago	New York			
I P-70GSR	Reclining Seats	%Chicago	New York			
I P70KR	Reclining Seats	%Chicago	New York			
2 P-85BR	Reclining Seats	%Chicago	New York			
I Diner		Chicago	New York			
I SL-Lounge	3 DBR, I DR, Bar	Chicago	New York	LW		224
I SL	10 Roomette, 5 DBR	Chicago	New York	LW		223
I SL	12-I DE Sat. & Nov. 27, 28, Dec. 24, 25, 26, 31, Jan. I, 2	Chicago	New York			222
I SL	12-I	Chicago	New York			221
I SL	12-I	Chicago	Washington	To 504 Harrisburg		220
I B-60	Papers, Wednesday	Louisville	Fort Wayne	From 305 Chicago		

7

J. Williams and Big Four Graphics
The Manhattan Limited often was assigned coaches from the P70GSR series. In this picture, taken in October, 1967, P70GSR No. 4240 is seen at Chicago, Illinois after it has received the new Pennsylvania Railroad's paint scheme, the simplified version with which the car ended its days in Pennsylvania Railroad passenger service.

The train, nevertheless, carried good equipment, but to a large extent both westbound and eastbound, No. 23 and No. 22, were laden with head-end cars, carrying a good deal of mail and express traffic between New York and Chicago. Nevertheless, as can be seen from the consist sheets, the train carried at least four through reclining seat coaches, although when P85BR and P70KR's were not available because of shopping or other shortages, *The Manhattan Limited* would receive other types of reclining seat coaches. Its diner provided basic fare and its sleeper-lounge car with bar kept patrons well saturated if they wished. The train also carried two through sleepers, a pre-war 10 roomette, 5 double bedroom *Cascade* series car and a heavyweight 12 section, 1 drawing room car. In addition, on weekends, it carried extra P70 coaches between New York and Pittsburgh on that portion of its journey and, eastbound, it was not unusual to find a coach or two added during heavy travel seasons between Chicago and Pittsburgh, usually cars of the straight P70 type.

The Manhattan Limited would labor on for the Pennsylvania Railroad on basically the schedule it had in 1952 until the advent of Amtrak, thus joining *The General* and *The Gotham Limited*, now renamed *The Pennsylvania Limited*, as Penn Central's three through New York-Chicago line trains, supplemented eastbound by *The Admiral*, until April 30, 1971 after which Amtrak took over all service. However, by the end, the train usually consisted of simply three headend cars of baggage, mail and express as well as three coaches, one with a snack bar. All of the amenities had disappeared years before.

Car Type	Description	From	To	Details	Car Des
	Train No. 23				
	Blue Ribbon				
	Manhattan Limited				
	Consist DE Saturday and November 27, 28, December 25, 26, 31, January 1 and 2				
1 MS-60	(X)	Philadelphia	Council Bluffs	From 611 Harrisburg	
1 MS-60	DE Sunday and Monday	Philadelphia	Chicago	From 611 Harrisburg	
1 MS-60		New York	Chicago		
1 MS-60	DE Sunday	New York	Chicago		
1 MS-60	(X)	P.C.C	Chicago		
1 B-60		New York	Chicago		
1 P-70GSR	Reclining Seats, Friday and Sunday	%New York	Chicago		
1 P-70GSR	Reclining Seats	%New York	Chicago		
1 P-70KR	Reclining Seats	%New York	Chicago		
2 P-85BR	Reclining Seats	%New York	Chicago		
1 Diner		New York	Chicago		
1 SL-Lounge	3 DBR, 1 DR, Bar	New York	Chicago	LW	230
1 SL	10 Roomette, 5 DBR	New York	Chicago	LW	231
3 P-70	Friday and Sunday	New York	Pittsburgh		
1 P-70	DE, Friday and Sunday only	New York	Harrisburg		

Harry Stegmaier Collection

Pennsylvania Railroad 12 section, 1 drawing room sleeper, *Launfal*, is seen in this photo at St. Louis, Missouri on July 22, 1952. Pennsylvania records show that *Launfal* was assigned to *The Manhattan Limited* in the 1950s on a regular basis and provided section space, as well as the one drawing room, in addition to the other cars carried by No. 22 and No. 23.

Harry Stegmaier

A normal assignment for postwar sleeper-lounge, *Colonial Houses*, in the 1950s, was on *The Manhattan Limited*. *Colonial Houses* contained 3 double bedrooms, a drawing room, plus a buffet lounge which kept *The Manhattan Limited* patrons from going thirsty on their New York to Chicago journey. *Colonial Houses* is seen here, after it had been renumbered and placed in New York to Washington parlor car service, at Landover, Maryland on May 26, 1969, being one of the last of the Pennsylvania Railroad's postwar *Colonial* series cars to survive into the Penn Central era. *Colonial Houses* was not retired until 1970 when it was finally scrapped by the Penn Central. These cars were first delivered to the Pennsylvania Railroad in May and June of 1949 and by the time this photograph was taken, it had completed two decades of service with the company

No. 28 and No. 29
THE BROADWAY LIMITED

The Broadway Limited is undoubtedly one of the great names in American streamliner history. By 1952, this famous train had been completely re-equipped with postwar lightweight sleeping cars. No. 29 and No. 28, west and east respectively, carried a BM70M railway post office car that handled urgent and special delivery as well as registered mail between New York and Chicago overnight. The train consisted of postwar lightweight sleepers, two of the 21 roomette *Inn* series, two of the 12 duplex single room, 4 double bedroom *Creek* series, three 4 double bedroom, 4 compartment, 2 drawing room *Imperial* cars, and three 10 roomette, 6 double bedroom sleepers. Both westbound and eastbound, it carried the 4 double bedroom, 4 compartment, 2 drawing room *Regal* series Santa Fe car which was handled west of Chicago on the Santa Fe's extra fare No. 19 and No. 20, the *Chief*, an all stainless steel speedster from Chicago to Los Angeles. *The Broadway Limited* was unique for its special cars. The train carried a twin-unit full dining car with a kitchen-dormitory car, usually Budd built, between New York and Chicago. In addition, the two *Harbor* series cars, *Harbor Cove* and *Harbor Rest*, which contained 2 double bedrooms as well as a bar, had been especially built for *The Broadway Limited*. These fine postwar cars, before they were later changed to a five double bedroom, bar-lounge configuration, contained as well two double bedrooms and lounge, a barber shop where the exalted patrons of the train could get a haircut, a shower bath, and a secretary's room where letters and telegrams could be dictated. Bringing up the rear were two famous flat end observation cars, *Mountain View* and *Tower View*, which contained, along with a double bedroom, two large master rooms. The master room was only found on a few cars in the United States. The Southern Railway's *Crescent* also had them. The master room was very large with three chairs for daytime use, a radio and two lower beds at night, as well as a private bathroom which included, uniquely, a shower which was almost unknown on American trains at that time. These cars would remain with the train until 1967. *The Broadway Limited* was Pennsylvania's finest train and, by the 1960s, had surpassed *The Twentieth Century Limited* as the best New York-Chicago method of travel by rail. However, with the Penn Central merger looming on the horizon, the Pennsylvania Railroad finally discontinued *The Broadway Limited* shortly before the final union with the New York Central was complete. Right until the end, service on *The Broadway Limited* was outstanding and one could still choose, in 1967, from duplex single rooms, double bedrooms, compartments, drawing rooms and roomettes, as well as a master room if one

Train No. 28
Blue Ribbon
Broadway Limited

Car Type	Description	From	To	Details	Car Des
1 BM70M	Letter End West	X Chicago	New York	SW	
1 SL	4 Cpt, 4DBR, 2DR	* Los Angeles	New York	LW Steam Jet A/C	PA28
1 SL	21 Roomette	Chicago	New York	LW Last Trip Dec. 12	292
1 SL	21 Roomette	Chicago	New York	LW	291
1 SL	12 Duplex SR, 4 DBR	Chicago	New York	LW	290
1 SL	12 Duplex SR, 4 DBR	Chicago	New York	LW	289
1 SL	4 Cpt, 4 DBR, 2 DR	Chicago	New York	LW	288
1 SL-Lge	2 DBR, Bar	# Chicago	New York	LW	286
1 Diner	)Twin Unit				
1 Kitchen-Dormitory	)Twin Unit	Chicago	New York	LW	
1 SL	4 Cpt, 4DBR, 2 DR	Chicago	New York	LW	285
1 SL	10 Rmte 6DBR	# Chicago	New York	LW	284
1 SL	10 Roomette, 6 DBR	# Chicago	New York	LW	283
1 SL	10 Roomette, 6 DBR	# Chicago	New York	LW	282
1 SL	4 Cpt, 4DBR, 2 DR	Chicago	New York	LW	281
1 SL-Obs	2 MR, 1 DBR	# Chicago	New York	LW	280

* From Santa Fe 20, Due Chicago 10:30 a.m.
X RPO apartment NOT in service Sunday, Chicago-Pittsburgh

Harry Stegmaier

Each *Broadway Limited* consist contained an RPO-Baggage car of the BM70M variety. These cars had a large RPO compartment plus a small baggage compartment in each car and were used for overnight priority mail between New York and Chicago. Cars like No. 6561, seen here in January, 1966, often operated on *The Broadway Limited* and carried the mail.

Car Type	Description	From	To	Details	Car Des
	Train 29				
	Blue Ribbon				
	Broadway Limited				
I BM-70M	Letter End East	xNew York	Chicago	SW	
I SL	10 Roomette, 6 DBR, December 25	zNew York	Los Angeles	LW	PA5
I SL	4 Compartment, 4 DBR, 2 DR	*New York	Los Angeles	LW, Steam Jet AC	PA29
I SL	21 Roomette	New York	Chicago	LW, Last Trip, December 11	W12
I SL	21 Roomette	New York	Chicago	LW	W11
I SL	12 Duplex SR, 4 DBR	New York	Chicago	LW	W10
I SL	12 Duplex SR, 4 DBR	New York	Chicago	LW	W-9
I SL	4 Compartment, 4 DBR, 2 DR	New York	Chicago	LW	W-8
I SL-Lounge	2 DBR, Bar	#New York	Chicago	LW	W-7
I Diner	) Twin Unit				
I Kitchen-Dormitory	) Twin Unit	New York	Chicago	LW	
I SL	4 Compartment, 4 DBR, 2 DR	New York	Chicago	LW	W-6
I SL	10 Roomette, 6 DBR	#New York	Chicago	LW	W-5
I SL	10 Roomette, 6 DBR	#New York	Chicago	LW	W-4
I SL	10 Roomette, 6 DBR	#New York	Chicago	LW	W-3
I SL	4 Compartment, 4 DBR, 2 DR	New York	Chicago	LW	W-2
I SL-Obs	2 MR, I DBR Bar Lounge	#New York	Chicago	LW	W-1

* to Santa Fe 19, leaving Chicago 1:30 p.m.
z to C&NW 1, leaving Chicago 12:10 p.m.
x RPO apartment NOT in service Sunday.

The Broadway Limited, until the very end, carried a twin unit diner such as No. 4620 and 4621. In these two photographs, each of the cars of the two unit set is seen in July, 1967 in Chicago, Illinois. Both cars were delivered to the Pennsylvania Railroad from the Budd Company in July, 1949. No. 4620 is a full length dining room, separated by a steward's desk in the middle of the car, while No. 4621 is a kitchen-dormitory car where the food was prepared and provided sleeping accommodations for the dining car crew. No. 4620-4621 served on *The Broadway Limited* and later on the former *General*, renamed *The Broadway Limited*, until Amtrak, then operated on lease to Amtrak on its own *Broadway Limited* until 1973 when Amtrak finally purchased both cars from the Penn Central.

desired to pay the cost. The train made its final run on December 12, 1967. However, *The Broadway Limited* name was then transferred to *The General*, which was simply by then a coach and Pullman train. By the time of the Penn Central debacle of 1970, it had disintegrated to second hand coaches from other railroads, a buffet-lounge and only 10 roomette, 6 double bedroom sleepers, although the train was still large enough to demand a twin-unit diner. It is unfortunate that *The Broadway Limited's* name had to be degraded in such a fashion and transferred to *The General* when it would have been better to simply let the name die when the last runs were made on the 12th of December, 1967.

Obviously, *The Broadway Limited* was Pennsylvania's speedster on the New York to Chicago run with its 6 p.m. departure from New York and 9:00 a.m. arrival in Chicago the next morning as well as a 4:30 p.m. departure eastbound from Chicago and a 9:30 a.m. arrival in New York. *The Broadway Limited* did not make many intermediate stops, except at crew change points such as Fort Wayne, Crestline and Pittsburgh. However, unlike the New York Central's *Twentieth Century Limited*, which did not pick up at its crew change stops, *The Broadway Limited* handled revenue passengers at those stops.

Harry Stegmaier

Two unique cars built especially for *The Broadway Limited* were twins, *Harbor Cove* and *Harbor Rest*, Pullman products delivered to the Pennsylvania Railroad in December, 1948 and containing 2 double bedrooms, a buffet, a 20-seat lounge plus rooms for a barber shop, a shower room and a secretary's room. These amenities only benefited a train with the prestige of *The Broadway*. In 1958, the car was rebuilt to contain 5 double bedrooms and a telephone room, a sign of the times. The barber shop, shower bath and secretary's room were all remodeled to create the additional 3 double bedrooms. They continued to serve on *The Broadway Limited* until its demise in December, 1967 and then could often be found on *The General*, renamed *The Broadway Limited*, until the cars were withdrawn from service by Penn Central in 1970. *Harbor Rest* is seen here in June, 1968, at Chicago, Illinois.

Harry Stegmaier Collection

Among the 12 duplex single room, 4 double bedroom Pullman sleepers regularly assigned to *The Broadway Limited* in the 1950s, was Pennsylvania Railroad's *Cedar Creek* built by Pullman Standard and delivered to the Pennsylvania Railroad in the spring of 1949. The car is seen here in December, 1965, after it had been

renamed *August A. Busch* in 1957, to honor the large brewing magnate of St. Louis, Missouri. The postwar 12 duplex single room, 4 double bedroom car differed on the outside from the prewar 12 duplex single room, 5 double bedroom *Brook* series cars by having large windows in the double bedrooms. *Cedar Creek*, later the *August A. Busch*, was often seen on *The Broadway Limited* in the 1950s and 1960s. The car served the Pennsylvania Railroad until 1968 when it was sold to Judge Roy Hofheinz for his motel complex in Houston which never materialized. The car was later scrapped.

Another regular on *The Broadway Limited* in the 1950s was postwar sleeper 4 double bedroom, 4 compartment, 2 drawing room *Imperial Peak*. The *Imperial Peak* was built for the Pennsylvania Railroad by American Car and Foundry and delivered to the company in the fall of 1948. The all multi-person, private room cars lasted on the Pennsylvania Railroad, and later on the Penn Central, until they were retired in 1971 and scrapped when Amtrak took over passenger service and decided not to purchase Pennsylvania Railroad's *Imperial* cars. *Imperial Peak* is seen here in March, 1966 still painted in the Pennsylvania Tuscan Red scheme with the full Pennsylvania name written out on the letterboard. As mainline trains were cut back,

these *Imperial* cars proved extremely versatile and were often seen on Seaboard Coast Line trains in the late 1960s in New York to Florida service, as well as on *The South Wind* and Illinois Central's *City of Miami* in the peak winter season in Florida.

10 roomette, 6 double bedroom sleeper *Little Miami Rapids* was built by the Pullman Company for the Pennsylvania Railroad and delivered in the spring of 1949. It was regularly assigned to *The Broadway Limited* in the early 1950s. In this photograph, taken in October, 1968, at Effingham, Illinois, *Little Miami Rapids* has fallen from its status as a regular on *The Broadway Limited* to serving on *The Spirit of St. Louis* or what remained of it by the Penn Central era. These 10 roomette, 6 double bedroom sleepers, for the most part, lasted well into the Penn Central era and this particular car was not scrapped until it was retired in 1970. Penn Central seemed to have run the cars until they dropped and then pulled another one out of storage and replaced it. Thus, some were scrapped earlier than the final Amtrak takeover in 1971 as was the case with *Little Miami Rapids*. Nevertheless, it still looks good with the full Pennsylvania

name on the letterboard and in Tuscan Red in this photograph in the fall of 1968.

The Broadway Limited carried the through New York to Los Angeles sleepers that were handled beyond Chicago on Santa Fe's No. 19 and No. 20, the all Pullman *Chief*. Santa Fe was rather insistent that the cars used all be Santa Fe cars because of their stainless steel appearance which would match the cars on Santa Fe's train. Thus, no Pennsylvania Railroad 4 double bedroom, 4 compartment, 2 drawing room sleepers were assigned to that daily New York to Los Angeles sleeping car route by 1952. Instead, six Santa Fe sleepers were assigned to this service. In this photograph, *Regal Manor*, a 4 compartment, 4 double bedroom, 2 drawing room Santa Fe sleeper, which was assigned to through New York to Los Angeles service via *The Broadway Limited* and the extra fare *Chief* in the 1950s, is seen at Chicago, Illinois on July 4, 1970. The author found the car assigned on that Independence Day to Santa Fe *The Texas Chief*. These *Regal* cars from the Santa Fe were beautiful

inside and rode exceptionally well for lightweight cars, which is what one would expect from the Santa Fe. *Regal Manor* was built by American Car and Foundry for the Santa Fe and delivered in the fall of 1950. Amtrak used the car briefly after it took over passenger service but then Santa Fe purchased the car from Amtrak and put *Regal Manor* into its business car fleet. The Santa Fe *Regal* cars could be seen on a daily basis on *The Broadway Limited* in the 1950s.

Al Chione, Harry Stegmaier Collection

Another unique car, like the *Harbor* cars, built for *The Broadway Limited* exclusively, were the two observation cars, *Mountain View* and *Tower View*, delivered in January, 1949 by the Pullman Company to the Pennsylvania Railroad. Each of the two postwar *View* cars contained two master rooms with showers, a double bedroom, and a 25-seat observation lounge served by a buffet. *Tower View* is seen here in Chicago in June, 1967, still carrying *The Broadway Limited* on the drumhead. Both cars would be retired in 1968 and both survive today. *Tower View* eventually ended up at Strasburg, Pennsylvania in the State of Pennsylvania Transportation Museum after serving on *The Broadway Limited* almost exclusively throughout its Pennsylvania Railroad career.

Mark Hildebrandt

This interior view is of one of the twin unit dining cars used on *The Broadway Limited*, although it was taken in 1969 after the Penn Central had taken over all service. These twin unit diners continued to operate on *The Broadway Limited* and still provided excellent meal service. One can see the 4-2 seating arrangement in the car in this photograph, as well as the steward's buffet which divides the two dining compartments of this full length diner.

Both: Mark Hildebrandt

These two views show the interior of Pennsylvania Railroad's 5 double bedroom, buffet, lounge sleeper *Harbor Cove*, especially built for *The Broadway Limited*. One can see the wall decorations as well as the plush lounge chairs and writing tables where one could also avail themselves of beverages and the hor d'ouveres which can be seen on the table in the one photograph. In the second photograph, one is looking toward the mirror in the lounge section. Notice the aisle to the left that leads to the double bedrooms as well as the buffet which provided plenty of beverages to keep travelers well quenched, even in the Penn Central era when these photographs were taken aboard *The Broadway Limited* in May, 1969. By 1970, the two cars would be retired. Neither car survived the scrapper's torch.

PENNSYLVANIA RAILROAD

BROADWAY
Limited

Harry Stegmaier Collection

The Broadway Limited dining car, as can be seen from this 1953 menu, provided first class restaurant service to the patrons of the flagship of the Pennsylvania Railroad's New York-Chicago line. One could choose from, among other things, a selection of cocktails before plunging into either a steak or prime ribs of beef. Perhaps the mixed grill, breast of chicken or Lake Superior whitefish were more appealing to some palettes. Anyone looking at this menu today can only think back to the better days when railroad dining car service was as good as any found in some of the finest restaurants in the country.

Broadway Limited

Dinner

Wine List

EXTRA DRY MARTINI	65
MANHATTAN	65
DAIQUIRI	65
SCOTCH OLD FASHIONED COCKTAIL	1.05
DOMESTIC BEER OR ALE	40
CANADIAN ALE	50
RED OR WHITE WINE (SPLIT)	65
SHERRY, IMPORTED	60
PORT, IMPORTED	60
BRANDY COGNAC (FRENCH)	85
CREME DE MENTHE	85
SOUTHERN COMFORT	70
B AND B	95
BENEDICTINE	95
DRAMBUIE	1.00

(For additional selections, please ask
Steward for Beverage List)

CANAPES   COTTAGE CHEESE   MIXED OLIVES

ORANGE FROSTED CRANBERRY JUICE   TOMATO JUICE
ONION SOUP, GRATED CHEESE   HOT OR JELLIED BEEF BROTH
HALF GRAPEFRUIT, MARASCHINO
FILETS OF HERRING IN SOUR CREAM

BROILED LAKE SUPERIOR WHITEFISH, MAITRE D'HOTEL   3.50
GARDEN GREEN PEAS   OVEN-BROWNED POTATOES

BREAST OF CHICKEN, KENTUCKY STYLE WITH CORN FRITTERS   4.10
ASPARAGUS, DRAWN BUTTER   CHATEAU POTATOES

LAMB CHOP MIXED GRILL, PENNSYLVANIA   4.50
(BACON-SAUSAGE-FRESH MUSHROOMS)
GRILLED TOMATO   MASHED POTATOES

ROAST PRIME RIBS OF BEEF AU JUS   4.35
ASPARAGUS SPEARS   CREAMY WHIPPED POTATOES

CHARCOAL GRILLED SIRLOIN STEAK   5.25
FRENCH FRIED ONION RINGS   CHATEAU POTATOES

SLICED TOMATOES, VINAIGRETTE

CREAM SCONES   DINNER ROLLS

CHILLED HALF GRAPEFRUIT   BAKED APPLE WITH CREAM
ORANGE SHERBET   COCOANUT CREAM PUDDING
VANILLA ICE CREAM, RUM FRUIT SAUCE
BLEU OR GRUYERE CHEESE WITH CRACKERS
PUMPKIN PIE WITH SHERRY WHIPPED CREAM

TEA   COFFEE
GRADE "A" MILK   BUTTERMILK

CANDY MINTS

Sidney N. Phelps, Manager, Dining Car Service, Pennsylvania Railroad

A la Carte

HALF GRAPEFRUIT, MARASCHINO 40
HOT OR JELLIED BEEF BROTH 40
FILETS OF HERRING IN SOUR CREAM 75

HEAD LETTUCE SALAD 65
PRR SALAD BOWL WITH RY-KRISP 95
SLICED CHICKEN SANDWICH 1.25
ROAST BEEF SANDWICH, GARNISHED 1.95

VANILLA ICE CREAM, RUM SAUCE 45
ORANGE SHERBET 40
HALF GRAPEFRUIT 40
BLEU OR GRUYERE CHEESE
WITH CRACKERS 45
PUMPKIN PIE WITH
SHERRY WHIPPED CREAM 50

POT OF COFFEE 35		TEA 30	
GRADE "A" MILK 25		BUTTERMILK 25	

Sea Food Special

ASSORTED RELISHES
CUP OF SOUP
SHRIMP CREOLE EN CASSEROLE
STEAMED RICE   GARDEN ASPARAGUS
HOT SCONES
SLICED TOMATOES, VINAIGRETTE
YOUR SELECTION OF DESSERT
TEA   COFFEE   MILK
CANDY MINTS
$3.50

10/15-11/4/53

Autumn Special

RELISHES
CHILLED TOMATO JUICE
BROILED HAM STEAK WITH FRIED EGGS
HASHED BROWNED POTATOES
SALAD
DINNER ROLLS
CHOICE OF DESSERT
TEA   COFFEE   MILK
$3.50

No. 38 and 39
THE CLEVELANDER

Pennsylvania's answer to New York Central's overnight New York to Cleveland service, *The Cleveland Limited*, was No. 39 westbound and No. 38 eastbound, *The Clevelander*. Westbound, No. 39, carried a number of head-end cars, especially between New York and Pittsburgh, including a working RPO car as well as a Pittsburgh to Cleveland RPO car. Coach passengers were accommodated in a PB70 combine and a P70KR reclining seat coach, while Pullman passengers could enjoy accommodations in a 21 roomette *Inn* car and a six bedroom bar-lounge sleeper as well as a prewar 10 roomette, five double bedroom car. The train also carried, as can be seen, two heavyweight sleepers between New York and Cleveland and, at Harrisburg, it picked up three cars from Washington to Cleveland, a reclining seat coach, a heavyweight sleeper and a *Cascade* series car, thus putting it in competition with B&O's No. 17 and No. 18, *The Cleveland Night Express*. Eastbound, the train did not handle the massive amount of head-end it did on its westbound trek because, at Pittsburgh, it had to pick up the coach and three sleepers, two lightweight and one heavyweight, as well as a sleeper-lounge from Akron, carried to Pittsburgh by *The Akronite* and, at Harrisburg, picked up the Roanoke-New York cars delivered by the Norfolk and Western to Hagerstown, and then on train No. 638 from Hagerstown to Harrisburg, that operated over the Shenandoah Valley route of the Norfolk and Western from Roanoke. In each direction, *The Clevelander* carried a dining-lounge car which provided a basic meal service. A larger menu was not needed since the train did not depart until 8:40 p.m. with a morning arrival in Cleveland at 8:30 and, eastbound, the train departed Cleveland late enough in the evening that many patrons had dinner before boarding so the evening menu offerings were, as can be seen from the illustration on

Both: Harry Stegmaier Collection
Top Right: The Clevelander regularly received for its through coaches, cars of the P70KR type. The P70KR coaches had been rebuilt by the Pennsylvania Railroad from old P70 coaches. Altoona Car Shop rebuilt the old P70s into P70KR coaches in April-June, 1940. This was the first batch that was followed by a second group in December, 1941. In this photo, P70KR coach No. 4292 is seen in 1951 at Orlando, Florida on an Atlantic Coast Line train. Some of the P70KR coaches received wide windows like No. 4292 while others still had single windows. These cars could be found on many Pennsylvania Railroad trains, both as fill in cars for the P85BR coaches, as well as in regular assignments, like No. 38 and No. 39, *The Clevelander*.

Center Right: The Clevelander was regularly assigned an *Inn* series sleeper that contained 21 roomettes. In this photograph, *Wilkensburg Inn* is seen in June, 1965 in Denver, Colorado in special service assignment. The *Inn* series sleepers on the Pennsylvania Railroad were primarily built by the Budd Company but a small group of seven cars, including the *Wilkensburg Inn*, were built by American Car and Foundry. Unlike the Budd built cars which were converted to coaches, the ACF cars always remained 21 roomette sleeping cars and all were retired in 1966 and 1967. *Wilkensburg Inn* was retired in 1966 and scrapped by the Pennsylvania Railroad.

Train 38
Blue Ribbon
The Clevelander

Car Type	Description	From	To	Details	Car Des
1 PB-70	Scheme 4	Cleveland	New York		
1 P-70KR	Reclining Seats	% Cleveland	New York		
1 SL	12-1	¢Cleveland	New York		389
1 SL	21 Roomette LW	Cleveland	New York		387
1 SL-Lge	6 DBR Bar LW	Cleveland	New York		386
1 Diner-Lounge		Cleveland	New York		
1 P-70KR	Reclining Seats	%Cleveland	Washington	To 536 Harrisburg	
1 SL	10 Rmte 5 DBR LW	Cleveland	Washington	To 536 Harrisburg	383
1 SL	8 Sec 1 DR 2 Cpt DE Sat	*Cleveland	Philadelphia	To 36 (86 Nov 27, Dec 25) Harrisburg	381
1 SL	10 Rmte 5 DBR DE Sat LW	*Cleveland	Philadelphia	To 36 (86 Nov 27, Dec 25) Harrisburg	380
1 SL	6 Sect 6 DBR	Cleveland	Philadelphia	To 36 (86 Nov 27, Dec 25) Harrisburg	381
1 P-85BR	Reclining Seats	% Akron	New York	From 10 Pittsburgh	
1 SL	12 Dup SR 5 DBR	* Akron	New York	From 10 Pittsburgh	110
1 SL-Lge	3 DBR 1 DR Bar	* Akron	New York	From 10 Pittsburgh	112
1 SL	10 Rmte 5 DBR LW	Akron	New York	From 10 Pittsburgh	113
1 SL	12-1	Akron	New York	From 10 Pittsburgh	114
1 SL	10 Rmte 6 DBR LW	xRoanoke	New York	From 638 Pittsburgh	W-6
1 SL	10 Sec 1 DR 1 Cpt, Nov. 29, Dec. 27, Jan. 1, 3	Roanoke	New York	From 638 Pittsburgh	RN1

* Will NOT operate Nov. 27, 28, Dec. 25, 26, 31, Jan. 1, 2
x Will NOT operate Nov. 28, 29, Dec. 26, 27, Jan. 1, 2, 3

Train No. 39
Blue Ribbon
The Clevelander

Car Type	Description	From	To	Details	Car Des
I MS-60	D.E. Monday & Holidays	New York	Harrisburg		
I MS-60	D.E. Sun. & Holidays	Baltimore	Pittsburgh	From 575 Harrisburg	
I MS-60	D.E. Monday	Harrisburg	Pittsburgh		
I MS-60	(X)	New York	Pittsburgh		
I MS-60	Saturday	New York	Pittsburgh		
I B-60	Papers Sunday	New York	Pittsburgh		
I BM70M	D.E. Sunday	New York	Pittsburgh	Letter End East	
I BM70K	D.E. Sunday Letter End. East	Pittsburgh	Cleveland	2 door type must operate	
I P-70	Sunday	New York	Harrisburg		
I PB-70	Scheme 4	New York	Cleveland		
I P-70KR	Reclining Seats	%New York	Cleveland		
I SL	12-1	¢New York	Cleveland		390
I SL	21 Roomette LW	New York	Cleveland		391
I SL-Lge	6DBR Bar LW	New York	Cleveland		392
I	Diner-Lounge	New York	Cleveland		
I SL	6 Section 6 DBR	New York	Cleveland		393
I SL	10 Rmte 5 DBR DE Saturday LW	*New York	Cleveland		394
I P-70KR	Reclining Seats	%Washington	Cleveland	From 539 Harrisburg	
I SL	8 Section I DR 2 Cpt DE Saturday	*Washington	Cleveland	From 539 Harrisburg	398
I SL	10 Rmte 5 DBR LW	Washington	Cleveland	From 539 Harrisburg	399

* Will NOT operate November 27, 28, December 25, 26, 31, January 1, 2

Harry Stegmaier Collection

Pennsylvania Railroad prewar 10 roomette, 5 double bedroom sleeper *Cascade Cliff*, was typical of the *Cascade* series cars assigned on a regular basis as lightweight sleepers to *The Clevelander*. These prewar lightweight cars were delivered to the Pennsylvania Railroad by Pullman Standard in June and July of 1940. *Cascade Cliff* lasted on the railroad until 1967 and then entered a varied career, first with the United States Army and then with Amtrak before being retired in 1975 and sold to the Golden Arrow Lines, where it was painted in New York Central colors and, as far as can be discerned, is still in existence today in operating condition. In this photo, the car is seen at San Francisco, California in September, 1963 while in charter service.

Bob's Photo

Another group of prewar cars assigned to No. 38 and No. 39, *The Clevelander*, were the 6 double bedroom, buffet lounge cars in the *Falls* series which the Pullman Company delivered to the Pennsylvania Railroad in the fall of 1940. *Pine Falls* contained a bar lounge, along with its 6 double bedrooms and thus provided the Pullman patrons on *The Clevelander* with bar service. *Pine Falls* is seen here at Montauk, Long Island, in June, 1969, still in its original Pennsylvania Railroad colors. The Long Island Railroad purchased these cars from the Pennsylvania Railroad for their parlor car trains to the Long Island resorts. *Pine Falls* was renamed *Pequott* and served the Long Island until its retirement in 1976.

page 7, somewhat limited for the 8:25 p.m. eastbound departure with an arrival in New York the next morning at 8:10.

The Clevelander, No. 38 eastbound and No. 39, westbound survived longer than some of Pennsylvania Railroad's other Blue Ribbon trains, as their better trains were designated on the main east-west route. The westbound *Clevelander* was finally combined with *The General* as far as Pittsburgh in June 1961, although the old schedule of No. 39 was protected by a coach-sleeper train from 1961 to 1964 between Philadelphia and Pittsburgh because the Pennsylvania Railroad had not obtained permission from the Public Utilities Commission to discontinue the train. In April of 1964, *The Clevelander* was finally terminated as a through train. Eastbound No. 38 had been combined with *The General* east of Pittsburgh since June, 1961 and it too died in April, 1964 ending all through Pennsylvania service on the New York to Cleveland route.

No. 48 and 49
THE GENERAL

The General was really, for all practical purposes, really an advance section of *The Broadway Limited*, somewhat akin to New York Central's *Commodore Vanderbilt*. *The General* handled, as can be seen from the consist sheets, some mail and express as well as passenger cars, both sleepers and coaches. Actually, the train had been an all Pullman train until it was combined with *The Trailblazer* but this book wishes to treat the train as a separate train from *The Trailblazer* because, between December 12 and January 20, *The General* ran between New York and Chicago as an all

Train 48
Blue Ribbon
The General

Consist—September 28th-December 12th, Inclusive AND January 21st-April 25th, inclusive

Car Type	Description		From	To	Details	Car Des
I MS-60	X-29 Wednesday LIFE		Chicago	Philadelphia	To 600 Harrisburg	
I MS-60	(X)		Chicago	P.C.C.	SW	
I B-60	Baggage Sealed		Chicago	New York	SW	
I SL	14 Section		¢Chicago	New York	SW	487
I SL	21 Roomette		Chicago	New York	LW	486
I SL	12 Duplex SR 4 DBR		Chicago	New York	LW	485
I SL	10 Roomette 6 DBR		#Chicago	New York	LW	484
I SL-Lge	6 DBR Bar		Chicago	New York	LW	
I Diner	)Twin Unit		Chicago	New York	LW	
I Kitchen-Dormitory	)Twin Unit					
I P-85BR	Reclining Seats		%Chicago	New York	LW	4
I P-85BR	Reclining Seats		%Chicago	New York	LW	3
I P-85BR	Reclining Seats		%Chicago	New York	LW	2
I POC85R	Observation-Buffet-Lounge		%Chicago	New York	LW	

Consist—December 13th-January 20th, Inclusive
Pullman Section (Will NOT operate December 25th)

Car Type	Description		From	To	Details	Car Des
I MS-60	X-29 Wednesday LIFE		Chicago	Philadelphia	To 600 Harrisburg	
I MS-60	(X)		Chicago	P.C.C.	SW	
I B-60	Baggage Sealed		Chicago	New York	SW	
I SL	14 Section		¢Chicago	New York	SW	487
I SL	21 Roomette		Chicago	New York	LW	486
I SL	12 Duplex SR 4 DBR		Chicago	New York	LW	485
I SL	10 Roomette 6 DBR		Chicago	New York	LW	484
I SL-Lge	6 DBR Bar		Chicago	New York	LW	483
I Diner	)Twin Unit		Chicago	New York	LW	
I Kitchen-Dormitory	)Twin Unit					
I SL	10 Roomette 6 DBR		Chicago	New York	LW	484
I SL	21 Roomette		Chicago	New York	LW	482
I SL	21 Roomette		Chicago	New York	LW	481
SL	Extra (X)		Chicago	New York		
I POC85R	Observation-Buffet-Lounge		%Chicago	New York	LW	

Coach Section

Car Type	Description		From	To	Details	Car Des
I PLB85	Baggage-Lounge. Sealed		Chicago	New York		
I P-85BR	(X) Reclining Seats		%Chicago	New York		
I P-85BR	Reclining Seats		*%Chicago	New York		8
I P-85BR	Reclining Seats		*%Chicago	New York		7
I P-85BR	Reclining Seats		*%Chicago	New York		6
I P-85BR	Reclining Seats		%Chicago	New York	Will not operate Dec. 25th	5
I P-85BR	Reclining Seats		%Chicago	New York		4
I Diner	)Twin Unit		Chicago	New York	LW	
I Kitchen-Dormitory	)Twin Unit					
I P-85BR	Reclining Seats		%Chicago	New York		3
I P-85BR	Reclining Seats		%Chicago	New York		2
I P-85BR	Reclining Seats		%Chicago	New York		1

* Will run December 18th-January 4th, Inclusive, except December 25th

Pullman train westbound consisting of headend cars, postwar lightweight sleepers, a twin-unit diner, a postwar *Falls* car with 6 double bedrooms and a bar, as well as a Pullman heavyweight betterment car with high-speed trucks containing 14 sections. This car was necessary to handle government traffic since the U. S. government would not pay more than the cost of a lower berth for people traveling on government business. Therefore, *The General* carried a 14 section sleeping car along with its lightweight, mostly postwar equipment. In addition, the prewar *Broadway Limited* cars, the bobtail observation cars, *Skyline View* and *Metropolitan View*, which contained two spacious master rooms with showers, a double bedroom and a bar-lounge as well as an observation, brought up the rear. The last assignment for these cars on a regular basis was on No. 48 and No. 49 during the

holiday travel seasons of 1952 and 1953 when it was not combined with *The Trail Blazer*. When combined with *The Trail Blazer*, the sleeping cars were run in the forward part of the train, with the twin unit diner in the middle and the *Trail Blazer's* coaches and observation-buffet-lounge coach bringing up the rear. Westbound No. 49 also handled the New York to Los Angeles sleeping car that was carried west of Chicago on the C&NW-Union Pacific's *Los Angeles Limited*. Eastbound, *The General* did not carry any transcontinental sleeping cars.

As an advanced section of *The Broadway Limited, The General* in both directions usually preceded *The Broadway Limited* by about an hour westbound and an hour and a half eastbound and made a number of extra stops that its more prestigious counterpart missed. Nevertheless, *The*

Train No. 49
Blue Ribbon
The General

Consist—September 28th-December 11th and January 21st-April 25th, Inclusive

Car Type	Description	From	To	Details	Car Des
I MS-60	(X)	New York	Council Bluffs	SW To CB&Q Chicago	
I MS-60	(X)	New York	Chicago	SW	
I B-60	Baggage Sealed	New York	Chicago	SW	
I SL	10 Roomette 6 DBR	*New York	Chicago	SW	PA5
I SL	14 Section	¢New York	Chicago	LW	494
I SL	21 Roomette	New York	Chicago	LW	493
I SL	12 Duplex SR 4 DBR	New York	Chicago	LW	492
I SL	10 Roomette 6 DBR	#New York	Chicago	LW	491
I SL-Lounge	6 DBR Bar	New York	Chicago	LW	490
I Diner	)Twin Unit				
I Kitchen-Dormitory)Twin Unit		New York	Chicago	LW	
I P-85BR	Reclining Seats	%New York	Chicago	LW	773
I P-85BR	Reclining Seats	%New York	Chicago	LW	774
I P-85BR	Reclining Seats	%New York	Chicago	LW	775
I P-85BR	Reclining Seats	%New York	Chicago	LW	775
I POC85AR	Observation-Buffet-Lounge	%New York	Chicago	LW	

Consist—December 12th-January 20th, Inclusive (Will NOT operate December 25th)

Car Type	Description	From	To	Details	Car Des
I MS-60	(X)	New York	Council Bluffs	SW To CB&Q Chicago	
I MS-60	(X)	New York	Chicago	SW	
I B-60	Baggage Sealed	New York	Chicago	SW	
I SL	10 Roomette 6 DBR	*New York	Chicago	SW	PA5
I SL	14 Section	¢New York	Chicago	LW	494
I SL	21 Roomette	New York	Chicago	LW	492
I SL-Lounge	6 DBR Bar	New York	Chicago	LW	490
I Diner	)Twin Unit				
I Kitchen-Dormitory)Twin Unit		New York	Chicago	LW	
I SL	10 Roomette 6 DBR	New York	Chicago	LW	491
I SL	21 Roomette	New York	Chicago	LW	479
I SL	21 Roomette	New York	Chicago	LW	478
SL	Extra (X)	New York	Chicago		
I SL-Obs	2 MR I DBR Bar-Lounge	New York	Chicago	LW	477

* To C&NW I leaving Chicago 12:01 p.m.

Both: Al Chione

No. 48 and 49, *The General*, was assigned a twin unit dining car which was certainly needed, since the train had been combined with *The Trail Blazer*, except for the period from December 12 to January 20 during the heavy Christmas holiday travel season. In these two photos, full dining car No. 4594 and kitchen-dormitory car No. 4595 are seen at Chicago in June of 1963. No. 4594 and 4595 differed from the Budd built diners usually found on *The Broadway Limited* in that they were built by the Pennsylvania Railroad's Altoona Car Shops in the fall of 1948. The company built cars were often found assigned to *The General*, even during the holiday travel season when it was separated from *The Trail Blazer*, and ran as a separate train. Plenty of dining car space was needed for the additional sleeping car patrons that crowded aboard at the Christmas season and rode the extra sleepers that were attached to the train.

Harry Stegmaier

The westbound *General* carried the through New York to Los Angeles sleeping car handled by the Pennsylvania Railroad as far as Chicago and then on the C&NW-Union Pacific *Los Angeles Limited* west of the windy city to Los Angeles. This 10 roomette, 6 double bedroom sleeper seen here is Union Pacific *Pacific Gardens*, which was regularly assigned in the pool arrangement for the New York-Los Angeles car that operated on the Union Pacific route to Los Angeles. One could leave New York on Sunday evening on *The General* and arrive Wednesday morning in Los Angeles without a change of cars in Chicago. *Pacific Gardens* was built by the Budd Company and delivered to the Union Pacific in early 1950. Almost all of these fine and well maintained cars were purchased by Amtrak They continued to serve Amtrak even into the 1990s on such trains as *The Capitol Limited* until those trains could be equipped with superliner cars. Here, in this photo, *Pacific Gardens* is seen at Chicago in September, 1969 and has had Pullman removed from its letterboard since the Union Pacific was now operating its own sleeping car service.

Harry Stegmaier Collection

No. 48 and No. 49, *The General*, carried a 6 double bedroom buffet lounge car in its consist next to the twin unit diner, both when it was combined with *The Trail Blazer* and during the Christmas season when it ran as a separate train. *Catalpa Falls*, seen here at Chicago on July 19, 1963, was part of the postwar order of eleven cars built by Pullman Standard and delivered to the Pennsylvania Railroad in the spring of 1949. These versatile cars lasted into the Penn Central era. *Catalpa Falls* was not retired until 1971 when Amtrak took over operations and could be found on *The General* until Amtrak day. It was then sold to George and Marsha Payne and today can be found leased out to and operating on a dinner train at York, Pennsylvania.

The prewar *Broadway Limited* received two of the four special observation cars built by Pullman Standard for that train as well as *The Liberty Limited*. The four pre-war *View* cars contained two master rooms, one double bedroom as well as a buffet lounge and round end observation. As such, they differed from the postwar *Tower View* and *Mountain View* which had a square end. The last permanent assignment for these Pullman Standard built cars that arrived on the company property in May, 1938, was on *The General* during the 1952 and 1953 Christmas seasons when it was decombined from *The Trail Blazer* and operated as a separate train. *Skyline View* and *Metropolitan View* were the two cars that were assigned to the prewar *Broadway Limited* and, after the war, were transferred to *The General*. After serving on *The General* through the Christmas season of 1953-54, *Skyline View* was put into special service and, in 1957, was renumbered and used as a parlor car on New York-Washington corridor trains until it was retired in 1961 and sold to Mac Lowry for his museum at Cuyahoga Falls, Ohio. This photograph shows the car on June 2, 1970 in Cuyahoga Falls. *Skyline View* still looks to be in pretty fine condition, considering that it is over 30 years old by the time this photo was taken and had been in storage, by this time, for over nine years at the museum. However, this was not the end of *Skyline View*. One can still find it today, although with one of its sides cut out, as part of the Quaker Square Hilton Hotel Complex in Akron, Ohio.

The General regularly received a 12 duplex single room, 4 double bedroom sleeper on its New York to Chicago route. These postwar 12 duplex single room, 4 double bedroom cars were built by Pullman Standard and received by the Pennsylvania Railroad in the early part of 1949. *Cherry Creek*, seen here, was regularly assigned to *The General* in the 1950s. Cars like *Cherry Creek* of the postwar variety differed from the prewar 12 duplex single room, 5 double bedroom cars in that the bedrooms had wide windows and also enclosed toilet facilities which the prewar *Brook* series cars did not have. *Cherry Creek* was finally retired in 1968 and eventually sold to Judge Hofheinz for his motel complex near the Astrodome which never was built, with most of the cars he purchased, including the *Cherry Creek*, being scrapped.

General, which had been established by the Pennsylvania Railroad back in 1937, was a fast, luxury train with a convenient 5:00 p.m. departure from New York and an arrival in Chicago the next morning at 8:20, only twenty minutes slower than the prestigious *Broadway Limited*. Eastbound No. 48 departed at 3 p.m. from Chicago and arrived at 8:25 the next morning, making the run in only 25 minutes more than No. 28. *The General* would carry on as the premier train of the Pennsylvania and later of the Penn Central after the discontinuance of *The Broadway Limited* on December 12, 1967. However, the name had been changed to *The Broadway Limited* upon the discontinuance of that train, although it was really *The General* with its old numbers from late 1967 on, much as was the case of *The Pennsylvania Limited*.

No. 54 and No. 55
THE GOTHAM LIMITED

The Gotham Limited was the Pennsylvania Railroad's late night departure entry in the east-west fleet, with both No. 54 departing Chicago and No. 55 departing New York very late at night as the last trains east and west, respectively. The westbound train served as an overnight New York-Pittsburgh train, while the eastbound train served as an overnight Chicago-Pittsburgh run, covering the remainder of their journeys in daylight, with both trains arriving at their terminals in Chicago and New York, respectively, in the late afternoon of the following day. Once one of Pennsylvania Railroad's better trains, and still part of the Blue Ribbon fleet, *The Gotham Limited* of 1952 was, nevertheless, primarily a train with a lot of head-

Both: Harry Stegmaier Collection

The Gotham Limited was, as has been mentioned in the text, a train that carried a good deal of headend equipment in its consist. Baggage car No. 9392, seen here, is typical of the Pennsylvania Railroad type baggage cars of the B60 class which populated a good deal of *The Gotham Limited* in the early 1950s. The car is, in this photograph, in Boston, Massachusetts and a good example of the headend equipment handled by No. 54 and No. 55.

The Gotham Limited also carried two RPO cars westbound in its consist, as well as one eastbound. RPO-Baggage car No. 6566, seen here in Louisville, Kentucky, was often found on trains like *The Gotham Limited* in the 1950s. These BM70M cars had a 60-foot mail compartment and a 10-foot baggage compartment. *The Gotham Limited* probably sorted a great deal of mail in its RPO cars during its career on the Pennsylvania Railroad.

Train No. 54
Blue Ribbon
Gotham Limited

Consist—DE, Saturday and November 27, 28, December 25, 26, 31, January 1, 2

Car Type	Description	From	To	Details	Car Des
Express	Perishable (X)	Chicago	Harrisburg and Gateway	From 62 Pittsburgh	
Express	Perishable (X)	Chicago	Hudson Cut Off	From 62 Pittsburgh	
Express	Perishable (X)	Chicago	Philadelphia	To 72 Pittsburgh	
1 Express	B-60	Chicago	Philadelphia	To 72 Pittsburgh	
1 Express	B-60 DE Saturday, Sunday, and Monday	Chicago	Hartford	To 96 Pittsburgh	
1 Express	X-29 Tuesday LIFE	Chicago	New London	To 96 Pittsburgh	
1 Express	B-60	Chicago	Boston	To 96 (Monday and Days after Holiday) Pittsburgh	
1 MS-60	(X)	Pittsburgh	New York		
1 BM70M	DE Monday	Pittsburgh	New York		
1 B-60		Chicago	New York		
1 P-70GSR	Reclining Seat Friday and Sunday	%Chicago	New York		
3 P-85BR	Reclining Seats	%Chicago	New York		
1 Diner		Chicago	New York		
1 SL-Lounge	5 DBR, Bar	Chicago	New York	LW	545
1 SL	21 Roomette	Chicago	New York	LW	544
1 SL	12-1	Chicago	New York	LW	543
1 SL	8 Section, 1 DR, 2 compartment	Chicago	Washington	To 554 Harrisburg	541
1 SL	6 Section, 6 DBR	Chicago	Pittsburgh		540
1 Milk	R-50 (X)	Kendallville	So. Edmeston	From Frt, Fort Wayne, To 96 Pittsburgh	
1 Milk	R-50 (X)	Berne	So. Edmeston	From PH-3 Fort Wayne, To 96 Pittsburgh	

Train No. 55
Blue Ribbon
Gotham Limited

Car Type	Description	From	To	Details	Car Des
1 MS-60	(X)	Baltimore	Chicago	From 535 Harrisburg	
1 MS-60		New York	Council Bluffs	To CB&Q Chicago	
1 MS-60	(X)	New York	St. Paul	To CMStP&P Chicago	
1 MS-60		New York	Chicago		
1 MS-60	DE Sunday	New York	Chicago	Registered Mails	
1 MS-60	Open DE Sunday	New York	Chicago		
1 BM70M	DE Sunday	New York	Chicago	Letter End West	
1 BM-70	30 ft apartment, DE Saturday & Sunday	*New York	Chicago	Letter End East	
1 MS-60	DE Sunday, Monday & Days after Holiday	Providence	Chicago	From 183 New York	
1 B-60	Saturday and Sunday	New York	Chicago		
1 P-70GSR	Reclining Seats, Friday, Saturday, Sunday	%New York	Chicago		
3 P-85BR	Reclining Seats	%New York	Chicago		
1 Diner		New York	Chicago		
1 SL-Lounge	5 DBR, Bar	New York	Chicago	LW	550
1 SL	21 Roomette	New York	Chicago	LW	551
1 SL	12-1	New York	Chicago		552
1 SL	8 Section, 1 DR, 2 Compartment	Washington	Chicago	From 535 Harrisburg	556

* RPO NOT in service New York-Pittsburgh.
Use baggage apartment for baggage.

Tom Hoffman, Harry Stegmaier Collection

As well as carrying three of the postwar P85BR coaches, *The Gotham Limited*, in both directions, also received one of Pennsylvania's Altoona car shop built P70GSR coaches on Fridays, Saturdays, and Sundays. However, when the P85BR coaches were in short supply, it was not unusual to find them replaced by P70GSR coaches on less important trains like *The Gotham Limited*. Altoona had rebuilt the P70GSR coaches from P70 coaches in the period before World War II. P70GSR coaches, like No. 4336 were rebuilt with reclining seats and air conditioning in the summer of 1939. A later group of P70GSR coaches had wide windows but this first group, like No. 4336, which is seen here on a special train in October, 1967 at Madison, Wisconsin, were not given wide windows. It was not unusual to regularly find cars like this on trains like *The Gotham Limited*. While not spectacular cars, they were certainly comfortable and at least gave the traveling public reclining seats in their journey on the Pennsylvania Railroad.

Harry Stegmaier

The Gotham Limited received heavyweight, rebuilt dining cars like No. 4476. The Pennsylvania Railroad had begun a massive modernization program of its dining car fleet in 1950. All of the work was done by the Altoona Car Shops. The idea behind the modernization program was to take the old D78R heavyweight dining cars, most of which had been built in the World War I era or in the 1920s, and streamline these cars both inside and out, turning them into dining cars with small lounge sections in each. When the project was finally completed the Pennsylvania Railroad had modernized 36 of the older dining cars, 34 into dining-lounge cars and two into coffee shop-tavern cars. These D78 class rebuilds became the backbone of the Pennsylvania Railroad dining car fleet in the 1950s and 1960s. Not all the cars were modernized in the same fashion, with some keeping their clerestory roofs while the majority received round, modernized roofs. In addition, seating capacities differed, depending on whether the cars had a "short lounge" or "long lounge" to use Pennsylvania Railroad terminology. After rebuilding, Number 4476, created out of a D78 dining car built in 1913, was classed D78fR with a modernized round roof. The D78fR class cars differed only in their interior because they had a larger kitchen but no pantry. No. 4476 was considered a "short lounge" car and seated 32 in the dining section and 10 in the lounge. This car would be the type that would have served breakfast and lunch on both No. 54 and No. 55. Because of its late night departures, the train did not serve dinner. On April 18, 1970, Pennsylvania Railroad dining car No. 4476 was seen on the scrap line at Altoona, Pennsylvania. These tank-like, heavyweight, rebuilt cars were common on Pennsylvania Railroad's secondary trains on the main line like *The Gotham Limited*.

Harry Stegmaier

12 section, 1 drawing room, Pullman sleeping cars like *Hess*, seen here on a Boy Scout special at Colorado Springs, Colorado in the early 1960s, were typical of the kinds of heavyweight Pullman equipment assigned to No. 54 and No. 55 in the early 1950s. While these cars provided plenty of section space, the train was short on room space, especially for two person accommodations. Cars like *Hess* lasted for quite a long period on the Pennsylvania Railroad, usually in special service. *Hess* was not retired until the early 1960s when it was converted to a maintenance of way car after sitting on the reclamation line for almost five years.

Harry Stegmaier

The prewar *Broadway Limited* midtrain lounge cars were regularly assigned to *The Gotham Limited* by 1952. Cars *Harbor Point* and *Harbor Springs* had been built by Pullman Standard and delivered to the railroad in May, 1938, containing 2 double bedrooms and a bar-lounge plus a secretary's room, barber shop and shower bath. They were quite modern for their day. However, the Pennsylvania Railroad rebuilt these two *Harbor* cars to contain 5 double bedrooms, replacing the luxury accommodation rooms with extra bedrooms. These cars were then assigned to other Pennsylvania Railroad trains after the re-equipping of *The Broadway Limited* after World War II, although they were converted during World War II, in April 1943, since things like shower baths and train secretaries were prohibited by wartime regulations. Initially, *Harbor Point* and *Harbor Springs* were assigned to *The Iron City Express*, but by 1952 were regulars on *The Gotham Limited* and stayed on that train for quite some time in the early and mid 1950s, although they were briefly transferred to *The Admiral* during that same time period. The cars were found to be excess by the Pennsylvania Railroad as it cut back passenger services and, thus, the 5 double bedroom, bar-lounge cars, *Harbor Point* and *Harbor Springs*, were sold by the company in 1964. *Harbor Springs* went to a private party in South Dakota, Mr. Wayne Kerslake, while *Harbor Point* is seen here, in this photograph, taken in July, 1968 in Guadalajara, Mexico. It was sold to the Ferrocarrilles Del Pacifico and named *Presa El Sabinito*, serving on trains like *El Costeno* and *El Mexicali* between Nogales and Guadalajara. The author found this car in Guadalajara in July, 1968, still in service thirty years after its delivery to the Pennsylvania Railroad.

end cars in both directions, with the westbound handling two RPO cars west of Pittsburgh, and the eastbound handling an RPO on the Pittsburgh-New York portion of its run. Passengers were accommodated in reclining seat coaches of various types, since the three P85BR cars that were to be assigned were often on other trains. If these cars were shopped, it was often No. 54 and No. 55 that got lesser coaches such as P70GSR's or P70KR coaches. Each train carried a heavyweight diner and lounge space was provided by the prewar *Broadway Limited* lightweight cars, *Harbor Point* and *Harbor Springs*, which had five double bedrooms, after being rebuilt from two double bedroom cars after World War II, and having the amenities such as the shower and the barbershop removed. In addition, each train carried a 21 roomette lightweight sleeper and a heavyweight 12 section, 1 drawing room car as well as an 8 section, 2 compartment, 1 drawing room sleeper between Washington and Chicago which the trains picked up and dropped at Harrisburg, respectively. These Washington cars were provided in order to give Washingtonians a late-night departure from the nation's capital or from

Chicago. *The Gotham Limited* was, therefore, by 1952 a mail and express train on a slower schedule than many of its New York-Chicago counterparts, with each train making numerous stops during the daylight portion of their runs. *The Gotham Limited* did provide a necessary late night service from both New York and Chicago as is evidenced by the fact that the train lasted until the coming of Amtrak in May, 1971. Most people would argue that the train was discontinued in April, 1956 but that is not true. No. 54 and No. 55 kept their numbers right down to Amtrak and operated on the same late night departure schedules from their terminals, although in 1956 when *The Pennsylvania Limited* was discontinued, the railroad saw fit to transfer that prestigious name to No. 54 and No. 55 and eliminate *The Gotham Limited* name. By the late 1960s it was just a few headend cars, a couple of coaches and a snack bar-coach. However, eastbound No. 54 carried a 10 roomette, 6 double bedroom sleeper through from Chicago to New York right down to May, 1971. This car was primarily provided to accommodate passengers from western connections which had arrived too late for them to ride the then-named

William P. Price, Harry Stegmaier Collection

In this fairly rare photograph, the rear of *The Gotham Limited* is brought up in the summer of 1951 by an ancient sleeping car built in October, 1927 for *The Colorado Limited*. Here in this photo, *Denver* brings up the rear of train No. 54 on Horseshoe Curve. These were fancy cars when built, containing 1 compartment, 1 drawing room and a large lounge area with a solarium in the rear and high windows. *Denver* later was bought by the Pennsylvania Railroad and, on this particular day, it was probably substituting for the regular lounge car which was not available due to mechanical problems. Ancient cars like *Denver* only lasted on the Pennsylvania Railroad for a short period after this photo was taken and it was finally dismantled at Altoona on September 24, 1952.

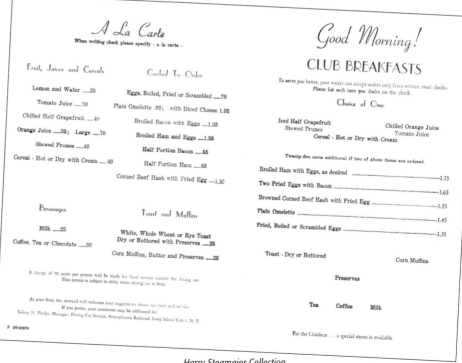

A La Carte
When writing check please specify - a la carte -

Fruit, Juices and Cereals

Lemon and Water __.20

Tomato Juice __.30

Chilled Half Grapefruit __.40

Orange Juice __.35; Large __.70

Stewed Prunes __.40

Cereal - Hot or Dry with Cream __.40

Cooked To Order

Eggs, Boiled, Fried or Scrambled __.70

Plain Omelette .80; with Diced Cheese 1.05

Broiled Bacon with Eggs __1.25

Broiled Ham and Eggs __1.35

Half Portion Bacon __.55

Half Portion Ham __.65

Corned Beef Hash with Fried Egg __1.30

Beverages

Milk __.25

Coffee, Tea or Chocolate __.30

Toast and Muffins

White, Whole Wheat or Rye Toast
Dry or Buttered with Preserves __.25

Corn Muffins, Butter and Preserves __.25

*A charge of 50 cents per person will be made for food service outside the dining car.
This service is subject to delay when dining car is busy.*

*As your host, the steward will welcome your suggestions about our food and service.
If you prefer, your comments may be addressed to:
Sidney N. Phelps, Manager, Dining Car Service, Pennsylvania Railroad, Long Island City 1, N. Y.*

F 5/9-6/4/52

Good Morning!

CLUB BREAKFASTS

*To serve you better, your waiter can accept orders only from written meal checks.
Please list each item you desire on the check.*

Choice of One:

Iced Half Grapefruit   Chilled Orange Juice
Stewed Prunes   Tomato Juice
              Cereal - Hot or Dry with Cream

Twenty-five cents additional if two of above items are ordered.

Broiled Ham with Eggs, as desired _____1.75

Two Fried Eggs with Bacon _____1.65

Browned Corned Beef Hash with Fried Egg _____1.55

Plain Omelette _____1.45

Fried, Boiled or Scrambled Eggs _____1.35

Toast - Dry or Buttered   Corn Muffins

Preserves

Tea   Coffee   Milk

For the Children . . . a special menu is available.

Harry Stegmaier Collection

The Gotham Limited, because of its late departures for both New York and Chicago, did not serve dinner but its dining car with lounge provided both breakfast and luncheon. Pennsylvania Railroad Commissary records show that trains like *The Gotham Limited* received what were known as "field menus." These were generally issued systemwide for about a month at a time and were given to blue ribbon and other trains that did not rank at the top of the scale in Pennsylvania Railroad's hierarchy of luxury. *The Gotham Limited*, being a secondary train, had a field menu such as this club breakfast menu from the summer of 1952, although no one could complain, given the wide selection of items that were available. Surely No. 54 and No. 55 left any patron hungry.

Broadway Limited, really *The General*. Because of its schedule, *The Gotham Limited* served a vital role during hours of day and night when other trains on the through New York-Chicago route did not operate. It might be added here that *The Gotham Limited* of the 1950s often had lesser equipment substituted for its usually assigned cars whenever they were needed for other more important trains and so lowly No. 54 and No. 55 got the short end of the deal.

No. 58 and 59
THE LIBERTY LIMITED

The Liberty Limited was Pennsylvania Railroad's attempt to compete with the Baltimore & Ohio in the Washington to Chicago market and, as such, it often received outstanding equipment. However, this was quite a difficult task since most of the government community as well as Washington and Baltimore area residents preferred the Baltimore & Ohio with its courtesy, service and the superb dining car meals which the B&O lavishly provided and could not be found on the Pennsylvania Railroad. *The Liberty Limited* was an overnight train between Washington and Chicago in both directions and since it was in direct competition with Baltimore & Ohio's overnight *Capitol Limited* as well as the new streamlined, all coach *Columbian*, the Pennsylvania Railroad tried to give the train the best equipment that it could find. This was proven by the fact that even before *The Broadway Limited* received a lightweight diner in the pre-World War II era, *The Liberty Limited* got one of the Budd lightweight diners in each direction. No. 58 and No. 59 carried modern reclining seat coaches, with the coach passengers served by a baggage-lounge car with a bar. As for sleeping cars, the train carried, because of its routing, two 14 section sleeping cars, modernized heavyweights with high speed trucks, to handle U.S. government traffic. These were modernized Pullmans and the train needed the section space because the government only reimbursed for lower berth space, at that time, for its employees. In addition to the 14 section cars, it carried a group of lightweight sleepers, a 21 roomette car, an 4-4-2 *Imperial* postwar car, a 12 duplex single room, 4 double bedroom car and a 6 double bedroom bar-lounge car in the *Falls* series as well as a 2 drawing room, 1 compartment, 1 double bedroom-observation-bar-lounge car which carried *The Liberty Limited* drumhead. Meals were provided by one of the Pennsylvania Railroad's twin unit full diner-kitchen-dormitory cars. *The Liberty Limited* was a mostly lightweight train with plenty of amenities. It was fast, it had modern equipment and a good schedule overnight between Washington and Chicago in both directions but, all this having been said, the Pennsylvania Railroad simply could not compete with the service, fine meals and the new lightweight equipment which the Baltimore & Ohio was acquiring, primarily secondhand.

Train No. 58
Blue Ribbon
Liberty Limited

Car Type	Description	From	To	Details	Car Des
1 PLB85	Baggage, Lounge, Bar	Chicago	Washington		
1 P-85BR	Reclining Seats	%Chicago	Washington		5811
1 P-85BR	Reclining Seats	%Chicago	Washington		5810
1 SL	14 Section	¢Chicago	Washington	SW	587
1 SL	14 Section DE Saturday	*¢Chicago	Washington	SW	586
1 SL	21 Roomette, DE Friday and Saturday	x¢Chicago	Washington	LW	585
1 SL-Lounge	6 DBR, Bar	#Chicago	Washington	LW	584
1 Diner	)Twin Unit	Chicago	Washington	LW	
1 Kitchen-Dormitory	)Twin Unit				
1 SL	4 Compartment, 4 DBR, 2 DR	Chicago	Washington	LW	583
1 SL	12 Duplex SR, 4 DBR	Chicago	Washington	LW	582
1 SL	21 Roomette	Chicago	Washington	LW	581
1 SL-Obs	2 DR, 1 Cpt, 1 DBR, Bar-Lounge	#Chicago	Washington	LW	580

* First trip on advice. Will NOT operate November 27, 28, December 24, 25, 26, January 1, 2
x First trip on advice. Will NOT operate November 27, December 24, 25, 31, January 1
Coach seats reserved

PENNSYLVANIA RAILROAD

Combinations and A La Carte

CHEESE OR CREOLE OMELETTE
Buttered Peas   Parsley Potatoes
Bread and Butter
Choice of Dessert
Tea   Coffee   Milk
$1.75

Cup of Soup
GRILLED CHOPPED SIRLOIN STEAK
Buttered Peas   Mashed Potatoes
Bread and Butter
Choice of Dessert
Tea   Coffee   Milk
$2.50

PRR SALAD BOWL WITH RY-KRISP .95
(Lettuce-Tomatoes-Scallions-Cucumbers-Radishes-Celery-Bleu Cheese-French Dressing)

Cream of Mushroom Soup with Crackers, Cup .30
Chilled Tomato Juice .30

Hearts of Lettuce, French Dressing

Sliced Chicken Sandwich with Lettuce,
Tomato Slices and Pickle Chips 1.25

Freshly Baked Apple Pie .35
Pear Helene .40   Caramel Custard .40
Butter Pecan or Vanilla Ice Cream .40
Gruyere or Bleu Cheese with Crackers .45

Pot of Coffee .40   Pot of Tea .30
Individual Milk .25   Sanka .35

MEAL CHECKS—Please write on check each item desired. Waiter is not permitted to accept oral orders.

ROOM SERVICE—A charge of 50 cents per person will be made for food service outside the dining car. This service is subject to delay when dining car is busy.

The steward will welcome your comments on our food and service.
If you prefer, write to Sidney N. Phelps, Manager,
Dining Car Service, Pennsylvania Railroad, Long Island City 1, N.Y.

Liberty Limited

DINNER

PRICE OF ENTREE INCLUDES COMPLETE MEAL

CHOICE OF ONE

Chilled Tomato Juice
Clear Consomme   Cream of Mushroom Soup
                                            Fresh Fruit Cup

GRILLED SWORDFISH STEAK, HOTELIER
Parsley Potatoes   Buttered Lima Beans   3.10

BAKED SUGAR CURED HAM, MADEIRA SAUCE
Buttered Broccoli   Mashed Potatoes   3.25

ROAST YOUNG CHICKEN, DRESSING, CRANBERRY SAUCE
Buttered Kernel Corn   Mashed Potatoes   3.25

CHARCOAL GRILLED SIRLOIN STEAK, MAITRE D'HOTEL
French Fried Onion Rings   Long Branch Potatoes   5.10

Hearts of Lettuce with Russian Dressing

Muffins

CHOICE OF ONE

                    Pear Helene   Freshly Baked Apple Pie   Caramel Custard
Gruyere or Bleu Cheese with Crackers   Vanilla or Butter Pecan Ice Cream

CHOICE OF ONE

Individual Milk   Pot of Tea
Pot of Coffee   Sanka

Mints

BEVERAGE SERVICE OFFERING ON OTHER SIDE   18-K-5

Harry Stegmaier Collection

The twin unit dining cars on *The Liberty Limited* provided a wide variety of meals as can be seen from this menu from the 1950s. The dinners included swordfish steak and sirloin steak plus some specials. While *The Liberty Limited* certainly left none of its patrons hungry, its menu in comparison to the rival Baltimore & Ohio menus on *The Capitol Limited* and *The Columbian*, was rather sparse and some of the very fine B&O dishes served is what attracted much of the patronage to that road. By the mid 1950s, Baltimore & Ohio, between Washington and Chicago had driven the nail into the coffin of trains like *The Liberty Limited*. However, *The Liberty Limited* was no slouch as far as the Pennsylvania Railroad was concerned and, thus, it received some of the railroad's better equipment.

B&O courtesy and service made *The Capitol Limited* the choice of people from Baltimore and Washington and the coach passenger usually chose *The Columbian* on rival B&O. Thus, *The Liberty Limited*, even though it tried to compete with the B&O, could not. In a sense, the train was already living on borrowed time in 1952 and, after the war in Korea ended and travel dropped off, *The Liberty Limited* would suffer a sudden decline. In April, 1956, *The Liberty Limited* lost its observation car and some of its sleeping cars and, in fact, for a short time, became a New York to Chicago train on the old schedule of No. 1 and No. 2, *The Pennsylvania Limited*, as far as Harrisburg where

Train No. 59
Blue Ribbon
Liberty Limited

Car Type	Description	From	To	Details	Car Des
I PLB85	Baggage, Lounge, Bar	Washington	Chicago		
I P-85BR	Reclining Seats	%Washington	Chicago		5911
I P-85BR	Reclining Seats	%Washington	Chicago		5910
I SL	14 Section	¢Washington	Chicago	SW	597
I SL	14 Section DE Saturday	*¢Washington	Chicago	SW	596
I SL	21 Roomette, DE Friday and Saturday	xWashington	Chicago	LW	595
I SL-Lounge	6 DBR, Bar	#Washington	Chicago	LW	594
I Diner	)Twin Unit	Washington	Chicago	LW	
I Kitchen-Dormitory	)Twin Unit				
I SL	4 Compartment, 4 DBR, 2 DR	Washington	Chicago	LW	593
I SL	12 Duplex SR, 4 DBR	Washington	Chicago	LW	592
I SL	21 Roomette	Washington	Chicago	LW	591
I SL-Obs	2 DR, I Cpt, I DBR, Bar-Lounge	#Washington	Chicago	LW	590

* First trip on advice. Will NOT operate November 27, 28, December 24, 25, 26, 31 January 1, 2
x First trip on advice. Will NOT operate November 28, December 24, 26, 31, January 2
Coach seats reserved

Mark Hildebrandt

The Liberty Limited, as Pennsylvania Railroad's main competition for the Baltimore & Ohio between Washington, Baltimore and Chicago, received some of the finest equipment on the Pennsylvania Railroad and this included a twin unit diner. Twin unit cars like No. 4616 and 4617, built by the Budd Company for the Pennsylvania Railroad in the postwar period, often could be found on *The Liberty Limited*. The cars were delivered in July, 1949 as twin unit cars, one car containing a full dining room and the other car providing the kitchen and dormitory space for the crew. 4616 and 4617 were photographed in Philadelphia in May, 1969 when they had been assigned to Nos. 48 and 49, *The General*, renamed *The Broadway Limited*. The twin unit combination provided dining car meals for both coach and Pullman car passengers on Pennsylvania's premier train between the nation's capital and the Midwest.

Harry Stegmaier Collection

Regularly assigned to *The Liberty Limited* in the 1950s as its mid-train Pullman lounge was 6 double bedroom buffet lounge car, *Aspen Falls*. *Aspen Falls* was built by Pullman and delivered to the Pennsylvania Railroad in the spring of 1949 in the series of postwar 6 bedroom, buffet lounges, eleven to be exact, that the Pennsylvania Railroad received. *Aspen Falls* not only provided double bedroom space on *The Liberty Limited* but it also gave Pullman passengers a place to relax, especially before dinner since the car was carried next to the twin unit dining car on No. 58 and No. 59. These *Falls* cars were extremely long lived and most of them made it until the end of the Penn Central era, with some cars actually being leased for a time by Amtrak. *Aspen Falls*, however, was the only one of the *Falls* series cars that Amtrak purchased and, when it was retired in 1975, it was sold to a private individual in Louisville, Kentucky. Amtrak used these cars, primarily, on Michigan division trains between Detroit and Chicago to serve as buffet lounge cars providing sandwiches, snacks and beverages to the coach passengers on those routes. *Aspen Falls* is seen here in Chicago in June, 1963.

the New York cars were combined with the Washington cars or dropped from No. 58 eastbound. A glance at *The Liberty Limited* menu shows that certainly the meals were mundane compared to the fine food provided by the Baltimore & Ohio. With passenger revenue on the train dropping drastically, the Pennsylvania Railroad was ready to pull out of the competition with the Baltimore & Ohio by the mid 1950s. By 1957, the Baltimore & Ohio carried 77% of all Pullman passengers on the Washington-Chicago route and 71% of the coach passengers. It was not much of a surprise then when, on October 27, 1957, No. 58 and No. 59, *The Liberty Limited*, were permanently dropped and Pennsylvania's only competition with B&O in the Washington-Chicago market were cars dropped at Harrisburg and picked up there by other through trains from a connection, primarily by No. 48 and 49, *The General*. The Baltimore & Ohio had won the battle in the Baltimore and Washington markets.

Bob's Photo

Lower Right: When the Pennsylvania Railroad decided to re-equip *The Liberty Limited* with postwar equipment, it chose to adorn the train with Pullman Standard sleeper-buffet lounge-observation cars. The *George Brooke Roberts*, seen in this photograph, was one of seven cars delivered early in 1949 to the Pennsylvania Railroad. It, like its half dozen sisters, contained 2 drawing rooms, a compartment and a double bedroom as well as a buffet lounge and observation room. The car is seen here while virtually new on May 28, 1949 in Washington, D.C. with *The Liberty Limited* drumhead on the rear. These flatend observation cars managed to last for some time on the Pennsylvania Railroad, but as service was cut more and more, they became surplus. When *The Liberty Limited* lost its observation cars in 1956, the railroad needed to find a spot for The *George Brooke Roberts* and so it was renumbered into the parlor car series for a time in the mid '50s but then went back into sleeping car service in 1958, being used on special charters. The car was finally retired in 1963 and sold to the ill-fated Hofheinz enterprise in Houston, Texas and eventually was scrapped.

Harry Stegmaier Collection

The Liberty Limited, of course, carried 14 section sleeping cars to handle the government traffic, but in addition, each *Liberty Limited* in 1952, was carrying two 21 roomette *Inn* series sleepers in each direction. Cars like *Warsaw Inn*, seen here in September, 1964 in Denver, Colorado, were part of the large number of 21 roomette sleepers fielded by the Pennsylvania Railroad. *Warsaw Inn*, like *Wilkensburg Inn* pictured earlier in the book, was built by American Car & Foundry for the Pennsylvania and delivered to the company in the spring of 1948. Like the other ACF built 21 roomette sleepers, seven to be exact, all were retired in the mid 1960s and not converted to coaches, as were the Pullman built cars. *Warsaw Inn* was scrapped in 1966.

Al Chione/Harry Stegmaier Collection

Multi-person accommodations were provided by cars like *Imperial Fields* on *The Liberty Limited*. The car is seen here in Chicago in June, 1963. These 4 double bed-room, 4 compartment, 2 drawing room cars were assigned to *The Liberty Limited*, with at least one car in each direction, on every trip. These cars were extremely valuable because, as passenger service went into a general decline in the mid 1950s and trains were removed and services disappeared as well, the Pennsylvania Railroad's *Imperial* cars proved extremely versatile for both special movement as well as for use on seasonal trains to Florida, such as the *City of Miami* and *The Florida Special*. Thus, most of the post-war *Imperial* cars remained on the Pennsylvania Railroad until the end of service in 1971, unlike the Pullman built pre-war cars. The post-war *Imperial* cars were built by ACF and delivered in the fall and winter of 1948. *Imperial Fields* lasted through the Penn Central era and could be seen as a regular on No. 48 and 49 into the summer of 1970. It was also seen in the winter of 1970 and 1971 on *The Florida Special*. The car was retired in 1971 and scrapped by the Penn Central.

No. 68 and 69
THE RED ARROW

The Red Arrow was Pennsylvania's premier overnight New York to Detroit train. As such, it was in direct competition with the highly touted New York Central all Pullman *Detroiter* and its Washington coach and sleepers, which were picked up and dropped at Harrisburg from connections, had to compete with Baltimore & Ohio's fine train No. 19 and 20, *The Ambassador*. Nevertheless, *The Red Arrow* was one of Pennsylvania Railroad's better trains. In both directions, No. 68 and No. 69 carried a dormitory car which was often a Pullman betterment sleeper with trucks and springs for high speed service. In addition, behind the dormitory came a combine car, three reclining seat coaches, two of them being of the P85BR lightweight variety and then a variety of sleepers, one a 12 section, 1 drawing room heavyweight betterment car plus two 21 roomette cars, and a 12 duplex single room, 4 double bedroom *Creek* car. Lounge service was provided by a 6 double bedroom bar-lounge cars and *The Red Arrow* received a modernized heavyweight or lightweight diner. In addition, the main train picked up cars at Harrisburg and dropped others there in Washington-Detroit service, carrying a modern reclining seat coach, a *Cascade* series 10 roomette, 5 double bedroom sleeper and an old heavyweight 8 section-solarium-lounge car in the *Club* series. In a sense, *The Red Arrow* was trying to compete in both the New York and Washington markets with two trains which had better patronage. New York Central's *Detroiter* was all Pullman and got the best of equipment including twin unit diners. In the Washington market, Baltimore & Ohio's *Ambassador* not only carried comfortable coaches, as well as a coach-lounge car, but a dining car and sleeping cars providing sections, duplex roomettes, roomettes and double bedroom space as well as a modern 5 double bedroom-observation-lounge sleeper built new for the Chesapeake & Ohio and acquired by the Baltimore & Ohio in 1950. In a sense, No. 68 and No. 69, *The Red Arrow* was outmatched in both markets by New York Central's *Detroiter*, and after that train's discontinuance by New York Central's *Wolverine*, and by B&O's *Ambassador* in the Baltimore and Washington to Detroit markets, respectively. It is not surprising then, that as time went on and patronage gradually declined, passengers went to the New York Central and the Baltimore & Ohio. *The Red Arrow* was up for discontinuance by the late 1950s. The Pennsylvania Railroad, in this particular case, did all that it could to basically hasten the demise of the train, first by cutting it back to a Philadelphia to Detroit routing, so that New York passengers had to change trains at Philadelphia and then, on July 26, 1959, the railroad discontinued the train between Detroit and Toledo, leaving it as a sorry little two-car local with one coach and a sleeping car operating from Toledo to Crestline where the cars were cut into *The General*. Obviously, such a train could not make money.

Train No. 68
Blue Ribbon
Red Arrow

Car Type	Description	From	To	Details	Car Des
1 Dormitory		Detroit	New York		
1 PB-70	Scheme 4	Detroit	New York		
1 P70GR	Reclining Seats, Friday and Sunday	%Detroit	New York		
2 P-85BR	Reclining Seats	%Detroit	New York		
1 SL	12-1	¢Detroit	New York		680
1 SL	21 Roomette	Detroit	New York	LW	681
1 Diner		Detroit	New York	LW	
1 SL-Lounge	6 DBR, Bar	Detroit	New York	LW	682
1 SL	12 Duplex SR, 4 DBR	Detroit	New York	LW	683
1 SL	21 Roomette, DE Saturday and Nov. 22, Dec. 24, 31	Detroit	New York	LW	684
1 P-85BR	Reclining Seats	%Detroit	Washington	To 574 Harrisburg	
1 SL-Lounge	10 Roomette, 5 DBR	Detroit	Washington	LW To 574 Harrisburg	685
1 SL-Lounge	8 Section, Bar	Detroit	Washington	To 574 Harrisburg	686
1 SL	10 Section, 3 DBR, DE Sun. and Nov. 23, Dec. 24, 25, 31, Jan. 1	Williamsport	New York	From 580 Harrisburg	76
1 SL	8 Section, 5 DBR	Erie	New York	From 580, Harrisburg	584

Each *Red Arrow* received, uniquely among Pennsylvania Railroad trains, one of the railroad's combines, like No. 5106, seen here at Sunnyside Yard in 1949. These combines provided both baggage space and additional coach seating space on trains like *The Red Arrow*.

The Red Arrow received one of Pennsylvania Railroad's heavyweight diners, which was rebuilt and modernized by the company shops at Altoona. This car classed D78dR retained its clerestory roof and was one of three cars with both the clerestory roof and a "long lounge" No. 4499 seated 24 in its dining section and 16 in the lounge. The car was originally built in 1926 and lasted into the

Penn Central era. Cars like No. 4499 were often found on *The Red Arrow* in the 1950s. The railroad considered *The Red Arrow* one of its more prestigious trains and gave the train good equipment for the New York to Detroit overnight service. Dining cars, like No. 4499, were excellent rebuilds and, when the railroad had no lightweight diners, these heavyweight rebuilds like No. 4499 probably were better choices than one of the single unit Budd diners, which were known as especially rough riders.

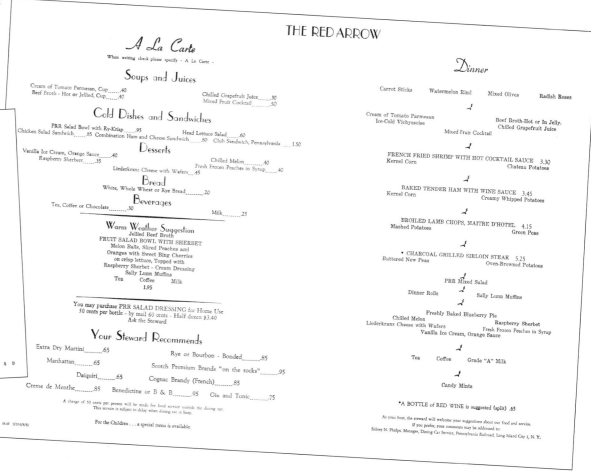

This oversized menu from the summer of 1952, with the Detroit Michigan downtown skyline on the cover, shows that the Pennsylvania Railroad considered *The Red Arrow* an important train in its repertoire. Not only did the train receive a special dinner menu with its own name on it like one of the better blue ribbon trains, but as can be seen from the menu, it served up a wide variety of dishes for the traveler to choose from, including broiled lamb chops for $4.15. What we would not give for those prices again today. The menu shows the esteem in which the railroad held *The Red Arrow* and the way in which the company tried its best to attract patrons to its New York-Detroit over-nighter and away from the rival New York Central's *Detroiter*.

Train No. 69
Blue Ribbon
Red Arrow

Car Type	Description	From	To	Details	Car Des
1 P-70	DE Friday and Sunday	New York	Harrisburg		
2 P-70	Friday and Sunday	New York	Harrisburg		
1 Dormitory		New York	Detroit		
1 PB-70	Scheme 4	New York	Detroit		
1 P70GR	Reclining Seats, Friday and Sunday	%New York	Detroit		
2 P-85BR	Reclining Seats	%New York	Detroit		
1 SL	12-1	¢New York	Detroit		690
1 SL	21 Roomette	New York	Detroit	LW	691
1 Diner		New York	Detroit	LW	
1 SL-Lounge	6 DBR, Bar	New York	Detroit	LW	692
1 SL	12 Duplex SR, 4 DBR	New York	Detroit	LW	693
1 SL	21 Roomette, DE Sat. and Nov. 22, Dec. 24, 31	New York	Detroit	LW	694
1 P-85BR	Reclining Seats	%Washington	Detroit	From 569 Harrisburg	
1 SL-Lounge	10 Roomette, 5 DBR	Washington	Detroit	LW From 569 Harrisburg	697
1 SL-Lounge	8 Section, Bar	Washington	Detroit	From 569 Harrisburg	698

One year later, on July 26, 1960, *The Red Arrow* disappeared from the Pennsylvania Railroad timetables forever. Nevertheless, in its heyday, *The Red Arrow* was a popular train for many people and the Pennsylvania Railroad gave the New York Central and, to a lesser extent, the Baltimore & Ohio, competition in their markets from New York and Washington, respectively, to the motor city.

Train No. 70
Blue Ribbon
The Admiral

Car Type	Description	From	To	Details	Car Des
1 MS-60	Sunday	Harrisburg	New York		
	Perishable (X)	Various	Hudson Cut-Off	To 14 (54 Sunday) Harrisburg	
	Perishable (X)	Chicago	Harrisburg		
	Milk and Perishable (X)	Chicago	Philadelphia	To 526 (602 Sunday) Harrisburg	
1 or more	MS-60 DE Monday	Chicago	Philadelphia	To 526 (602 Sunday) Harrisburg	
1 BM-70M	DE Sunday	Chicago	Pittsburgh		
1 MS-60	X-29	Chicago	Pittsburgh		
1 MS-60	(X)	Chicago	Pittsburgh		
1 MS-60	Wednesday LIFE	Chicago	Pittsburgh		
1 Express	X-29, Sunday	Pittsburgh	Harrisburg		
1 MS-60	Sunday	Pittsburgh	Harrisburg		
1 MS-60	Sunday (X)	Pittsburgh	Reading	To Reading RR Harrisburg	
2 MS-60	Sunday	Pittsburgh	New York		
1 M-70	Sunday	Pittsburgh	New York		
1 Express	B-60, Sunday	Pittsburgh	New York		
1 B-60	Saturday	Chicago	New York		
1 PB-70	Scheme 4	Chicago	New York		
2 P-70KR	Reclining Seats	%Chicago	New York		
1 Diner		Chicago	New York		
1 SL-Lounge	3 Compartment, 1 DR, Bar	Chicago	New York	SW	704
1 SL	21 Roomette	Chicago	New York	LW	703
1 SL	12 Duplex SR, 5 DBR, DE Saturday	Chicago	New York	LW	702
1 SL	12-1	Chicago	New York	SW	701
1 SL	10 Roomette, 6 DBR	*San Francisco	New York	LW	P287
1 SL	10 Roomette, 6 DBR	xSan Francisco	New York	LW	CZ11

* From C&NW 28, due Chicago 1 P.M. — Alternate Dates
    Even - September, October, January, March
    Odd - November, December, February, April

x From CB&Q 18, due Chicago 1:30 p.m. — Alternate Dates
    Even - November, December, February, April
    Odd - September, October, January, March

No. 70 and 71
THE ADMIRAL

The Admiral, No. 70 and No. 71, was a train, by 1952, as is obvious from the consist, that carried a massive amount of headend. Its schedule was somewhat odd. Westbound, it departed in mid-evening from New York at 8:00 p.m. after most of the main trains of the fleet had left and thus served as an interim New York-Chicago train between the bulk of the Pennsylvania's east-west service and the late departing *Gotham Limited*. Its arrival was in Chicago the next afternoon at 1:15 p.m.

Eastbound, *The Admiral* was sandwiched in between *The Broadway Limited* and *The Pennsylvania Limited*, with a 5:30 p.m. departure from Chicago and a late morning arrival at 11:45 a.m. in New York City, only 14 minutes ahead of *The Pennsylvania Limited*. The longer running times for No. 70 and No. 71 can be explained by the fact that it made a large number of stops that were bypassed by other east-west trains. Eastbound No. 70 was laden with headend as it evidenced by the consist, including a Chicago to Pittsburgh RPO car which was also handled by

Harry Stegmaier Collection
The Admiral carried a great deal of headend equipment in both directions. The train could often be found with a large number of mail storage cars in its consist. Baggage Railway Express Agency cars like 9181, a B60, often served as MS-60 mail storage cars on *The Admiral* and, particularly the eastbound train, could be found with a large number of cars among its headend equipment. No. 9181 was photographed in Dallas, Texas in October of 1966.

Train No. 71
Blue Ribbon
The Admiral

Car Type	Description	From	To	Details	Car Des
1 MS-60		Harrisburg	Pittsburgh		
1 MS-60	(X) Sunday	Philadelphia	Pittsburgh	From 525 Harrisburg	
1 B-60	Papers, Saturday	New York	Pittsburgh		
1 MS-60	(X)	New York	Pittsburgh		
1 MS-60	(X)	New York	Pittsburgh		
1 BM-70	DE Sunday and Monday	Pittsburgh	Chicago	Letter End East	
1 BM-70M	DE Sunday	Pittsburgh	Chicago	Letter End West	
1 MS-60	Semi-Open, DE Sunday and Holidays	New York	Chicago		
1 B-60	Baggage Saturday	New York	Chicago		
1 PB-70	Scheme 4	New York	Chicago		
2 P-70KR	Reclining Seats	%New York	Chicago		
1 Diner		New York	Chicago		
1 SL-Lounge	3 Compartment, 1 DR, Bar	New York	Chicago	SW	710
1 SL	21 Roomette	New York	Chicago	LW	711
1 SL	12 Duplex SR, 5 DBR, DE Saturday	New York	Chicago	LW	712
1 SL	12-1	New York	Chicago	SW	714
1 SL	12-1	Washington	Chicago	SW From 575 Harrisburg	717
1 SL	12 Duplex SR, 5 DBR, Friday	New York	Pittsburgh	LW	715
1 SL	12-1	New York	Akron	SW To 9 Pittsburgh	94
1 SL	10 Roomette, 5 DBR	New York	Akron	LW To 9 Pittsburgh	95
1 SL-Lounge	3 DBR, 1 DR, Bar, Will NOT Operate December 24, 31	New York	Akron	LW To 9 at Pittsburgh	96
1 SL	12 Duplex SR, 5 DBR, DE Saturday and Nov. 22, 23, Dec. 23, 24, 30, 31	New York	Akron	LW To 9 Pittsburgh	97
1 P85BR	Reclining Seats	%New York	Akron	To 9 Pittsburgh	

Harry Stegmaier

Eastbound No. 70 also was designated to handle the through Oakland to New York through sleeping car that arrived on *The California Zephyr* every other day. On the days *The California Zephyr* car was not carried, the car from Oakland to New York was received from *The San Francisco Overland*. Pennsylvania Railroad contributed only one car to *The California Zephyr* pool. This was Budd built *Silver Rapids*, a 10 roomette, 6 double bedroom Pullman sleeper that was delivered to the Pennsylvania Railroad in November of 1948. Viewed here in 1969, *Silver Rapids* has been given Penn Central lettering on each end. *Silver Rapids* could be found occasionally in the consist of *The Admiral* and the car was quite useful to the Pennsylvania Railroad long after the through sleeping car service was discontinued. It lasted into the Penn Central era and was often assigned as the eastbound sleeper on No. 54, *The Pennsylvania Limited*, out of Chicago in the 1969 to 1971 period. By that time, only No.48 and 49 carried sleeping cars, with the exception of the eastbound Pennsylvania Limited, No. 54, formerly *The Gotham Limited*. This car was assigned to that train for one reason by that late date, to handle passengers from western trains that had arrived too late to make the connection with No. 48, *The General*, now named *The Broadway Limited*. After its service on Penn Central, *Silver Rapids* was purchased by Amtrak and served Amtrak into the 1980s. This excellent sleeping car is one of a kind and had the extra long and wide beds that were found on all of *The California Zephyr* sleeping cars.

Harry Stegmaier Collection

The Admiral carried in its consist a prewar 12 duplex single room, 5 double bedroom *Brook* series sleeper in both directions. *Mineral Brook* was one of the cars regularly assigned to *The Admiral* in the 1950s. Built by Pullman Standard for *The Liberty Limited*, it was delivered to the Pennsylvania Railroad in the spring of 1938. This prewar, lightweight sleeper is seen here in June of 1960 in Chicago. *Mineral Brook* served the Pennsylvania Railroad until it was finally retired in 1966 and sold to the Hofheinz Enterprises in Houston which scrapped the car after their planned venture never materialized.

Harry Stegmaier

Another regular car on *The Admiral* in the 1950s was Pullman built, prewar, lightweight, 6 double bedroom buffet-lounge car, *Spruce Falls*, which provided first-class lounge seating and bar service to the Pullman patrons of that train. Pullman Standard had delivered the car to that railroad in September of 1940 and its served

the Pennsylvania Railroad for 28 years, both in regular and later in charter service, until it was finally sold to the Long Island Railroad in 1968 for its many parlor car trains operated, especially on weekends, to the resorts on the eastern tip of Long Island. The Long Island renamed the car *Pantigo* and kept it until it was finally retired in 1975 and sold for scrap. *Spruce Falls*, then, lasted in service 35 years from the date the Pennsylvania Railroad received it. By the end of its career, however, it was a long way from the days when it was the first-class lounge car on *The Admiral*. In this photograph, the car is still seen in its Tuscan Red scheme, with Pennsylvania Railroad lettering, when it was photographed by the author at Jamaica, New York on the *Advance Cannonball* on June 6, 1969.

westbound No. 71. Eastbound, the passenger accommodations on No. 70 were a combine, two P70KR coaches, older cars than the new P85BR's, and a heavyweight diner, as well as a prewar *Colonial* series 3 compartment, 1 drawing room-bar-lounge sleeper. In both directions, the train also carried two lightweight sleepers, one a 21 roomette car and the other a prewar *Brook* series 12 duplex single room, 5 double bedroom sleeper as well as a heavyweight 12 section, 1 drawing room car. No. 70 differed from No. 71 in one significant way. Eastbound No. 70 was chosen as the train to carry the San Francisco to New York through sleeping car that operated west of Chicago every other day on *The San Francisco Overland* and on alternate days on *The California Zephyr*. The San Francisco car but not *The California Zephyr* car was switched shortly thereafter to *The Pennsylvania Limited* in the fall of 1952. Westbound, behind the through New York-Chicago cars and headend equipment, the train carried a Washington to Chicago heavyweight sleeper, picked up at Harrisburg, as well as all of the through cars for Akron, Ohio that were detached at Pittsburgh and made up *The Akronite*. In fact, Pennsylvania Railroad timetables listed No. 71 as *The Admiral-Akronite*. Because of its schedule, *The Admiral* was one of those trains, as passenger traffic declined in the mid 1950s, that was expendable. On October 26, 1958, the westbound *Admiral* was discontinued after having been cut back to a Pittsburgh-Chicago routing although through cars were still delivered to the train from the east by other Pennsylvania Railroad trains at Pittsburgh. Somehow or another, eastbound No. 70 survived, despite every effort the railroad could make to discontinue it, right down until the advent of Amtrak in May 1971. By then the train was reduced to some headend cars, a coach or two and a snack bar coach, with threatening notices in the timetable issued by Penn Central that the train was up for discontinuance. Like the renamed *Gotham Limited* and *The Manhattan Limited*, the eastbound *Admiral* survived some of the more prestigious Blue Ribbon trains on the Pennsylvania Railroad, probably due to its heavy lading of headend during the 1960s.

No. 76 & 77
THE TRAIL BLAZER

This author has decided to treat *The Trail Blazer* as a separate train for two reasons, one of those being that it was Pennsylvania Railroad's premier New York-Chicago all coach overnight train for many years and carried very heavy passenger loads all through the 1940s and into the 1950s, In 1950, the Pennsylvania Railroad combined it with *The General* between New York and Chicago in the summer months. By 1952, this combination with *The General* was a permanent arrangement except for the period between December 12 and January 20, when *The Trail Blazer* operated as a separate train because of the heavy holiday loads westbound, and often eastbound as a separate section of No. 48. *The Trail Blazer* cars simply brought up the rear of *The*

Train No. 77						
Car Type	Description		From	To	Details	Car Des
MS-60	(X)		New York	Chicago		
I PLB-85R	Baggage-Lounge, Sealed		%New York	Chicago		
P-85BR	Reclining Seats (X)		%New York	Chicago		
I P-85BR	Reclining Seats		*%New York	Chicago		770
I P-85BR	Reclining Seats		*%New York	Chicago		771
I P-85BR	Reclining Seats Will NOT operate December 25th		%New York	Chicago		772
I P-85BR	Reclining Seats		%New York	Chicago		773
I Diner	)Twin Unit					
I Kitchen-Dormitory	)Twin Unit		New York	Chicago		
I P-85BR	Reclining Seats		%New York	Chicago		774
I P-85BR	Reclining Seats		%New York	Chicago		775
I P-85BR	Reclining Seats		%New York	Chicago		776
I P-85BR	Reclining Seats		*%New York	Chicago		777
I POC-85AR	Observation, Buffet, Lounge		%New York	Chicago		

* WILL operate December 18th-January 4th, inclusive, except January 25th.

The Trail Blazer was the Pennsylvania Railroad's premier overnight coach train between New York and Chicago but, except for the holiday season in 1952, it was combined with *The General* and operated on the rear of that train. The standard postwar coach equipment for *The Trail Blazer* were the postwar P85BR coaches that were built by both the Pennsylvania Railroad shops, as well as by ACF. Coach 4137 is typical of the P85BR class of cars. These coaches were the most modern on the Pennsylvania Railroad in the postwar era and were the staple cars on the important mainline Pennsylvania Railroad passenger train, seating 44 passengers in reclining seats and providing them with spacious washrooms. However, most of these cars were retired between 1965 and 1968 because the steel, it was found, had rotted from underneath and the cars were in rather sad shape. Nevertheless, in the early 1950s, coach passengers on the Pennsylvania Railroad who had seats in a P85BR car, certainly enjoyed luxury compared to many of the other standard coaches that the railroad provided to its patrons.

General, when not run as a separate train, usually four reclining seat coaches, P85BR cars, as well as an Altoona-built observation-buffet-lounge car for coach passengers, which was equipped with a small kitchen serving basic meals for those who did not wish to avail themselves of *The General's* dining car. However, during the holiday season, the westbound *Trail Blazer* continued to operate in 1952 and 1953 as a separate train for over a month and, thus, it will be treated separately here.

The consist of the train during the holiday period gives some idea of the makeup of the train before the it was combined with *The General*. Besides carrying a storage mail car behind its diesel units, *The Trail Blazer* had a combination baggage-lounge car on the headend for its coach passengers, followed by another reclining seat coach and one of Pennsylvania's twin-unit dining cars, then another four or five coaches, with extra cars being added as needed, and the rear brought

up by the Altoona-built 1130 series observation-buffet-lounge car serving light meals. After 1953, *The Trail Blazer* was combined with *The General* on a permanent basis. It's name would remain in the timetable until July 26, 1959. *The Trail Blazer* was simply the coach portion of *The General* after 1953. Nevertheless, at one time, it had been the darling coach train of the Pennsylvania Railroad. It was a victim of more people turning to the automobile rather than a decline in the quality of the train itself that would eventually doom *The Trail Blazer* to a status where it could no longer operate as a separate train. In a sense, its spirit continued on to Amtrak day in May, 1971 in the coaches and the coach buffet-lounge that was provided on *The General*, renamed *The Broadway Limited*.

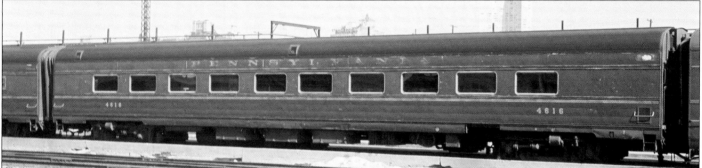

The Trail Blazer, once it was combined with *The General*, did not have its own twin unit diner but its patrons could avail themselves of the dining car that served the Pullman passengers on *The General*, as well as *The Trail Blazer's* coach patrons. However, during the holiday season, from December 12 to January 20, when *The Trail Blazer* was operated as a separate train, it carried a twin unit diner in its consist since the train often swelled to very large proportions during this heavy travel season. In this photograph, one sees full dining room car No. 4616 and kitchen-dormitory car No. 4617, still in Pennsylvania Railroad Tuscan Red at Chicago, Illinois in the late 1960s. This twin unit diner-kitchen-dormitory set had been built by the Budd Company and delivered to the Pennsylvania Railroad in July of 1949. These versatile cars were purchased by Amtrak in 1973, after an initial decision had been made not to take the cars. Nevertheless, Amtrak had a need for large dining rooms on some of its more popular trains and, after leasing the cars for two years, it purchased this twin unit diner set from the Penn Central.

The Trail Blazer, whether combined with *The General* or not, carried an observation-buffet-lounge car for the use of its coach passengers. Even when combined with *The General*, the coach section of *The Trail Blazer* was run on the rear of the train and, thus, still merited the observation-buffet-lounge car. These cars were primarily drawn from the company built cars that Altoona car shops had delivered in January and February, 1948. Each car had a buffet and a large lounge with tables, seating 53 passengers and the buffet was equipped to provide light meal service for those who cared not to avail themselves of the full dining car. Here, flatend observation car No. 1132 is seen on *The South Wind* at New Smyrna Beach, Florida on August 3, 1951. These cars finished their careers, running on *The General* and serving as the coach-buffet-lounge cars on that train until 1967, being run next to the headend equipment and not on the rear. Except for car 1135, which was retired in 1961, No. 1132 and three other sisters were not retired until 1967, when they were scrapped by the Pennsylvania Railroad.

FOR THE BEST IN TRAVEL

"Spirit of St. Louis"

ALL-PULLMAN FLEET LEADER

ST. LOUIS · PHILADELPHIA · NEW YORK
ST. LOUIS · BALTIMORE · WASHINGTON

Enjoy the last word in comfort on this luxury leader of the Southwest Fleet. Fully equipped with five types of private rooms in latest all-room sleeping cars, each with its own lighting and temperature controls. Restful berths in section-type cars. Colorful Lounge and Observation Cars with easy chairs, magazine libraries, writing desks and convenient buffets. Palate-tempting meals served in a beautifully decorated Master Dining Car.

Smooth electric power all the way.

THE SOUTHWEST FLEET

"SPIRIT OF ST. LOUIS"
All-Pullman Fleet Leader

THE JEFFERSONIAN
All-Coach Reserved-Seat Streamliner

THE PENN TEXAS
Pullman and Coach Streamliner

THE AMERICAN
Pullman and Coach Train

THE ST. LOUISAN
Pullman and Coach Train

For Schedules Consult Table 3.

K.L. Miller Collection
Extolling the virtues of the "Southwest Fleet" noting the "Smooth electric power all the way." From Timetable Form 1, January 25, 1953.

INTRODUCTION

While the Pennsylvania main line trains on the St. Louis and Cincinnati segments of the railroad could not match the larger number which were operated on the New York to Chicago, Cleveland and Detroit runs. Nevertheless, the Pennsylvania Railroad in 1952 was still operating what could be considered, at that time, a substantially large number of through trains. While the Chicago main line boasted no less than 10, actually 11 if *The Trail Blazer* is counted as a separate train, the St. Louis main line boasted only 7 trains on through schedules and this presumes that one counts the westbound *Metropolitan*, No. 25, No. 27 west of Pittsburgh, and eastbound St. Louis to Pittsburgh, No. 6, *The Allegheny*, as part of the through train service. Six of these trains were through New York to St. Louis operations, with *The Cincinnati Limited* operating to its namesake city. The all-

Pullman *Spirit of St. Louis* was the pride of the route with *The Penn Texas*, which handled through cars for Texas points, running second. They were supplemented by the all coach, streamlined *Jeffersonian*, and older trains such as *The St. Louisan*, and an old name from the Pennsylvania Railroad timetable, *The American*. In addition, while no passenger cars ran through, Nos. 25-27, *The Metropolitan*, carried passenger equipment on all portions of its run, and while there was no eastbound counterpart, No. 6, *The Allegheny*, operated St. Louis to Pittsburgh with a connection to New York on Pennsylvania Railroad's Pittsburgh to New York train, *The Duquesne*. As well as these mainline operations, the Pennsylvania Railroad's competition for New York Central and Baltimore & Ohio in the Cincinnati market was *The Cincinnati Limited*, streamlined after World War II with the flood of new equipment which the

Harry Stegmaier Collection

Pennsylvania Railroad's No. 25, *The Metropolitan*, on this day in the summer of 1948, is probably running in two sections as is evidenced by the lack of headend traffic on the train. A helper is required to assist one of Pennsylvania Railroad's unique T-1 class duplex locomotives as it rounds Horseshoe Curve westbound with No. 25, *The Metropolitan*, on that summer day over 50 years ago.

Pennsylvania Railroad acquired. The St. Louis main line then was second only to the Chicago main in quantity of trains, but certainly not in the quality of the trains which were operated. Except for *The Broadway Limited*, they were a match in equipment and appointment and were given the same care as the Chicago, Detroit and Cleveland trains.

No. 3 and No. 4
THE PENN TEXAS

No.3 and No. 4, Pennsylvania Railroad's *Penn Texas*, had been inaugurated after World War II as *The Sunshine Special* and this train had then been renamed *The Penn Texas* as *The Sunshine Special*. This train lasted only a short time as a through Pennsylvania Railroad-Missouri Pacific train. It's first run was on July 7, 1946 and provided through train service between New York and Dallas. Other points such as Houston and El Paso were served by through sleeping cars, and there was a New York to Mexico City car via San Antonio. On April 25, 1948, the through operation was discontinued and replaced by a train which would carry the through sleeping cars for Texas points, first named *The Texas Eagle*, since its primary connection in St. Louis was the new streamlined Missouri Pacific train of that name. On December

12, 1948, it took on the name that it would carry until its final demise, *The Penn Texas*. As can be seen from the consist sheet, the train was not heavy with headend cars but did carry a full RPO car, a combine, plus three reclining seat coaches westbound and two eastbound. The major portion of the sleeping car traffic were the through cars to other railroads. The two Pennsylvania Railroad online sleeping cars, a prewar *Cascade* series 10 roomette, 5 double bedroom sleeper, and a heavy-weight 12 section, 1 drawing room sleeper were added between New York and St. Louis to pick up overflow traffic between these points that *The Spirit of St. Louis* could not handle. In addition, the westbound train carried a New York to Columbus 10 roomette, 6 double bedroom *Rapid* series sleeper. The five through cars were the key. These were all still operating in 1952, although the Oklahoma City car which had been a briefly in the train, was now history. The Missouri Pacific bound cars were handled west of St. Louis on Missouri Pacific No. 1, the first section of *The Texas Eagle*, bound for south Texas points. The El Paso car was carried by Missouri Pacific No. 21, the second section of *The Texas Eagle* which operated to Fort Worth and Dallas. Another sleeping car was handed over and received from the combined Frisco-Missouri-

Train No. 3
Blue Ribbon
Penn Texas

Car Type	Description	From	To	Details	Car Des
1 MS-60	Tuesday NEWSWEEK	Dayton	St. Louis		
1 BM-70M	DE Sunday	New York	St. Louis	Letter End East	
1 Express	R-50, DE Sunday, Monday and Days after holidays	New York	New Orleans	To IC St. Louis	
1 PB-70	Scheme 4	New York	St. Louis		
1 P-70GSR	Reclining Seats	%New York	St. Louis		
2 P-85ER	Reclining Seats	%New York	St. Louis		
1 Diner		New York	St. Louis	LW	
1 Recreation-Bar		New York	St. Louis		
1 SL	10 Roomette, 5 DBR	New York	St. Louis	LW	36
1 SL	12-1	New York	St. Louis		37
1 SL	14 Roomette, 4 DBR or				
	10 Roomette, 6 DBR	*New York	San Antonio	LW	15
1 SL	14 Roomette, 4 DBR	¢New York	El Paso	LW	MP2
1 SL	10 Roomette, 6 DBR	&New York	San Antonio	LW	MP3
1 SL	10 Roomette, 6 DBR	&New York	Houston	LW	MP4
1 SL	10 Roomette, 6 DBR	&Washington	Houston	LW From 575 Harrisburg	MP5
1 SL	10 Roomette, 6 DBR	New York	Columbus	LW	39
1 MS-60	(X)	Pittsburgh	Indianapolis	To 67 Columbus	

* To Frisco 1, leaving St. Louis 5:30 p.m.
$ To MP 1, leaving St. Louis 5:30 p.m.
& To MP 21, leaving St. Louis 5:30 p.m.

Harry Stegmaier Collection

Pennsylvania Railroad 10 roomette, 6 double bedroom Pullman *Eagle Cove* is seen here in the consist of *The Penn Texas* in the mid 1950s. The car is painted in Missouri Pacific *Eagle* colors of blue and cream to match up with the colors of *The Texas Eagles*, which will carry it beyond St. Louis. *Eagle Cove* was delivered to the Pennsylvania Railroad in the late summer of 1950 from American Car and Foundry. The car was renamed *Loyalsock Rapids* in 1964 and painted in the Tuscan Red scheme after through car service had ended. The car was normally assigned, in the early 1950s, to the New York-Houston route, operated via St. Louis and, thus, was regularly seen on *The Penn Texas*. Later, as *Loyalsock Rapids*, it went on to the Penn Central and served until it was finally retired in 1971 and was scrapped.

Harry Stegmaier

Missouri Pacific *Roaring River*, seen here in later days, not in *Eagle* colors but in the solid blue scheme, better known as Jenks Blue after the president of the Missouri Pacific by that time, was a Budd built car that was delivered to the Missouri Pacific in August of 1948. Many of the Missouri Pacific cars were 14 roomette, 4 double bedroom or 14 roomette, 2 double bedroom, 1 drawing room cars but the railroad did purchase some of the standard 10 roomette, 6 double bedroom sleepers, particularly for through car service. *Roaring River* was normally assigned to the Washington, D. C. to Houston, Texas through car line in the early 1950s and,

thus, could often be seen in the consists of No. 3 and 4 on the Pennsylvania Railroad. *Roaring River* was finally retired by the Missouri Pacific in 1969 and sold off to the National Railways of Mexico. which renamed the car *Luxemburgo*.

Kansas-Texas Railroad's streamlined competition in the Texas market, *The Texas Special*, which operated through Dallas and Fort Worth to San Antonio. All of these through sleeping cars were modern 10 roomette, 6 double bedroom or 14 roomette, 4 double bedroom cars, supplied mostly by the western roads. The Pennsylvania supplied a few 10 roomette, 6 double bedroom cars but it owned none of the 14 roomette, 4 double bedroom style. Unlike the through transcontinental cars on the Chicago route, which were terminated in the 1950s, through sleeping cars via the St. Louis route lasted much longer. The first car to go was the Frisco car, which operated west of St. Louis on *The Texas Special* to San Antonio. This car was dropped on October 1, 1958, because *The Texas*

Top: The Missouri Pacific seems to have had a special preference for 14 roomette, 4 double bedroom cars, whereas many of the other American railroads purchased the standard 10 roomette, 6 double bedroom sleepers. In this photograph, taken at San Antonio, Texas in May of 1966, Missouri Pacific *Eagle Summit* is seen in the consist of *The Texas Eagle. Eagle Summit* was built by the Pullman Company and arrived on Missouri Pacific property in the first half of 1948. This 14 roomette, 4

double bedroom sleeper was often in the consist of *The Penn Texas* in the 1950s and was normally assigned to New York-El Paso, and later, New York Dallas, after the sleeper was discontinued all the way to El Paso. *Eagle Summit.* was not retired until 1967 when the Missouri Pacific shipped it to to the Ferrocarril Del Pacifico which renamed the car *Rio Presidio* and operated it on trains like *El Norteno* and *El Mexicali.*

The Texas & Pacific Railroad also contributed equipment to the through car line operated via *The Penn Texas.* This almost completely controlled subsidiary of the Missouri Pacific, however, did own its own passenger cars because it was easier for tax purposes and accounting purposes to put some of the costs over on the Texas & Pacific.

In this photograph, *Eagle Beach*, a Texas & Pacific 14 roomette, 4 double bedroom sleeper, built by the Pullman Company and delivered in the first half of 1948, is seen repainted from *Eagle* colors into the solid and easier to maintain solid blue Jenks scheme. *Eagle Beach* was normally assigned to the New York-El Paso and later the New York-Dallas sleeping car line like Missouri Pacific *Eagle Summit.* One should note that the Texas & Pacific logo, not the Missouri Pacific logo, is on this car which was photographed in May, 1965. Texas & Pacific finally retired the car and sold it to the Ferrocarril Del Pacifico in 1967, which renamed the car the *Rio Piaxtia* and operated it into the 1980s, both as a Pacifico Railways car and later as part of the overall Nacionales De Mexico combined passenger train service.

Train No. 4
Blue Ribbon
Penn Texas

Car Type	Description	From	To	Details	Car Des
1 Express	B-60 Tuesday NEWSWEEK	Dayton	New York		
1 MS-60	B-60, Tuesday, NEWSWEEK	Dayton	New York		
1 M-70	DE Monday	St. Louis	Pittsburgh	Letter End West	
1 PB-70	Scheme 4	St. Louis	New York		
2 P-85BR	Reclining Seats	%St. Louis	New York		
1 Diner		St. Louis	New York	LW	
1 Recreation-Bar		St. Louis	New York		
1 SL	10 Roomette, 5 DBR	St. Louis	New York	LW	40
1 SL	12-1	St. Louis	New York	LW	41
1 SL	14 Roomette, 4 DBR or 10 Roomette, 6 DBR	$San Antonio	New York	LW	25
1 SL	14 Roomette, 4 DBR	@El Paso	New York	LW	PR-9
1 SL	10 Roomette, 6 DBR	*San Antonio	New York	LW	PR15
1 SL	10 Roomette, 6 DBR	*Houston	New York	LW	PR12
1 SL	10 Roomette, 6 DBR	*Houston	New York	LW To 504 Harrisburg	PR11

$ From Frisco 1, due St. Louis 8:10 a.m.
@ From MP 2, due St. Louis 8:10 a.m.
* From MP 22, due St. Louis 8:20 a.m.

Here, in the consist of *The Penn Texas* in the early 1950s, is Frisco Lines 14 roomette, 4 double bedroom sleeping car *August Chouteau*. The car is labeled, as might be noted, for *The Texas Special* and, while it was not in regular through car assignment, the Frisco and its compatriot, the Missouri-Kansas-Texas, were not particular about what cars seemed to have been used in through car assignments. The *August Chouteau* is on *The Penn Texas* as it backs into St. Louis Union Station. It is in through car service between New York and San Antonio, being handled beyond St. Louis on the combined Frisco-Missouri-Kansas-Texas jointly operated *Texas Special*. This 14 roomette, 4 double bedroom sleeper was built by the Pullman Company for the Frisco when it upgraded its passenger equipment after World War II. The *August Chouteau* operated on *The Texas Special* until that train's demise in the late 1950s, after which it was leased for private charters and or operated on trains like *The Meteor* to Oklahoma City. By the mid 1960s, the Frisco was pulling out of the passenger game altogether, and the car was sold to the Canadian National Railways, which renamed it *Sisiboo Falls* in 1965 and put it into general service. By the 1970s, after a stint on *The International Limited* between Chicago and Toronto, as well as the Toronto to Montreal *Cavalier*, the car was restricted to the latter train as well on *The Ocean Limited* and *The Scotian* to the Maritime provinces, a long way from this October 5, 1956 photo when it was in through car service in the consist of *The Penn Texas*.

The Missouri-Kansas-Texas, in conjunction with The Frisco, operated *The Texas Special* between St. Louis and the Texas cities of Dallas, Fort Worth, with its final terminus in San Antonio. Thus, the Missouri-Kansas-Texas also bought 14 roomette, 4 double bedroom sleepers from the Pullman Company and these were often seen in the consist of *The Penn Texas*. One such car that was often used in this service was Missouri-Kansas-Texas sleeper *Benjamin R. Milam*. This car was delivered in the first half of 1948 to the Missouri-Kansas-Texas. After the through *Texas Special* was discontinued from St. Louis to Texas, the Missouri-Kansas-Texas began operating their own version of *The Texas Special* from Kansas City to Texas over their own line. The Frisco had pulled out of the joint train arrangement because of the horrible condition of Missouri-Kansas-Texas track, which caused the train to be consistently late. Thus, the *Benjamin Milam* continued running on the Missouri-Kansas-Texas *Texas Special* until that train was finally discontinued in the early 1960s. Unlike the Frisco cars, many of which were sold to the Canadian National, the Missouri-Kansas-Texas retired and scrapped all of its 14 roomette, 4 double bedroom cars in 1965 except for the *Benjamin Milam* which had already been retired and scrapped a year earlier.

Special had fallen upon hard times and was, by 1958, consistently hours late because of the horrible track conditions on the Missouri-Kansas-Texas. In fact, the Frisco would no longer operate the train from St. Louis after February, 1959. The El Paso car, because of its long routing, was not as popular as the other cars that ran via the Missouri Pacific and was cut back on January 24, 1958 to a New York to Dallas-Fort Worth route. The Washington to Houston car was finally dropped on June 10, 1959, partially a victim of declining patronage but also of the very popular slumbercoach service which the Baltimore & Ohio and Missouri Pacific had established between the nation's capital and Texas. The other three cars that operated west of St. Louis on *The Texas Eagle* lasted until 1961. The airplane had virtually taken away most of the traffic from these cars by that date, and in June, 1961, all three cars were dropped between New York, San Antonio, Dallas, and Houston. The interline Baltimore & Ohio-Missouri Pacific Slumbercoach service and a sleeper from the nation's capital lasted longer than the Pennsylvania Railroad's through cars. It is interesting to note, in looking at the consist of *The Penn Texas*, that it was one of the few Pennsylvania Railroad's Blue Ribbon trains with long consists that did not have a twin-unit diner. A train such as *The Penn Texas* seemed to warrant one, because of its size. However, most of these cars were already assigned to other trains, and it simply received a regular dining car. The Pennsylvania seemed to favor putting Budd built dining cars on this route on Nos. 3 and 4. To make up for the lack of dining space, and to provide plenty of lounge area for people to have a drink or two if they were waiting to be called for dinner, the Pennsylvania Railroad had transferred the very unique recreation cars from *The Jeffersonian* to *The Penn Texas*, providing a full car devoted to lounge, recreation and bar space. *The Penn Texas* had a long life with westbound No. 3 not being discontinued until the Penn Central dismissed the train in June, 1970. Eastbound No. 4 continued right down until Amtrak, although it was renamed *The Spirit of St. Louis* in October, 1970 when service between New York and St. Louis was cut to one through train in each direction.

No. 25-27
THE METROPOLITAN
No. 6
THE ALLEGHENY

One of the strangest trains on the New York to St. Louis route was *The Metropolitan*, No. 25, which continued west of Pittsburgh as No. 27 and went on through to St. Louis. This train primarily served two purposes. Throughout its entire route, as can be seen from the consist sheet, *The Metropolitan* was a heavy headend train, especially west of Pittsburgh, and could usually be seen even east of Pittsburgh carrying not only an RPO car, plus an RPO-baggage car with another 30 ft.

			Train 25			
Car Type	Description		From	To	Details	Car Des
1 BM-70M	DH DE Sunday and Monday		Harrisburg	Pittsburgh	Return of 64's car	
1 MS-60	DE Monday		Harrisburg	Pittsburgh		
1 X-29	Mail and Express, DE Sunday and Mon.		Washington	Pittsburgh	From 571 Harrisburg	
1 Express	X-29 Sunday		Harrisburg	Pittsburgh		
1 Express	X-29 Sunday		Harrisburg	St. Louis	To 27, Pittsburgh	
1 Express	B-60, Sunday and Days after holidays		Boston	St. Louis	From 163, New York, To 27 Pittsburgh	
1 Express	B-60, Sunday and Days after holidays		Boston	Pittsburgh	From 163, New York	
1 Express	B-60, Sunday and Days after holidays		Boston	Chicago	From 163, New York, To 99 Pittsburgh	
1 MS-60	(X)		New York	Cincinnati	To 203, Pittsburgh	
1 MS-60	Semi-open, DE Monday		New York	Pittsburgh		
1 BM-70M	Letter End East		New York	Pittsburgh		
1 BM-70M	30 foot apartment, DE Monday		New York	Pittsburgh	Letter End West	
1 B-60	Monday		New York	Pittsburgh		
4 P-70KR	Reclining Seats		%New York	Buffalo		
1 Diner-Lounge			New York	Pittsburgh		
1 PL	28-1		New York	Pittsburgh		
1 P-70KR	Reclining Seats		%New York	Buffalo		
1 P-70KR	Reclining Seats		%Washington	Pittsburgh	From 571, Harrisburg	

Seen here on the deadline at Altoona, Pennsylvania in 1971, is Pennsylvania Railroad's Railway Express Agency Express Refrigerator Car No. 2561. The railroad operated a large number of these R50 class cars in passenger train service and *The Metropolitan* was regularly assigned three of them west of Pittsburgh, with most of the cars coming from New England points and being added to the train at Pittsburgh. This car is a classic example of some of the Pennsylvania Railroad's unique headend equipment. It has been preserved at the railroad museum in Altoona, Pennsylvania.

Train No. 27

Car Type	Description	From	To	Details	Car Des
1 MS-60	DE Monday	Indianapolis	St. Louis		
1 MS-60	(X)	Indianapolis	St. Louis		
1 Express	X-29 Sunday	New York	St. Louis	From 85 Pittsburgh	
1 Express	X-29 Sunday	Harrisburg	St. Louis	From 25 Pittsburgh	
1 Express	B-60, Messenger, Sunday and Days after Holidays	Boston	St. Louis	From 25 Pittsburgh	
1 Express	B-60 Messenger	Pittsburgh	St. Louis		
1 MS-60	(X) Sun., Mon. and Days after Holidays	Pittsburgh	St. Louis		
1 MS-60	Open, DE Monday	Pittsburgh	St. Louis		
1 BM-70M	Letter End East	Pittsburgh	St. Louis		
1 B-60	Baggage an d Mail	Pittsburgh	St. Louis		
1 P-70	Sunday	Pittsburgh	St. Louis		
2 P-70GSR	Reclining Seats	%Pittsburgh	St. Louis		
1 SL	12-1	Pittsburgh	St. Louis		270
1 SL-Lounge	8 Section, Buffet (Lounge End West)	Pittsburgh	Louisville	To 306 Indianapolis	271
1 Express	X-29	xNew York	Indianapolis	From 95 Pittsburgh	
1 Express	B-60, Messenger	xBoston	Indianapolis	From 95 Pittsburgh	
1 Express	R-50	xHartford	St. Louis	From 95 Pittsburgh	
1 Express	B-60, Messenger	xProvidence	St. Louis	From 95 Pittsburgh	
1 Express	B-60	xSouth Norwalk	St. Louis	From 95 Pittsburgh	
1 Express	B-60	xReading	St. Louis	From 95 Pittsburgh	
1 Express	R-50	xDelmar	St. Louis	From 95 Pittsburgh	
1 Express	B-60	xPhiladelphia	St. Louis	From 95 Pittsburgh	
1 Express	R-50	xPhiladelphia	Indianapolis	From 95 Pittsburgh, To 33 Columbus	
1 Express	B-60, DE Saturday and Sunday	@Columbus	St. Louis		
1 MS-60	DE Saturday and Sunday	@Columbus	St. Louis		
1 MS-60	DE Sunday	@Columbus	Indianapolis		
1 Express	X-29, DE Sunday and Monday	@Dayton	St. Louis		
1 MS-60	(X)	@Springfield	St. Louis	From 101 Richmond	
1 MS-60	(X)	Pittsburgh	St. Louis		
1 Rider		xPittsburgh	St. Louis		
1 X-29	Papers, Thursday or Friday	Wilkes Barre	Dayton	From 93 Pittsburgh	
1 MS-60	DE Monday	Pittsburgh	Dayton		
1 MS-60	(X)	Pittsburgh	Columbus		
1 Express	X-29, Sunday	New York	Columbus	From 85 Pittsburgh	
1 MS-60	(X)	@Springfield	Indianapolis	From 101 Richmond	
1 B-60	Mail and Express	@Springfield	Indianapolis	From 101 Richmond	

x DE Sunday, Monday and Days after Holidays
@ Move in Express 27

The Metropolitan carried an RPO car over most of its route both east and west of Pittsburgh. East of Pittsburgh, the train had two RPO cars between New York and Pittsburgh. West of Pittsburgh, it always carried one RPO car. The car, seen here, is an M70BA car built in 1910-1911 and modernized. These cars often substituted for the regularly assigned BM70 cars which The Metropolitan was normally assigned. No. 6, *The Allegheny*, also carried a BM70M car from St. Louis to Pittsburgh eastbound. One could find various types of baggage-RPO cars or straight RPO cars substituting for the assigned type of car as long as the RPO compartment met the size required by the Railway Postal Service. Thus, a BM70BA car might easily substitute for a BM70M. No. 6511 was 60 years old when this photograph was taken of the car in Washington, D. C. in September, 1973. By then, it was covering the last RPO route in the United States between New York and Washington.

While *The Metropolitan* was normally assigned P70KR type reclining seat coaches, or P70GSR reclining seat coaches, west of Pittsburgh, as was *The Allegheny* on its eastbound run to Pittsburgh. Nevertheless, the railroad often substituted other types of coach equipment, both for the normally assigned cars and as extra cars for *The Metropolitan*. Thus, it would not have been unusual to see a car like this P70FBR car, No. 1721, in the consist of *The Metropolitan* or *The Allegheny* in the early 1950s. The P70FBR cars were built after World War II by the Altoona car shops from older P70 cars and were given air conditioning, but the fact was that when the railroad rebuilt many of its older P70s, it did not equip them with reclining seats. Nevertheless, P70FBR cars like 1721 would probably have been in the consist of *The Metropolitan* on a fairly regular basis east of Pittsburgh, in particular, when extra cars were needed or regular cars were not available.

Train No. 6					
Car Type	**Description**	**From**	**To**	**Details**	**Car Des**
1 MS-60	(X)	Dayton	Pittsburgh		
2 MS-60	X-29	St. Louis	Pittsburgh		
1 Express	B-60	St. Louis	New York	To 18, Pittsburgh	
1 Express	B-60 DE Saturday and Sunday	St. Louis	Harrisburg	To 18, Pittsburgh	
1 Express	B-60	St. Louis	Philadelphia	To 18, Pittsburgh	
1 Express	B-60, Messenger, GOLD STAR	St. Louis	Pittsburgh		
1 MS-60	X-29	St. Louis	Philadelphia	To 46, Pittsburgh	
1 MS-60	(X)	St. Louis	New York	To 46, Pittsburgh	
1 MS-60	B-60 Open	St. Louis	New York	To 46, Pittsburgh	
1 BM-70M		St. Louis	Pittsburgh	Letter End West	
2 P-70GSR	Reclining Seat	%St. Louis	Pittsburgh		
1 SL	12-1	St. Louis	Pittsburgh		61
1 SL-Lounge	8 Section, Buffet	Louisville	Pittsburgh	From 305, Indianapolis	65
1 MS-60	X-29, DE Monday	Indianapolis	Pittsburgh		

Early in the 1950s, Altoona Car Shop decided to rebuild two of the older dining cars, into two unique coffee shop-tavern cars, No. 1157 and No. 1158. No. 1157 and No. 1158 had interiors patterned almost exactly after the streamlined *Congressional* cars and the railroad intended them for service on the New York to Washington corridor. However, in 1954, the cars were assigned to New York-Pittsburgh service, replacing *The Metropolitan's* diner. The coffee shop-tavern car, seen here, No. 1158, was now classified D78edR with a long lunch counter and seated 17 in the coffee shop section, 18 in the dining section, and 6 in the lounge. The car was photographed at Cuyahoga Falls, Ohio after it had been taken off the roster by the Pennsylvania Railroad in 1961 and been purchased by the Mack Lowry Museum. This photo shows the car on June 2, 1970, and it still looks fairly decent after years of retirement and storage. They were an attempt by the railroad to provide economy meal service on trains like No. 25 between New York and Pittsburgh. The cars were later put into service on the New York-Washington corridor.

apartment, but usually with 10 to 12 other head-end cars. West of Pittsburgh, the train was loaded down with masses of headend equipment, and had a very slow schedule. The passenger cars were sandwiched somewhere in the middle. In fact, there was so much headend equipment on No. 27 that a separate rider coach had to be provided for the crew between Pittsburgh and St. Louis to watch and keep track of all of the headend traffic that followed the passenger cars. In addition, as should be evident from the consist sheets, this train switched headend equipment in and out, at virtually every sizable intermediate point. This made for a very slow schedule on No. 27.

East of Pittsburgh, No. 25 was a very important New York to Pittsburgh train with an early morning departure from New York and, a late afternoon arrival in Pittsburgh, where it laid over so that all of the headend equipment could be switched into the departing No. 27, which usually departed after 6 o'clock in the evening. In addition to all of the headend equipment, No. 27 also carried 2 reclining seat coaches as well as a heavy-weight 12 section, 1 drawing room sleeping car for anybody who cared to ride the slow and dowdy *Metropolitan*. This sleeping car was patronized mostly by passengers traveling from intermediate points, which were completely bypassed by Pennsylvania Railroad's other through trains, and by pass riders. In addition to the Pittsburgh to St. Louis cars, the train also conveyed the 8 section-

buffet lounge car between Pittsburgh and Louisville, which was handed over to No. 306 at Indianapolis. This provided some class to *The Metropolitan* west of Pittsburgh because it did provide beverage service as well as snack service to first-class passengers. There was no dining car service west of Pittsburgh.

Between New York and Pittsburgh, however, *The Metropolitan* was a very popular train because of the time of day it operated. The consist sheet is actually deceiving, because while the railroad often regularly assigned four P70KR reclining seat coaches, the train was often seen and photographed with many more coaches than those four, usually straight P70 air conditioned coaches. In addition, No. 25 east of Pittsburgh carried a dining-lounge car and a parlor car with 28 seats and a drawing room to provide first class service over the route for daytime travelers. No. 25, *The Metropolitan*, played a key role in New York to Pittsburgh service but west of Pittsburgh, despite its passenger equipment, it was primarily a mail and express train. It might be noted here that Pennsylvania's own Altoona-built coffee shop-tavern cars, No. 1157 and No. 1158, replaced the dining-lounge car on this train in 1954, operating on it for a period of time until the train was finally dropped. The interiors of these cars were modeled almost exactly after *Congressional* Coffee Shop-Tavern cars. No. 25, *The Metropolitan*, lasted until February, 1956 when it was replaced on the New

Coffee Shop Tavern
BREAKFAST

Price Includes Choice of Orange, Tomato or
Pineapple Juice, Toast with Preserves and Beverage.

HOT CAKES WITH SYRUP AND BACON SLICES	1.35
CRISP BACON SLICES WITH EGGS, FRIED OR SCRAMBLED	1.35
GRILLED TENDER HAM WITH EGGS, "AS DESIRED"	1.45
TWO FARM FRESH EGGS, ANY STYLE	1.05

Continental Breakfast	Keystone Special
Double Orange Juice	Orange Juice
Danish Pastry with Butter	Two Doughnuts
Tea Coffee Milk	Cup of Coffee
75¢	**50¢**

Additional Suggestions - A la Carte
FRUIT, CEREAL, JUICE

Orange Juice .20; Large .35   Stewed Prunes .30
Pineapple Juice .20   Chilled Melon .30
        Tomato Juice .20   Cooked or Dry Cereal .30

TOAST AND PASTRY

Doughnuts (2) .15
Danish Pastry with Butter .25
Toasted English Muffin with Butter .25
Toast - Dry or Buttered - with Preserves .25

BEVERAGES

*Coffee, Tea, Sanka or Milk .20
*Second cup .10

MEAL CHECKS—i.e.—write on check each item desired. Waiter is not permitted to accept oral orders.

The steward will welcome your comments on our food and service.
If you prefer, write to Sidney N. Phelps, Manager,
Dining Car Service, Pennsylvania Railroad, Long Island City 1, N.Y.

4G5

PENNSYLVANIA RAILROAD

The menu shown here is a general service menu from the Pennsylvania Railroad in the 1950s but is indicative of the kind of breakfast that a coffee shop-tavern car such as 1157 or 1158 might have provided to the patrons of No. 25. The menu is quite extensive and one can see that, despite the loss of its dining car, *The Metropolitan* provided an extensive variety of choices to its patrons at economy prices in its coffee shop-tavern cars.

York-Pittsburgh route by the ill-fated and disastrous experimental train built by General Motors. *The Aerotrain* lasted only a short time and operated westbound pretty much on the schedule of *The Metropolitan*. The short-lived experiment over, the Pennsylvania Railroad resumed running No. 25 as a standard train, but renamed it *The Duquesne* to handle the early morning New York to Pittsburgh schedules. Like other Pennsylvania trains, *The Metropolitan* survived until Amtrak in May, 1971 except with another name, *The Duquesne*, borrowed from another train.

No. 25-27, *The Metropolitan* had strictly no eastbound counterpart but the schedule was balanced by the operation of train No. 6, *The Allegheny*, between St. Louis and Pittsburgh, as well as another eastbound schedule strictly from Pittsburgh to New York that did not connect with *The Allegheny*. This was train No. 72, *The Juniata*, which handled the same equipment as the westbound *Metropolitan*. Train No. 6, *The Allegheny*, departed St. Louis late at night and arrived in Pittsburgh at lunchtime the following day. Passengers could then connect with Pennsylvania Railroad's No. 74, *The Duquesne*, for Philadelphia and New York. As the least favored train on the

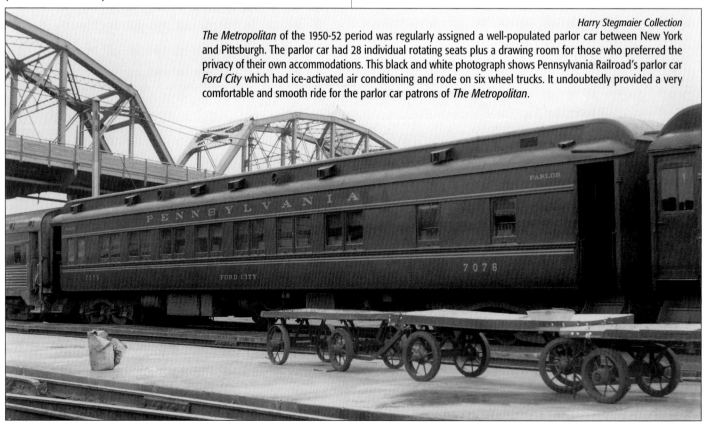

The Metropolitan of the 1950-52 period was regularly assigned a well-populated parlor car between New York and Pittsburgh. The parlor car had 28 individual rotating seats plus a drawing room for those who preferred the privacy of their own accommodations. This black and white photograph shows Pennsylvania Railroad's parlor car *Ford City* which had ice-activated air conditioning and rode on six wheel trucks. It undoubtedly provided a very comfortable and smooth ride for the parlor car patrons of *The Metropolitan*.

entire St. Louis route, train No. 6 carried a substantial amount of headend traffic, including a St. Louis to Pittsburgh RPO car, plus 2 reclining seat P70GSR coaches and a 12 section, 1 drawing room sleeper, as well as, from Indianapolis to Pittsburgh, the 8 section-buffet lounge sleeper from Louisville. No. 6 ran on a slow schedule but was not overburdened with the tremendous amount of headend traffic west of Pittsburgh that No. 27, *The Metropolitan*, carried. Trains like No. 6, *The Allegheny*, and its westbound counterpart, No. 27, *The Metropolitan*, were found expendable between Pittsburgh and St. Louis by the mid 1950s and both were discontinued as part of the general overall cutback in passenger services by the Pennsylvania Railroad.

No. 30 and No. 31
THE SPIRIT OF ST. LOUIS

Undoubtedly, No. 30 eastbound and No. 31 westbound, *The Spirit of St. Louis*, was Pennsylvania's premier train on the St. Louis to New York route. While not as illustrious as *The Broadway Limited*, this train, named after Charles Lindbergh's famous plane in his trans-Atlantic crossing, nevertheless, was certainly the best Pennsylvania had to offer in the New York-St. Louis market. As such, *The Spirit of St. Louis* was an all-Pullman train with mostly new lightweight equipment. The train carried only one regular

headend car. It also carried 2 heavyweight sleeping cars, 14 section, high speed betterment Pullman rebuilds, to handle government traffic, one between New York and St. Louis, and another operating between the nation's capital and St. Louis, the latter transferred to and from the main train at Harrisburg. Between New York and St. Louis, Nos. 30 and 31 handled a number of lightweight cars, including a 21 roomette *Inn* series sleeper, a *Creek* series 12 duplex single room, 4 double bedroom car and a 4 double bedroom, 4 compartment, 2 drawing room *Imperial* car. These cars were complemented by a mid-train 6 double bedroom *Fall* series lounge-sleeper with a bar and, of course, a twin-unit dining car. In addition, each train carried a Washington to St. Louis 10 roomette, 6 double bedroom sleeper to go along with the heavyweight 14 section car. It is interesting to note that *The Spirit of St. Louis* observation-lounge sleeper which contained 2 drawing rooms, 1 compartment and 1 double bedroom as well as a bar, operated not to and from New York but between Washington and St. Louis in both directions. Another interesting note, which will become significant, is the fact that this train handled a substantial amount of Indianapolis traffic as did *The Jeffersonian*. Three sleeping cars handled by the all-Pullman *Spirit of St. Louis* operated to Indianapolis, one a prewar *Cascade* series 10 roomette, 5 double bedroom car operated to and

Train No. 30
Blue Ribbon
Spirit of St. Louis
Will NOT operate November 27, 28, December 24, 25, 26, 31

Car Type	Description	From	To	Details	Car Des
1 Milk	R-50 (X)	Salamanca	New York	SW From 574, Harrisburg	
1 Milk	R-50 (X)	Centerville	New York	SW From 580, Harrisburg	
1 MS-60	X-29	St. Louis	New York	SW	
1 SL	14 Section	¢St. Louis	New York	SW	310
1 SL	21 Roomette	St. Louis	New York	LW	309
1 SL	12 Duplex SR, 4 DBR	St. Louis	New York	LW	308
1 SL	4 Compartment, 4 DBR, 2 DR	St. Louis	New York	LW	307
1 SL-Lounge	6 DBR, Bar	#St. Louis	New York	LW	306
1 Diner	) Twin Unit				
1 Kitchen-Dormitory	) Twin Unit	St. Louis	New York	LW	
1 SL	21 Roomette	Indianapolis	New York	LW	305
1 SL	10 Roomette, 6 DBR	#Indianapolis	New York	LW	304
1 SL	10 Roomette, 5 DBR, DE Saturday	Indianapolis	Washington	LW To 530, Harrisburg	303
1 SL	14 Section	¢St. Louis	Washington	SW To 530, Harrisburg	302
1 SL	10 Roomette, 6DBR	#St. Louis	Washington	LW To 530 Harrisburg	301
1 SL-Obs.	2 DR, 1 Compartment, 1 DBR	#St. Louis	Washington	LW To 530 Harrisburg	300

Pennsylvania Railroad's *Spirit of St. Louis* was still an all-Pullman train in 1952, although it would lose that status in 1953 with the discontinuance of *The Jeffersonian* and the addition of *The Indianapolis Limited* to the Pennsylvania Railroad timetable. This meant that the train would then receive coaches in New York to St. Louis operation. *The Indianapolis Limited*, was really just a Pullman-coach second section of *The Spirit of St. Louis*. The all-Pullman *Spirit of St. Louis* merited a twin-unit dining car in the 1952 era and cars like Pennsylvania Railroad's No. 4608, a full dining car, and No. 4609, a kitchen-dormitory car, were often found on Pennsylvania Railroad Nos. 30 and 31. The railroad provided this large amount of dining car space for *The Spirit of St. Louis* because it was its premier train on the New York-St. Louis run and, for this reason, the railroad deemed it necessary to operate a twin-unit diner to handle all the Pullman patrons still carried aboard the train in 1952. Cars No. 4608 and 4609 were built by American Car & Foundry for the Pennsylvania Railroad and delivered in early 1949. The full dining car, No. 4608, had a 68 seat dining room and a 4 seat waiting lounge and was operated with the 4609. Of the five twin units built by ACF in this group, only 4608 and 4609 made it into the Penn Central era, the rest being retired or scrapped between 1966 and 1968. No. 4608 and 4609 were finally retired by the Penn Central in 1970 and went to the scrapper's torch.

As can be seen from the color cover of this *Spirit of St. Louis* menu, the twin unit diners on the train provided the Pullman passengers with a large selection to which to choose. *The Spirit of St. Louis* left none of its patrons hungry but the fact is that Pennsylvania Railroad menus, in general, simply did not provide the variety of choice or some of the exquisite cuisines found on other railroads such as The Baltimore & Ohio, The New York Central or The Santa Fe.

PENNSYLVANIA RAILROAD

Spirit of St. Louis

DINNER

Radishes - Celery - Olives

CHOICE OF ONE

Bismarck Herring
Bacon and Bean Soup

Chilled Tomato Juice
Chicken Broth with Noodles

FRIED FILET OF SOLE, TARTAR SAUCE
Buttered Peas   Parsley Potatoes   3.25

BAKED SUGAR CURED HAM, ORANGE SAUCE
Braised Red Cabbage   Parsley Potatoes   3.50

ROAST YOUNG CHICKEN, DRESSING, CRANBERRY SAUCE
Buttered Peas   Rissolee Potato   3.60

CHARCOAL GRILLED SIRLOIN STEAK, MAITRE D'HOTEL
French Fried Onion Rings   Rissolee Potato   5.25

Cole Slaw with Green Peppers

Honeybran Muffins

CHOICE OF ONE

Freshly Baked Apple Pie
Gruyere or Bleu Cheese with Crackers   Stewed Pears

Vanilla or Strawberry Ice Cream
Caramel Custard

CHOICE OF ONE

Pot of Coffee
Individual Milk

Tea with Lemon or Cream
Sanka

Mints   15E5

Train No. 31
Blue Ribbon
Spirit of St. Louis
Will NOT Operate November 27, 28, December 24, 25, 26, 31

Car Type	Description	From	To	Details	Car Des
I Express	B-60, DE Saturday, Sunday, Monday and Days after holidays	New York	St. Louis	SW	
I SL	14 Section	¢New York	St. Louis	SW	320
I SL	21 Roomette	New York	St. Louis	LW	319
I SL	12 Duplex SR, 4 DBR	New York	St. Louis	LW	318
I SL	4 Compartment, 4 DBR, 2 DR	New York	St. Louis	LW	317
I SL-Lounge	6 DBR, Bar	#New York	St. Louis	LW	316
I Diner	) Twin Unit				
I Kitchen-Dormitory	) Twin Unit	New York	St. Louis	LW	
I SL	21 Roomette	New York	Indianapolis	LW	315
I SL	10 Roomette, 6 DBR	#New York	Indianapolis	LW	314
I SL	10 Section, I DR, I Cpt., DE Saturday and November 27, December 26, January I	New York	Roanoke	SW, To 645, Harrisburg	K20
I SL	10 Roomette, 6 DBR	New York	Roanoke	LW, To 645, Harrisburg	KI7
I SL	10 Roomette, 5 DBR, DE Saturday	Washington	Indianapolis	LW, From 531, Harrisburg	313
I SL	14 Section	¢Washington	St. Louis	SW, From 531, Harrisburg	312
I SL	10 Roomette, 6 DBR	#Washington	St. Louis	LW, From 531, Harrisburg	311
I SL-Obs	2 DR, I Compartment, I DBR, Bar	#Washington	St. Louis	LW, From 531, Harrisburg	310

from Washington, while a 21 roomette car and a 10 roomette, 6 double bedroom car operated from New York in both directions. This led to an important change. In the spring of 1953, *The Spirit of St. Louis* would take over *The Jeffersonian's* coaches, now added to this previously all-Pullman train between New York and St. Louis, while the

Indianapolis traffic would be handled by a new train, a coach and Pullman Blue Ribbon *Indianapolis Limited*. The Pennsylvania Railroad was always a big player in the New York and Washington to Indianapolis market, with much faster schedules than the competing New York Central. *The Spirit of St. Louis* was the premier

David E. Staplin

Each *Spirit of St. Louis* consist contained a 4 double bedroom, 4 compartment, 2 drawing room sleeper drawn from the *Imperial* series, which provided multi-person private room accommodations for the patrons of the St. Louis line. *Imperial Trees*, seen here in Chicago in September 1969, was one of the Pennsylvania Railroad *Imperial* cars regularly assigned to *The Spirit of St. Louis* in the 1950s. *Imperial Trees* came from a postwar order for the railroad and was delivered to the company between September and December, 1948. All of these cars were built by American Car & Foundry and most of them, because of their 4 double bedroom, 4 compartments and 2 drawing room accommodations, proved valuable even after cutbacks in passenger service, both for charters and for leasing to other railroads during heavy traffic periods. All of the postwar ACF built *Imperial* cars lasted until 1971, when all but two were scrapped by the Penn Central after Amtrak took over passenger service.

Each *Spirit of St. Louis* carried among its sleepers two 10 roomette, 6 double bedroom cars on a regular basis, with the westbound train having three cars, one being the New York to Roanoke sleeper. One 10 roomette, 6 bedroom car operated from New York to Indianapolis while another operated from Washington to St. Louis. Regularly assigned to *The Spirit of St. Louis* in the 1950s was Pennsylvania Railroad's *Conestoga Rapids*, shown in this picture taken in May, 1965 in Louisville, Kentucky. *Conestoga Rapids* had been delivered to the Pennsylvania Railroad by the Pullman Company in the postwar era, arriving on the property in early 1949. *Conestoga Rapids* contained 10 roomettes and 6 double bedrooms and was normally assigned by Pullman and the Pennsylvania Railroad to the New York to Indianapolis sleeping car line in the 1950s. *Conestoga Rapids* made it into the Penn Central era until it was finally retired in 1971 and went into work train service as Penn Central 27057.

Each *Spirit of St. Louis* consist carried one of Pennsylvania Railroad's postwar *Creek* series 12 duplex single room, 4 double bedroom cars in its consist. These cars were assigned to the New York to St. Louis route on *The Spirit of St. Louis*. One regularly assigned car to *The Spirit of St. Louis* was Pennsylvania Railroad's *Crystal Creek*, seen here in Chicago in June, 1963. *Crystal Creek* arrived on the Pennsylvania property from Pullman in early 1949 and served on *The Spirit of St. Louis* in the 1950s on a regular basis. Later it operated on other trains and in charter service in the 1960s. It was finally retired in 1968, sold to the Hofheinz Enterprises in Houston, and when that collapsed, was scrapped. However, a fall 1969 photo shows that the car was still in Chicago in October of 1969 before being transferred to Texas.

Harry Stegmaier Collection

In this photograph, a very long *Spirit of St. Louis* is seen backing into St. Louis Union Station early in the 1960s. On the rear is one of the unique flatend observation cars which was purchased by the Pennsylvania Railroad for its top trains. On the rear is 2 drawing, 1 compartment, 1 double bedroom buffet-lounge-observation car *Frank Thomson*, which came from Pullman Standard in early 1949. This car was regularly assigned to *The Spirit of St. Louis* to carry the drumhead for the train. When the train finally lost its observation cars, the *Frank Thomson* and some of its other sister cars went into corridor parlor car service in 1957 but returned to sleeping car service in 1958. The *Frank Thomson* remained on the property until 1963 when it was sold to the Hofheinz Enterprises in Houston, Texas. However, luckily it was saved and, is now in the hands of a private individual who is restoring it in Arizona. In this photograph, the car is still carrying the drumhead of *The Spirit of St. Louis*.

train on the St. Louis route. Although the train lost its all-Pullman status in April, 1953, it carried on through the lean years until 1971. In October, 1970, eastbound No. 30 was dropped but No. 4, *The Penn Texas* was renamed *The Spirit of St. Louis* when the Pennsylvania Railroad's successor, the Penn Central, cut New York-St. Louis trains to one in each direction. Westbound, No. 31, continued as *The Spirit of St. Louis* until Amtrak day in May 1971, the most long lived train in the New York-St. Louis market.

No. 32 and No. 33
THE ST. LOUISAN

The St. Louisan, trains No. 32 eastbound and No. 33 westbound, were Pennsylvania Railroad trains that fitted somewhere below the level of quality found on *The Spirit of St. Louis* but were a cut above secondary trains on the run like *The American* and *The Metropolitan*. The westbound *St. Louisan* departed New York in the early afternoon and arrived in St. Louis early the next morning, while the eastbound *St. Louisan* departed St. Louis in the early evening, made an overnight run to Pittsburgh, and then served as a daylight train between Pittsburgh and New York, arriving there in late afternoon. Both trains carried a good deal of headend equipment, with westbound No. 33 also carrying an RPO car between New York and St. Louis. Eastbound No. 32 carried an RPO between St. Louis and Pittsburgh. In addition, this train

Train 32
Blue Ribbon
The St. Louisan

Car Type	Description	From	To	Details	Car Des
1 MS-60	X-29, Wednesday, NEWSWEEK	Dayton	Harrisburg		
1 B-60	Mail and Express, Tuesday NEWSWEEK	Dayton	New York		
1 MS-60	(X)	Dayton	New York		
1 MS-60	(X)	Dayton	Pittsburgh		
1 Express	R50, or X-29, DE Sunday and Monday	Dayton	Pittsburgh		
1 Express	B-60, Messenger	St. Louis	Boston	To 96 (74 Mon. and Days after Holidays) Pittsburgh	
1 BM-70M	Letter End East	St. Louis	Pittsburgh		
2 P-70	DE Friday	Harrisburg	New York		
3 P-70	Friday	Harrisburg	New York		
1 B-60		St. Louis	Pittsburgh		
1 Baggage Dormitory		St. Louis	New York		
1 P-70GR	Reclining Seats	%St. Louis	New York		
1 P-85BR	Reclining Seats	%St. Louis	New York		
1 Diner		St. Louis	New York	LW	
1 SL-Lounge	3 DBR, 1 DR, Bar	St. Louis	New York	LW	327
1 SL	21 Roomette	St. Louis	New York	LW	326
1 SL	6 Section, 6 DBR	St. Louis	New York		325
1 SL	8 Section, 5 DBR	Louisville	New York	From 327 Indianapolis	324
1 SL	12-1	Cincinnati	New York	From 202 Pittsburgh	202
1 SL	6 Section, 6 DBR	St. Louis	Washington	To 554 Harrisburg	323

The St. Louisan was one of the Pennsylvania Railroad's trains which received one of the unique Baggage-Dormitory cars which the Pennsylvania Railroad had purchased in the postwar era. In this photograph, taken in 1948 at Sunnyside Yard on Long Island, New York, is No. 6691, a Baggage-Dormitory car that the railroad ordered and received from American Car & Foundry in the spring of 1948. No. 6691 provided a big baggage compartment plus dormitory space for the crew. This ACF product remained a Baggage-Dormitory car until 1964 when it was converted into a baggage-RPO car, No. 6596, which somehow survived through the Penn Central era, was purchased by Amtrak in 1976, and was out of service after 1977.

carried one of the rare Pennsylvania Railroad baggage-dormitory cars, as well as reclining seat coaches, two of which were the new streamlined lightweight P85BR cars. In addition, each train carried a 6 section, 6 double bedroom sleeper between New York and St. Louis, as well as a lightweight 21 roomette car from the *Inn* series, complemented by a *Colonial* series 3 double bedroom, 1 drawing room, bar-lounge-sleeper, as well as a lightweight diner, often a prewar or postwar Budd built lightweight car. *The St. Louisan* also carried a Washington to St. Louis sleeping car, with No. 33 having a standard 12 section, 1 drawing room sleeper, while No. 32 carried a 6 section, 6 double bedroom sleeper. No. 33 and No. 32 also carried the New York to Louisville car, a 6 section, 6 double bedroom sleeper westbound and an 8 section, 5 double bedroom sleeper eastbound, which were handed over or received from a connecting train at Indianapolis. The train was a strange mix-

Train 33
Blue Ribbon
The St. Louisan

Car Type	Description	From	To	Details	Car Des
1 MS-60	Tuesday NEWSWEEK	Dayton	Kansas City	To MP 5 St. Louis	
1 B-60	Mail & Express, Wednesday NEWSWEEK	Dayton	St. Louis		
1 MS-60	(X)	Dayton	St. Louis		
1 MS-60		Dayton	St. Louis		
1 MS-60	(X)	Philadelphia	St. Louis	From 611 Harrisburg	
			Kansas City		
			Texarkana		
			Los Angeles		
1 MS-60	DE Sunday, Monday and Days after Holidays	New York	St. Louis	Preferential Mails	
1 MS-60	(X)	New York	St. Louis		
			Kansas City		
			Texarkana		
			Los Angeles		
1 Express	X-29	zNew York	St. Louis		
1 Express	B-60 Messenger	zNew York	St. Louis		
1 BM-70M	DE Sunday	xNew York	St. Louis	Letter End East	
1 Baggage-Dormitory		New York	St. Louis		
1 P-70GSR	Reclining Seats, Sat, Sun. and Mon.	%New York	St. Louis		
1 P-70GR	Reclining Seats	%New York	St. Louis		
2 P-85BR	Reclining Seats	%New York	St. Louis		
1 Diner		New York	St. Louis	LW	
1 SL-Lounge	3 DBR, 1 DR, Bar	New York	St. Louis	LW	330
1 SL	21 Roomette	New York	St. Louis	LW	331
1 SL	6 Sections, 6 DBR	New York	St. Louis		332
1 SL	6 Sections, 6 DBR	New York	Louisville	To 326 Indianapolis	333
1 SL	12-1	Washington	St. Louis	From 533 Harrisburg	334
1 SL	12-1	*Washington	Chicago	From 533 Harrisburg	50
1 P-70KR	Reclining Seats	%Washington	Pittsburgh	From 533 Harrisburg	
1 P-70	Friday and Sunday	New York	Harrisburg		
1 MS-60	(X)	Pittsburgh	Indianapolis		
1 Express	R-50	yPhiladelphia	Indianapolis		
1 MS-60	(X)	Springfield	Indianapolis	From 27 Columbus	
1 Express	B-60 DE Sun., Mon., Holidays and Days after Holidays	New York	Dayton	From 205 Columbus	

x Mail apartment NOT in service New York-Pittsburgh; receives mail New York and Harrisburg
z DE Sunday, Monday and days after Holidays
y DE Monday, Tuesday, and 2 Days after Holidays
* To 63 Pittsburgh (23 Saturday and November 27, 28, December 25, 26, 31 and January 1, 2)

Harry Stegmaier Collection

Regularly assigned coaches on *The St. Louisan* included P70GR coaches like No. 4365, seen here in Chicago in June, 1963. Altoona had rebuilt these cars in the late 1930s and equipped them with 68 reclining seats and roller bearing trucks, as well as a mechanical air conditioning system. No. 4365 was typical of the kind of coaches that sometimes populated No. 32 and No. 33 in the 1950s, with one P70GR being assigned in each direction to the train.

Dining car service on *The St. Louisan* was provided by heavyweight, rebuilt diners such as No. 4472, which had been modernized by Altoona Car Shops in the early 1950s. No. 4472 had been built as a dining car in 1922 and was classed as a D78fR dining-lounge car after it emerged from the Altoona Car Shops in December, 1951. The car now seated 32 in the dining section and 10 in the lounge, which can be seen at the far end in this June, 1963 photo taken in Chicago, Illinois. While the menus were not spectacular, *The St. Louisan's* dining car provided the patrons of the train with plentiful choices of food.

Each of the consists of No. 32 and No. 33 contained a 6 section, 6 double bedroom, heavyweight sleeper between New York and St. Louis. Cars like *Poplar Heights* were often found on *The St. Louisan* during the 1950s. These heavyweights did not have to be betterment cars. A car like *Poplar Heights* held down the New York-St. Louis 6 section, 6 double bedroom car routing on Nos. 32 and 33 in the 1950s. The car was still in service when this photograph was taken in January, 1963.

As one of the lesser trains on the New York to St. Louis route, certainly in comparison to *The Spirit of St. Louis, The St. Louisan* did not receive top but, nevertheless, very good equipment. Prewar cars like *Colonial Statesmen* contained 3 double bedrooms and 1 drawing room to go along with their lounge section which contained a bar to keep the Pullman passengers well watered if they so desired. This car was originally built for *The General* and delivered in 1938.

ture of heavyweight headend equipment, heavy-weight rebuilt coaches, streamlined coaches, streamlined sleepers and heavyweight sleepers all mixed together. It provided not only through service between New York and St. Louis, but convenient daytime service on the New York to Pittsburgh leg of its run. It also acted as a night train between Pittsburgh and St. Louis in both directions. After the Pennsylvania Railroad had cut back some of its lesser trains on the line, *The St. Louisan* became a candidate for discontinuance by the late 1950s on a route already served by *The Spirit of St. Louis* and *The Penn Texas*. On April 26, 1959, the westbound *St. Louisan* was dropped in its entirety, but the eastbound *St. Louisan* continued operating, although the portion between Pittsburgh and New York had been dropped on February 22, 1959. After that date, *The St. Louisan* through cars were delivered at Pittsburgh to No. 54, now named *The Pennsylvania Limited*. This practice continued well into the 1960s before the final demise of the train. During that interim era, *The St. Louisan* still carried a through St. Louis-New York sleeper and coach, as well as a sleeper-bar-lounge between St. Louis and Pittsburgh, and provided a convenient overnight train for St. Louis-Pittsburgh travelers. It was finally discontinued in the mid 1960s.

No. 40 and 41
THE CINCINNATI LIMITED

Probably the most prestigious operation on the New York-St. Louis main after *The Spirit of St. Louis* were Pennsylvania trains No. 40 and No. 41, *The Cincinnati Limited*. The Pennsylvania Railroad had equipped these trains with almost all streamlined equipment by 1950-51 and, they were the preferred New York-Cincinnati train for most travelers, although still some chose the competing *Ohio State Limited* on the New York Central, traveling on a roundabout route via Cleveland to reach Cincinnati and New York, respectively. It is interesting to note that *The Cincinnati Limited* carried no Washington sleeping cars since Washington-Cincinnati traffic belonged almost exclusively to the Baltimore & Ohio with its *National Limited* and *Diplomat*. *The Cincinnati Limited* did not carry much headend traffic but did handle a through railway post office car between New York and Cincinnati in both directions as well as an extra RPO-baggage car between Pittsburgh and New York eastbound and a mail storage car westbound. Coach passengers were accommodated in new P85BR lightweight streamlined coaches. Amenities were provided for them by two unique cars built strictly for *The Cincinnati Limited*, coach-bar lounge cars No. 1151 and No. 1152, post-war streamlined products. The sleeping cars

Car Type	Description	From	To	Details	Car Des
	Train No. 40				
	Blue Ribbon				
	Cincinnati Limited				
1 BM-70	30 foot apartment, DE Sat. & Sun.	Pittsburgh	New York	Letter End West	
1 BM-70	30 foot apartment	xCincinnati	New York	Letter End East	
2 P-85BR	Reclining Seats	%Cincinnati	New York		
1 Coach-Lounge-Bar, 28 Reclining Seats, 21 Lounge Seats		Cincinnati	New York	LW	
1 SL	12-1	¢Cincinnati	New York		409
1 SL	21 Roomette	*Cincinnati	New York	LW	408
1 SL	21 Roomette	Cincinnati	New York	LW	407
1 SL-Lounge	6 DBR, Bar	#Cincinnati	New York	LW	406
1 Diner	)Twin Unit				
1 Kitchen-Dormitory	)Twin Unit	Cincinnati	New York		
1 SL	12 Duplex SR, 4 DBR	Cincinnati	New York	LW	405
1 SL	10 Roomette, 6 DBR	Cincinnati	New York	LW, Car returns to Columbus in No. 3	404
1 SL	Extra (X)	Cincinnati	New York		
1 SL	10 Roomette, 6 DBR	Nashville	New York	LW, From L&N 8, Cincinnati	L403
1 SL	10 Roomette, 6 DBR	Louisville	New York	LW, From L&N 8, Cincinnati	L402
1 SL-Obs	2 DR, 1 Compartment, 1 DBR Bar-Lge	#Cincinnati	New York	LW	400

* Will not operate November 27, 28, December 24, 25, 26, 31, January 1, 2.
x RPO Portion NOT in service Sundays

Train No. 41
Blue Ribbon
Cincinnati Limited

Car Type	Description	From	To	Details	Car Des
1 MS-60	(X)	New York	Cincinnati		
1 BM-70	30 foot apartment	xNew York	Cincinnati	Letter End West	
2 P-85BR	Reclining Seats	%New York	Cincinnati		
1	Coach-Lounge-Bar, 28 Reclining Seats, 21 Lounge Seats	New York	Cincinnati	LW	
1 SL	12-1	¢New York	Cincinnati		410
1 SL	21 Roomette	*New York	Cincinnati	LW	411
1 SL	21 Roomette	New York	Cincinnati	LW	412
1 SL-Lounge	6 DBR, Bar	#New York	Cincinnati	LW	414
1 Diner	)Twin Unit				
1 Kitchen-Dormitory	)Twin Unit	New York	Cincinnati		
1 SL	12 Duplex SR, 4 DBR	New York	Cincinnati	LW	415
1 SL	10 Roomette, 6 DBR	New York	Memphis	LW, To L&N 99, Cincinnati	K416
1 SL	10 Roomette, 6 DBR	New York	Nashville	LW, To L&N 99, Cincinnati	K417
1 SL	10 Roomette, 6 DBR	New York	Louisville	LW, To L&N 99, Cincinnati	K419
1 SL-Obs	2 DR, 1 Compartment, 1 DBR Bar-Lge	#New York	Cincinnati	LW	420

* Will not operate November 27, 28, December 24, 25, 26, 31, January 1, 2.
x RPO Portion NOT in service Sundays. Daily New York-Pittsburgh

Harry Stegmaier

Especially built for *The Cincinnati Limited* were two coach-bar-lounge cars, No. 1151 and No. 1152. They provided both 28 coach seats and a 21 seat lounge that was serviced by a bar. The Budd Company built these cars for the Pennsylvania Railroad and delivered them in September, 1949, specifically for service on *The Cincinnati Limited* in order that that train might have lounge car space for its coach passengers. These coach-bar-lounge cars usually were operated just behind the two regularly assigned coaches on the train. *The Cincinnati Limited* coach-bar-lounge cars had long lives. They served the Pennsylvania Railroad as coach-bar-lounge cars until the Penn Central merger. In 1969, Penn Central rebuilt both cars into parlor-bar-lounge cars for service on the New York-Washington corridor, with No. 1152, seen here in this photograph, being given the name *John Adams*. This car was purchased by Amtrak in 1974 from the Penn Central and converted to a full buffet-lounge. It could often be seen in the 1990s on Amtrak's *Capitol Limited*. Its sister, renamed *Thomas Jefferson* in 1969, was retired by Amtrak in 1977.

on the train, with one exception, a 12 section, 1 drawing room heavyweight Pullman betterment car with high speed trucks, included two 21 roomette *Inn* series sleepers, a modern 12 duplex single room, 4 double bedroom *Creek* car and three through cars westbound that were handed over to the Louisville & Nashville at Cincinnati, as well as two interline cars eastbound. Both the New York to Nashville sleeper and the New York to Louisville sleeper were handled in both directions on *The Cincinnati Limited*, but the westbound train carried an additional New York to Memphis interline sleeper that was handled by the Louisville

& Nashville beyond Cincinnati. This car returned eastbound on other trains. Pennsylvania Railroad provided most of the 10 roomette, 6 double bedroom cars for these routings but the Louisville & Nashville did contribute three 10 roomette, 6 double bedroom sleepers, all of them painted in Tuscan Red to match the colors of *The Cincinnati Limited*. The rear of the train was graced by a blunt end, 2 drawing room, 1 compartment, 1 double bedroom bar lounge-observation car carrying *The Cincinnati Limited* drumhead, a postwar lightweight car that gave the train real class. Mid-train bar lounge service was provided by a *Falls* series

THE CAPITOL, WASHINGTON, D.C.

PENNSYLVANIA RAILROAD

Cincinnati Limited

COMBINATION SUGGESTIONS	DINNER

KEYSTONE FEATURE

Cup of Soup

CHICKEN SALAD SANDWICH, GARNISHED

Your Selection of Dessert

Tea   Coffee   Milk

$1.75

TRAVELER'S SPECIAL

Cup of Soup or Tomato Juice

HAM OR BACON WITH FRIED EGGS

Potatoes or Head Lettuce, French Dressing

Bread and Butter

Choice of Dessert

Tea   Coffee   Milk

$2.30

A LA CARTE

When writing check please specify - A La Carte

COLD DISHES AND SANDWICHES

Head Lettuce Salad .65

PRR Salad Bowl with Ry-Krisp .95

Imported Sardine Sandwich with Sliced Tomatoes
and Cole Slaw 1.15

BEVERAGES

Pot of Coffee .35   Tea .30   Grade "A" Milk .25

40-41
10/15-11/4/53

The steward will welcome your comments on our food and service.
If you prefer, write to Sidney N. Phelps, Manager.
Dining Car Service, Pennsylvania Railroad, Long Island City 1, N. Y.

DINNER

RELISHES

Carrot Sticks   Cottage Cheese   Radish Roses

APPETIZERS

Tomato Juice

Hot or Jellied Beef Broth

Half Grapefruit, Maraschino

Onion Soup, Grated Cheese

Orange Frosted Cranberry Juice

ENTREES

FRENCH FRIED SHRIMP WITH COCKTAIL SAUCE	3.30
Garden Green Peas Oven-Browned Potatoes	
FRIED CHICKEN, MARYLAND STYLE, CORN FRITTER	3.60
Asparagus, Drawn Butter Mashed Potatoes	
ROAST LOIN OF PORK WITH PAN GRAVY	3.50
Freshly Stewed Apples Whipped Potatoes	
SIRLOIN STEAK FROM THE CHARCOAL BROILER	5.25
French Fried Onion Rings Chateau Potatoes	

Sliced Tomatoes, Vinaigrette

Cream Scones   Dinner Rolls

DESSERTS

Pumpkin Pie with Sherry Whipped Cream

Vanilla Ice Cream, Chocolate Sauce   Chilled Half Grapefruit

Orange Sherbet   Cocoanut Cream Pudding   Baked Apple with Cream

Bleu or Gruyere Cheese with Crackers

BEVERAGES

Tea   Coffee   Grade "A" Milk

Candy Mints

BOTTLE of RED or WHITE WINE is suggested (Split) .65

Harry Stegmaier Collection

This *Cincinnati Limited* menu, from the fall of 1953, shows that its twin-unit diner served pretty much the same kind of meals that all of Pennsylvania's blue ribbon trains did. Pennsylvania Railroad menus seemed to be very much alike in many cases, with four entrees for dinner on blue ribbon trains plus special items. As one of the premier trains, *The Cincinnati Limited* got its own menu with the name of the train printed on it, rather than a simple field menu like some of the secondary blue ribbon trains.

Harry Stegmaier

Each *Cincinnati Limited* carried a postwar 6 double bedroom-bar-lounge car in the *Falls* series. Regularly assigned to *The Cincinnati Limited* in the 1950s was Pennsylvania Railroad's *Palm Falls*, which had arrived on the property in the first half of 1949 from the Pullman Company. *Palm Falls* is seen here in September, 1969 after it had received Penn Central lettering but was still in Tuscan Red. This photo shows the aisle side of the car as it sits in Chicago, Illinois. The 6 double bedroom-bar-lounge sleepers on *The Cincinnati Limited* were operated just in front of the twin-unit diner, providing lounge car accommodations and bar service for Pullman passengers, as well as a spot for those waiting for dinner. *Palm Falls*, as a postwar car, lasted through the Penn Central era until Amtrak. It was finally retired in 1971 and sold to the Bethlehem Steel Corporation for private use.

postwar 6 double bedroom-bar lounge sleeper and meals were provided in one of Pennsylvania Railroad's twin-unit dining cars, one unit being a full diner and the other a kitchen-dormitory car.

The Cincinnati Limited was an overnight train, departing New York westbound in the late afternoon at 5:25 and arriving in Cincinnati. Eastbound train No. 40 departing Cincinnati in

Harry Stegmaier Collection

The Louisville & Nashville Railroad, because of its through passenger car service with the Pennsylvania Railroad, purchased three 10 roomette, 6 double bedroom sleepers that were painted in Tuscan Red to match the Pennsylvania Railroad colors. In this photograph, *Green River*, one of the three sleepers, is seen as part of *The South Wind* consist in May, 1965. During the early 1950s, *Green River* was regularly assigned to the through sleeping car route between New York and Louisville, which was handled east of that city by *The Cincinnati Limited* and, thus, it was a regular on Nos. 40 and 41. *Green River* lasted on the Louisville & Nashville until Amtrak, although it was repainted into their blue color scheme. In 1973, Amtrak purchased the car for its own operations.

Harry Stegmaier Collection

Each *Cincinnati Limited* carried, in its consist, one of the postwar observation-lounge-sleepers that the Pennsylvania Railroad had Pullman build for them after World War II. These cars arrived on the company property in March and April, 1949. *Samuel Rea*, which was a regular observation-lounge-sleeper on *The Cincinnati Limited*, contained 2 drawing rooms, 1 compartment, 1 double bedroom, as well as a buffet-lounge, seating 25. Of the seven cars of this type, The *Samuel Rea* lasted the longest, since it served as a backup car for *Tower View* and *Mountain View* on *The Broadway Limited*. In fact, in this photograph, taken in June, 1963, *Samuel Rea* is seen in Chicago with a *Broadway Limited* drumhead on the rear and, thus, it must have been assigned that day while one of the *View* cars were being serviced. *Samuel Rea* hung around the property until 1968 when it was sold by the Penn Central to the Indiana Railway Museum. It still survives today, but certainly, it is a long way from the days when it carried the drumhead of one of Pennsylvania Railroad's premier blue ribbon trains.

late afternoon and arrived in New York the next morning. No. 40 and No. 41 were unique in their history in that they lasted until Amtrak, although consolidations and downgrading of the train left them as simply a coach and sleeping car connecting trains between Columbus and Cincinnati for main line New York to St. Louis trains such as *The Spirit of St. Louis*. By the early 1960s, all of the through cars operated with the Louisville & Nashville had disappeared as well. Nevertheless, No. 40 and No. 41, *The Cincinnati Limited*, were first-class trains and provided their patrons excellent service between New York and Cincinnati. Somehow or another, they managed to survive until Amtrak.

No. 64 and No. 65
THE JEFFERSONIAN

The Jeffersonian, by 1952, was no longer the darling of Pennsylvania Railroad management which it had been before World War II. Inaugurated shortly after *The Trail Blazer* had proved how profitable overnight coach passenger traffic could be, *The Jeffersonian* once boasted a streamlined steam locomotive and rebuilt wide windowed passenger cars but, by 1952, the railroad had other plans for *The Jeffersonian*. In fact, this train would be gone within a year. Train No. 65 westbound and No. 64 eastbound operated from St. Louis and New York, respectively, usually anywhere from five to twenty minutes behind *The Spirit of St. Louis* and really ran as the coach section of that train. The westbound train departed New York five minutes behind *The Spirit of St. Louis* at 6:15 p.m. and arrived the next afternoon in St. Louis at 1:40 p.m. while eastbound No. 64 departed that city at 1:00 p.m. and was in New York the next morning at 10:05 a.m. By this time, No. 64 and No. 65 were carrying a good deal of headend traffic for the Pennsylvania and could often be found with up to ten cars of headend, something unheard of in their heyday. The train was a favorite of the Pennsylvania Railroad to handle lots of mail storage equipment, as well as an RPO car between New York and Pittsburgh westbound and between St. Louis and Harrisburg eastbound. In addition, the train was primarily made up of the new streamlined, lightweight P85BR

Train No. 64
Blue Ribbon
The Jeffersonian
Consist—Except November 27, 28, December 24, 25, 26, 31

Car Type	Description	From	To	Details	Car Des
Baggage Cars Deadhead		St. Louis	New York		
1 BM-70M	DE Saturday and Sunday	*St. Louis	Harrisburg	Letter End West	
1 BM-70M	Saturday	*St. Louis	New York	Letter End West	
1 Express	B-60 Saturday, U.S. NEWS	Dayton	New York		
1 MS-60	B-60 Saturday	Dayton	New York		
1 B-60	Baggage	Dayton	New York		
1 Dormitory		St. Louis	New York		
1 PLB-85BR	Baggage-Lounge-Bar	xSt. Louis	New York		
1 P-85BR	Reclining Seats	%St. Louis	New York		645
1 P-85BR	Reclining Seats	%St. Louis	New York		644
1 Diner		St. Louis	New York	LW	
1 P-85BR	Reclining Seats	%zIndianapolis	New York		6440
1 P-85BR	Reclining Seats	%zIndianapolis	Washington	To 530 Harrisburg	6420
1 P-85BR	Reclining Seats	%St. Louis	Washington	To 530 Harrisburg	643
1 P-85BR	Reclining Seats	%St. Louis	New York		642
1 P-85BR	Reclining Seats	%St. Louis	New York		641
1 POC-85AR	Observation, Buffet, Lounge	%St. Louis	New York		

* RPO portion NOT in service east of Indianapolis Saturday
 RPO portion NOT in service east of Pittsburgh on other days
 Will contain Harrisburg mail east of Pittsburgh

x Operates whenever there are more than five coaches including Washington coach operated
z Operate December 18th-January 4th, inclusive, except December 24, 25, 26, 31

Train No. 65
Blue Ribbon
The Jeffersonian
Consist—Except November 27, 28, December 24, 25, 26, 31

Car Type	Description	From	To	Details	Car Des
I Express	R-50, Sunday	Delmar	St. Louis	From 525 Harrisburg	
I MS-60	Tuesday GRIT	Williamsport	St. Louis	From 570 Harrisburg	
I MS-60	(X)	Philadelphia	St. Louis	From 527 (525 Sunday), Harrisburg	
			Kansas City		
			Texarkana		
			Los Angeles		
I MS-60	(X)	Philadelphia	St. Louis		
			Kansas City		
			Texarkana		
			Los Angeles		
I BM-70M	DE Sunday	New York	Pittsburgh	Letter End West	
I Express	X-29, DE Sunday, Monday and Days after Holidays	Pittsburgh	St. Louis		
I MS-60	(X)	Pittsburgh	St. Louis		
I BM-70M	DE Monday	New York	St. Louis		
I MS-60	DE Sunday, Semi-Open	New York	St. Louis		
I BM-70M	Sunday	New York	St. Louis	Letter End East	
I B-60	Baggage	New York	St. Louis		
I Dormitory		New York	St. Louis		
I PLB-85BR	Baggage-Lounge-Bar	xNew York	St. Louis		
I P-85BR	Reclining Seats	%New York	St. Louis		654
I P-85BR	Reclining Seats	%New York	St. Louis		653
I Diner		New York	St. Louis	LW	
I P-85BR	Reclining Seats	*%New York	Indianapolis		655
I P-85BR	Reclining Seats	*%Washington	Indianapolis	From 531 Harrisburg	656
I P-85BR	Reclining Seats	%Washington	St. Louis	From 531 Harrisburg	652
I P-85BR	Reclining Seats	%New York	St. Louis		651
I P-85BR	Reclining Seats	%New York	St. Louis		650
I POC-85AR	Observation, Buffet, Lounge	%New York	St. Louis		
I B-60	Mail-Express Saturday, U.S. NEWS	Dayton	Chicago	To 215 Richmond	
I MS-60	Tuesday, U.S. WORLD	Dayton	Chicago		

x Operates whenever there are more than five coaches including Washington coach operated

* Operate December 18th-January 4th, inclusive, except December 24, 25, 26, 31

coaches, although by 1952, cars of a lesser breed would sometimes replace them on Nos. 64 and 65. In addition to the through coaches, there was a Washington to St. Louis coach as well as a Washington to Indianapolis coach. The train also carried a dormitory car for the crew, usually by this time a heavyweight sleeper, as well as a lightweight dining car, Budd built in most cases, and one of the Pennsylvania Railroad's Altoona built 1120 to 1130 series observation-buffet-lounge cars. Whenever the train carried more than five coaches, it also had a headend lounge, one of those rare Pennsylvania Railroad baggage-lounge cars with a bar to quench the thirst of the economy minded traveler. The normal complement of the train were four New York-St. Louis coaches, a New York to Indianapolis coach and Washington to St. Louis and Indianapolis reclining seat coaches. The company was already planning to dismiss this train and replace it with *The Indianapolis Limited*. The Indianapolis coach and sleeping car traffic could be handled by a separate train while the St. Louis coach traffic would simply be added to *The Spirit of St. Louis*. This was done in April, 1953 and *The Jeffersonian* was discontinued on April 25 of that year. Once the proud all-coach streamliner of the New York to St. Louis run, it would be replaced by another Blue Ribbon train, *The Indianapolis Limited* in April of 1953, with its coaches being split between the new train and *The Spirit of St. Louis*.

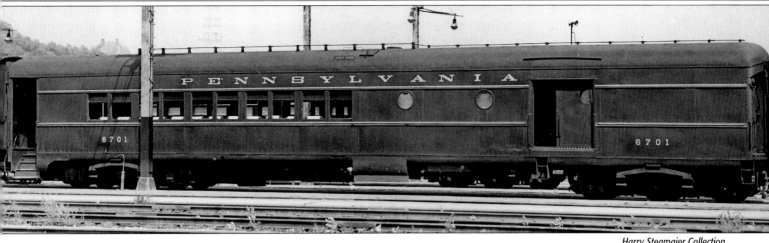

Harry Stegmaier Collection

By fall 1952, *The Jeffersonian* was entering its last few months of operation, a far cry from the days when it was Pennsylvania Railroad's premier coach passenger train on the New York-St. Louis route. It would be discontinued in April, 1953 and replaced by *The Indianapolis Limited*, at the same time that coaches were added to *The Spirit of St. Louis*. By 1952, as is obvious from the consist sheets, the train had been relegated to carrying a good deal of Pennsylvania Railroad's east coast to St. Louis headend, including an RPO car and, thus, it looked like just about any other train, even though it had been re-equipped with modern equipment after World War II. Unique to the train was the fact that whenever more than five P85BR coaches, which were still the usually assigned type of car, were operated , the train received one of Pennsylvania's rare baggage-bar-lounge cars, operated between the dormitory car and the first coach on the train. These cars were heavyweights that had been rebuilt and modernized by the Pennsylvania Railroad. In this photograph, Pennsylvania Railroad baggage-bar-lounge car, No. 6701, is seen in the 1950s. These were unique cars and *The Jeffersonian* was one of the few trains that still operated them regularly.

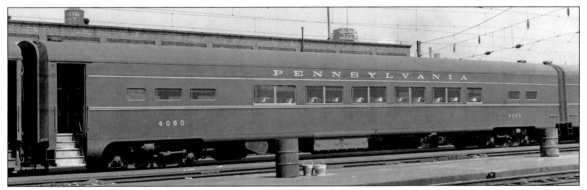

Both: Bob's Photo,
Harry Stegmaier Collection
The Pennsylvania Railroad had re-equipped *The Jeffersonian* after World War II with the new P85BR reclining seat coaches. These cars seated 44 passengers and had very large lounges and restrooms at each end. The P85BR coaches were part of a major upgrading of the train only four years before its discontinuance. Each *Jeffersonian* carried four New York-St. Louis coaches, plus a New York-Indianapolis coach, as well as a Washington to Indianapolis and Washington to St. Louis coach. The train operated four regular New York-St. Louis coaches, with the Indianapolis cars running only during the heavy holiday travel season in December and January. However, extra coaches could always be added. Whenever there were more than five coaches, the baggage-bar-lounge cars were operated as well. P85BR No. 4080, seen here in 1948 at Sunnyside Yard on Long Island, was one of the group of P85BR's built by American Car & Foundry. The P85BR's were split between two different companies with ACF building P85BR's for the Pennsylvania Railroad in 1947. These ACF built P85BR's were numbered from 4068 to 4091. The Pennsylvania Railroad's own shops at Altoona built another group of P85BR cars from kits supplied by American Car & Foundry, numbered 4100-4169. These were ready in the fall of 1947. No. 4080, in this photograph, is one of the cars that was actually built by ACF and not by the Pennsylvania Railroad, as were most of the cars. Unfortunately, almost all of the P85BR coaches, whether built by ACF or Altoona Car Shops, developed major problems by the 1960s in their body work. The Pennsylvania Railroad converted one car in 1965 to a modernized 60-seat coach which lasted well into the Penn Central era. However, the rebuilding of that one car was so expensive and the bodies of the other cars were in such bad shape, that the railroad gradually got rid of the cars. No. 4080 was retired in 1965 and scrapped. In the second photograph is one of the P85BR cars built from kits supplied by American Car & Foundry at the Altoona Car Shops. They were virtually identical to the ACF built cars but had the same problems. In this photograph, No. 4134 is seen in March, 1947 just after it has been delivered to the company in Washington, D.C. No. 4134 was retired in 1965 and scrapped. In fact, virtually all of the P85BR cars were

gone by 1968, with a few exceptions. Nevertheless, they were the best passenger coaches on the Pennsylvania Railroad when they were first received in the late 1940s. *The Jeffersonian* and *The Trail Blazer* always were usually first in line for the new P85BR cars.

Unlike *The Trailblazer*, *The Jeffersonian* did not get a twin-unit diner, but by 1952 usually received one of Pennsylvania Railroad's rebuilt, modernized, heavyweight cars like No. 4473, seen here at Chicago in the 1960s. No. 4473 had been built as a dining car in 1922 and its modernization was completed by Altoona in January, 1952. It was now classified as a D78fR dining car with lounge, seating 32 in the dining section and 10 in the "short lounge." These heavyweight, rebuilt diners were regulars on *The Jeffersonian* in the years just before the train's discontinuance.

Each *Jeffersonian* received one of the Pennsylvania Railroad's Altoona built observation-lounge cars to serve coach passengers. Classed POC85AR cars, these observation-buffet-lounge cars were built by the Altoona Car Shops of the Pennsylvania Railroad early in 1948, specifically for service on trains like *The Jeffersonian* and *The Trail Blazer*. Car No. 1135, seen here at Mack Lowry's Museum in Cuyahoga Falls, Ohio, on June 2, 1970, was the first of the five cars to be retired in 1961. The other cars lasted until 1967, being run on the headend of *The General* as coach-bar-lounge cars for that train's coach passengers. All of the other cars of the same class were scrapped in 1967, after being retired by the Pennsylvania Railroad. Each POC85AR car had an observation section and a 53-seat buffet-lounge.

No. 66 and No. 67
THE AMERICAN

Pennsylvania Railroad's *American* was a long, old-time train that had been in the timetable for decades. By 1952, it had fallen upon hard times. Overshadowed by the more prestigious *Spirit of St. Louis*, *Penn Texas*, and *Jeffersonian*, *The American* was the equivalent of *The Gotham Limited* on the Chicago run. Westbound No. 67 was Pennsylvania Railroad's late night train from New York which provided overnight service to Pittsburgh in an already crowded market with competition from *The Iron City Express* and, of course, the all-Pullman *Pittsburgher*. It then provided daytime service west of Pittsburgh to St. Louis where it arrived at the dinner hour the next day. Eastbound, No. 66 was the daytime early morning train out of St. Louis at 9:00 a.m., with a daylight run to Pittsburgh and then an overnight trek to New York, where it arrived early the next morning. The train handled quite a bit of coach traffic over the daylight portion of its route but, surprisingly, this train did not, even though it was a train of lowly status by 1950, carry an enormous amount of headend. That was left to trains like *The Metropolitan* and *The Allegheny*. *The American*, however, did have a 70-foot section RPO and a baggage-mail car in both directions as well as a second RPO car with a 30-foot apartment, between New York and Pittsburgh westbound. The westbound train also carried two mail-storage cars. Coach traffic was accommodated in a combine and two or more reclining seat coaches, mostly of the P85BR variety, but being a train of lesser status, when the P85BR lightweight streamlined cars were not available, one could find any different number of types of P70's on the train. Through cars included a heavyweight dining car, and a pre-war 3 double bedroom, 1 drawing room lounge-sleeper as well as a 21 roomette *Inn* series car and a 12 section, 1 drawing room heavyweight sleeper. In addition to these cars, a heavyweight 8 section, 5 double bedroom sleeper operated on the train between Washington and St. Louis. No. 66 and No. 67 both were responsible for conveying the New York to Wheeling sleeper to and from Weirton Junction, where it was picked up for the short hop to the bustling steel city of Wheeling, West Virginia by a connecting train. This was an interesting car. It was always listed as a 10 roomette, 5 double bedroom sleeper for sales purposes as was clear from the public timetables and Pullman records. In reality, it was a 10 roomette, 6 double bedroom car that specifically had to be

Harry Stegmaier

Probably the least favored, by 1952, of all of the Pennsylvania Railroad trains on the New York-St. Louis route, with the exception of *The Metropolitan*, was No. 66 & No. 67, *The American*. With passenger traffic declining systemwide, trains like *The American* were superfluous when there were two other blue ribbon trains on the route. Decades earlier, *The American* had been the pride of the Pennsylvania Railroad on its New York-St. Louis mainline but, by 1952, it had fallen into a very secondary position. While the consist book shows that the train received reclining seat coaches nevertheless, when they were not available, trains like *The American* would get a substitute car, often, for example, a car like No. 3960, a non-reclining seat but modernized and air-conditioned coach, rebuilt by Altoona Car Shops before World War II, and classed P70FAR. These were very versatile cars and, in fact, No. 3960 is seen here on June 11, 1966 at Bayhead Junction, New Jersey in commuter train service. It was not unusual to find cars like the P70FAR substituting for the P70GR's and P85BR's on trains like No. 66 and No. 67.

Train No. 66
Blue Ribbon
The American

Will NOT operate December 25th

Car Type	Description	From	To	Details	Car Des
1 BM-70M	DE Sunday	*St. Louis	New York	Letter End West	
1 PB-70	Scheme 4	St. Louis	New York		
1 P-70GR	Reclining Seats	%St. Louis	New York		
2 P-85BR	Reclining Seats	%St. Louis	New York		
1 Diner		St. Louis	New York		
1 SL-Lounge	3 DBR, 1 DR, Bar	St. Louis	New York	LW	
1 SL	21 Roomette	St. Louis	New York	LW	666
1 SL	12-1	St. Louis	New York		665
1 SL	8 Section, 5 DBR	St. Louis	Washington	To 504 Harrisburg	662
1 SL	12-1, DE Saturday and Nov. 22, Dec. 24, 31	Indianapolis	Washington	To 504 Harrisburg	661
1 SL	10 Roomette, 6 DBR	xWheeling	New York	LW, from 702 Weirton Jct.	660
1 PB-70	Baggage-Mail-Express	Wheeling	Pittsburgh	From 702, Weirton Jct.	
	Baggage Deadhead (X)	Steubenville	Pittsburgh		

* RPO portion NOT in service Pittsburgh-New York

x Will be TEXAS EAGLE color for protection of the through Texas lines in Nos, 3 and 4 and should be held to 10 Roomette-5 DBR on diagrams in event it is necessary to take car out of line to protect a Texas line.

painted in *Eagle* colors. The Pennsylvania Railroad and the Pullman Company were using the New York-Wheeling sleeping car line to keep cars painted in *Eagle* colors at work, while at the same time using them as protection for the through sleeping car lines handled by *The Penn Texas*. Thus, the 10 roomette, 6 double bedroom car was always listed for sales purposes as a 10 roomette, 5 double bedroom car because, if it was needed to replace a shopped car on the through Texas routes on *The Penn Texas*, then the Pennsylvania Railroad

could pull out a 10 roomette, 5 double bedroom *Cascade* series sleeper and substitute it on the New York-Wheeling run. No. 66 and No. 67, *The American*, had lost most of its purpose in the minds of Pennsylvania Railroad management. The train survived a few more years, plodding along on the New York to St. Louis main but, in the big changes of April 1956 when the railroad sought to cut its ever soaring deficits in passenger service, No. 66 and No. 67 disappeared from the Pennsylvania Railroad timetable forever.

The American carried a full dining car with a lounge section on its through trek from New York to St. Louis. Its schedule required the train to serve breakfast, lunch and dinner in both directions. Dining cars like No. 4498, created by Altoona Car Shops from a 1924 built diner in May, 195, now a class D78fR car with a round roof and dining section seating 32 and a "short lounge" seating 10. Cars like this could often be found on trains like No. 66 and No. 67 during the early 1950s before the train's final demise in April, 1956.

Train No. 67
Blue Ribbon
The American

Car Type	Description	From	To	Details	Car Des
1 MS-60	(X)	New York	St. Louis		
			Kansas City		
			Texarkana		
			Los Angeles		
1 BM-70	30 foot apartment, DE Sat. & Sun.	New York	Pittsburgh	Letter End East	
1 BM-70M	DE Sunday	New York	Pittsburgh	Letter End West	
1 MS-60	Open DE Saturday and Sunday	New York	St. Louis		
1 B-60	Saturday	New York	St. Louis		
1 PB-70	Scheme 4	New York	St. Louis		
2 P-85BR	Reclining Seats	%New York	St. Louis		
1 Diner		New York	St. Louis		
1 SL-Lounge	3 DBR, 1 DR, Bar	New York	St. Louis	LW	671
1 SL	21 Roomette	New York	St. Louis	LW	672
1 SL	12-1	New York	Wheeling		673
1 SL	8 Section, 5 DBR	Washington	St. Louis	From 539 Harrisburg	676
1 SL	10 Roomette, 6 DBR	zNew York	Wheeling	LW To 701 Weirton Jct.	701
1 PB-70	Baggage-Mail-Express	Pittsburgh	Wheeling	To 701 Weirton Jct.	
1 B-60	Papers Saturday	New York	Altoona		
1 MS-60	Wednesday and Thursday GRIT	Williamsport	Pittsburgh	From 578 Harrisburg	
1 MS-60	DE Monday	Grand Rapids	Indianapolis	From 500 Richmond	

* Will be TEXAS EAGLE color for protection of the through Texas lines in Nos, 3 and 4 and should be held to 10 Roomette-5 DBR on diagrams in event it is necessary to take car out of line to protect a Texas line.

Harry Stegmaier Collection

The American carried, in both directions, the New York to Wheeling sleeping car. Timetables always listed this as a 10 roomette, 5 double bedroom car and, in fact, the space in the car was always sold as such. However, both the consist book and Pullman Company records indicate that this car had to be a 10 roomette, 6 double bedroom sleeper, painted in *Eagle* colors. The railroad and the Pullman Company were using the New York-Wheeling car line as a place where the 10 roomette, 6 double bedroom sleepers in *Eagle* colors could be put to revenue use but quickly pulled out and put in *Penn Texas* service if the regular cars were not available. Thus, the car line was always sold as a 10 roomette, 5 double bedroom for space. The New York-Wheeling car was always added to and detached from *The American* at Weirton Junction, a short hop from Wheeling, and was primarily operated for the benefit of the businessmen of that then thriving industrial city. In this photograph, Pennsylvania Railroad *Eagle Chief* is seen in Denver, Colorado on July 10, 1963. It was one of the large number of Pennsylvania Railroad's sleepers that were specifically bought and painted for the through car service operated in conjunction with the Missouri Pacific to Texas. The car was built by American Car & Foundry and delivered to the Pennsylvania in the late summer of 1950. *Eagle Chief* could, of course, be found as the New York to Wheeling sleeper on *The American* in the 1950s. Once the through car service was finally eliminated, the *Eagle* cars were painted Tuscan Red and given new names, with *Eagle Chief* becoming *Park Rapids* in 1964 and lasting until it was retired in 1971 and scrapped.

MODERN MAGIC...

in the locomotive cab ahead!

Even when powerful fog-piercing headlights are unable to cut through the zero visibility of cloudbursts, blizzards or freezing sleet, engineers on the Pennsylvania know what's in front of them... thanks to modern electronic signals visible in the cab which show a counterpart of the wayside interlocking or automatic block signals. Whenever this signal in the cab calls for a slower speed or other restriction, the engineman is alerted by a warning whistle in the cab in addition to the change in the signal indication before his eyes. Now, the newest and most advanced safety development—an electronic speed control device—is being installed in

Pennsylvania locomotives. With this apparatus, if for any reason the engineman should not within six seconds take action to slow his train and then maintain it at the reduced speed called for by the signals, an automatic governor takes command and *STOPS* the train. Searching for—and finding—ways and means to achieve greater safety and better service is a continuous job on the Pennsylvania. All along the line, in a program costing hundreds of millions of dollars, the Pennsylvania is providing its customers and the Nation with the finest, safest and most dependable rail transportation ever achieved.

 PENNSYLVANIA RAILROAD

Harry Stegmaier Collection

This early 1953 Pennsylvania Railroad field menu was typical of the type that one would have found on trains like *The American*. It should be noted that this menu, according to Pennsylvania Railroad Commissary files, was basically used for both lunch and dinner on trains like *The American*. While not providing the patrons with the steak dinners and lamb chops of some of the more favored Blue Ribbon trains, it nevertheless gave patrons a choice of a number of entrees as well as some specials. But, of course, as one looks at this menu, one can see that there was nothing spectacular about field menus that were used on trains like *The American*.

Menu

Combinations and A La Carte

Appetizers

Soup du Jour .40   Hot Beef Broth .40
Grapefruit Juice .30   Chilled Tomato Juice .30

YOU'LL LIKE

BROWNED CORNED BEEF HASH WITH MUSTARD SAUCE
Garden Peas
Chef's Salad
Corn Muffins
Choice of Dessert
Tea   Coffee   Milk
$1.95

TRAVELER'S SPECIAL

Cup of Soup or Tomato Juice
HAM OR BACON WITH FRIED EGGS
Potatoes or Head Lettuce, French Dressing
Corn Muffins
Choice of Dessert
Tea   Coffee   Milk
$2.30

PRR SALAD BOWL WITH RY-KRISP
95¢

Desserts

Apple Pie	.40
Half Grapefruit	.40
Bleu Cheese, Wafers	.45
Holiday Ice Cream	.35
Chocolate Ice Cream	.35

Beverages

Pot of Coffee	.30
Pot of Tea	.30
Grade "A" Milk	.25
Chocolate	.30

CLUB MEALS

Choice of One:

Cup of Soup   Hot Beef Broth
Grapefruit Juice   Chilled Tomato Juice

BROILED HALIBUT STEAK, PARSLEY BUTTER 2.25
Garden Peas   Baked Potato

BREADED VEAL CUTLET, TOMATO SAUCE 2.60
Whipped Potatoes   Green Peas

GRILLED SLICE OF COUNTRY HAM 2.60
Buttered Lima Beans   Baked Potato

ROAST TURKEY, GIBLET GRAVY, CRANBERRY JELLY 2.65
Garden Peas   Mashed Potatoes

Corn Muffins

PRR Mixed Salad
30c additional

Choice of One:

Holiday Fruit Ice Cream
Freshly Baked Apple Pie   Bleu Cheese with Wafers
Chilled Half Grapefruit   Chocolate Ice Cream

Tea   Coffee   Grade "A" Milk

<u>MEAL CHECKS</u>
To serve you better your waiter can accept orders only from written meal checks. Please list each item you desire on the check.

<u>ROOM SERVICE</u>
A charge of 50 cents per person will be made for food service outside the dining car. This service is subject to delay when dining car is busy.

As your host, the steward will welcome your suggestions about our food and service.
If you prefer, your comments may be addressed to:
Sidney N. Phelps, Manager, Dining Car Service, Pennsylvania Railroad, Long Island City 1, N. Y.
F 1/2-12/53

Harry Stegmaier Collection

The Pennsylvania Railroad operated, on a regular basis, a 21 roomette sleeper on *The American* between St. Louis and New York, in both directions. *Vincennes Inn*, seen here in September, 1964 in Denver, Colorado, was one of the seven *Inn* series sleepers that was built by American Car & Foundry instead of the Budd Company for the Pennsylvania Railroad. The car was regularly assigned to *The American* in the 1950s. *Vincennes Inn* was not converted to a corridor coach like the other Budd built *Inn* cars but was retired in 1967 and scrapped. It was regularly on *The American* as the New York-St. Louis car and later as the Washington to St. Louis 21 roomette sleeper before the train's demise in April, 1956.

Harry Stegmaier

Each consist of *The American* carried a 3 double bedroom, 1 drawing room-bar-lounge car which was operated just behind the dining car, primarily for the use of Pullman patrons. The 3 double bedroom, 1 drawing room-bar-lounge sleepers on *The American* were drawn from the prewar series of cars built by Pullman Standard for the Pennsylvania Railroad and delivered to the company in May of 1938. The regular cars assigned to *The American* in the 1950s were *Colonial Mansions, Colonial Governors* and *Colonial Trails* but, when one of these cars was not available, then *Colonial Congress*, which was an extra car, would substitute for them on No. 66 and No. 67. *Colonial Congress* stayed on the railroad until 1962 when it was sold to the Ferrocarril Del Pacifico, which used it between Nogales and Guadalajara. That Mexican company renamed the car, *Presa Del Humaya*. As such, the car is seen at Nogales in early 1969 in the consist of *El Norteno*, which often carried two of these former Pennsylvania Railroad sleeper-bar-lounges back to back, as well as two diners in the late 1960s and early 1970s. The outside appearance of the car is little changed except for the paint scheme from the days when it graced the likes of Pennsylvania Railroad's *American* between New York and St. Louis.

On a summer's day in 1948, the two unit E-7A/E-7B combination of train No. 75, *The Duquesne*, is getting an assist over the Alleghenies from a steam helper locomotive that was added at Altoona. Trailing behind the E's are ten headend cars followed by the passenger cars of this popular daytime New York to Pittsburgh train. One can see in the consist several of the box express cars, as well as a refrigerated express car, plus the working RPO that *The Duquesne* handled on its westbound trek in that summer long ago. Undoubtedly, trailing on the rear of the train but out of the picture, is a parlor car and a parlor-buffet-lounge car.

INTRODUCTION:

The Pennsylvania Railroad, on its two main lines, New York-Pittsburgh-Chicago, with off-shoots to Detroit and Cleveland, as well as New York-Pittsburgh-St. Louis with its Cincinnati diverting line, provided a substantial intermediate train service. Of course, the through main line trains which covered the main routes, provided local service in the sense that they hit the largest communities such as Harrisburg and Altoona but, in addition, the Pennsylvania Railroad ran a number of strictly New York-Pittsburgh trains.

As well as the through main line trains, the railroad operated in both directions, a daylight New York to Pittsburgh run, *The Duquesne*, providing both coach and first class service. Overnight service was provided by two different trains, the famous all Pullman *Pittsburgher*, between New York and Pittsburgh, and the old *Iron City Express* from New York to Pittsburgh, which ran about an hour ahead of *The Pittsburgher* with both coaches and sleeping cars. In addition, the Pennsylvania Railroad ran an overnight train from Philadelphia to Pittsburgh, *The Philadelphia-Pittsburgh Night Express* westbound and *The Pittsburgh-Philadelphia Night Express* eastbound. The railroad also operated an overnight train, *The Statesman*, between Washington and Pittsburgh. By 1952, this train was almost always combined into *The Pittsburgh Night Express* at Harrisburg and detached from *The Philadelphia Night Express* at Harrisburg eastbound with the cars continuing on to Washington as *The Statesman*. In addition to these trains, on the eastern end of the Pennsylvania Railroad, service was also provided not only by the through main line trains such as *The Metropolitan* and *The Manhattan Limited*, but by several mail and express trains which did carry passengers and will be treated in a later chapter, for example, No. 13, No. 85 on Sundays, from New York's Penn Station to Pittsburgh calling at a lot of towns that other trains simply skipped such as Miflin,

Pennsylvania and Cresson, Pennsylvania.

Eastbound, between Pittsburgh and New York, *The Duquesne* and the night trains were supplemented by an additional daylight run, No. 72, *The Juniata*, as well as the afternoon train from Pittsburgh, *The New Englander*, which carried through sleeping cars for Boston and Springfield. Thus, in addition to the Pittsburgh to New York *Duquesne*, eastbound daylight service was also provided by *The Juniata* and *The New Englander*. In addition to those trains between Pittsburgh and New York in the daylight hours, mail trains No. 14, an early morning mail and express train from Pittsburgh to New York, and late afternoon, No. 18, a mail and express train from Pittsburgh to New York, also carried passengers in the coaches that were sandwiched amidst their large amounts of headend traffic. Therefore, on the eastern part of the line, the company had two overnight New York-Pittsburgh trains as well as a Philadelphia to Pittsburgh overnight train and a Washington to Pittsburgh overnight train plus *The Duquesne* in daylight. They were supplemented eastbound by four additional trains, two mail and express trains, *The Juniata* and *The New Englander*.

West of Pittsburgh on the Chicago main line, the Pennsylvania Railroad ran a Blue Ribbon overnight train, *The Golden Triangle*, between Pittsburgh and Chicago, popular for sleeping car traffic and carrying coach passengers as well. In addition to its Chicago cars, *The Golden Triangle* also carried coaches and sleeping cars which were detached and added to the train at Mansfield, Ohio. These cars provided a through Pittsburgh to Detroit overnight service that arrived in Detroit ahead of *The Red Arrow* each morning and departed much later in the evening than the through Detroit to New York train. As well as the overnight service between Pittsburgh and Chicago provided by *The Golden Triangle*, there was also a daytime train, *The Fort Pitt*, operating from Pittsburgh to Chicago in both directions, carrying a large amount of headend traffic along with coaches and a unique parlor-cafe car. This train made all of the local stops on the Chicago mainline between Pittsburgh and Chicago calling at such towns as Salem, Ohio, and Upper Sandusky, Ohio and Valparaiso, Indiana as well as many other places in between. Thus, the Pennsylvania Railroad had a daylight train and a night train in both directions on its main line strictly between Pittsburgh and Chicago. These two schedules were supplemented by a very odd, unnamed train, No. 44, a Chicago to Pittsburgh mail and express train, which eastbound carried coaches and a sleeping car on its long trek between Chicago and Pittsburgh. While this train was primarily operated for headend business, it nevertheless did provide some passenger accommodations and strictly had no westbound counterpart unless one considers it to be the eastbound counterpart of Pittsburgh-Chicago mail and express train No. 99 which did not carry passengers except, occasionally, on holidays when other trains did not run.

The Pennsylvania Railroad did not provide any strictly local Pittsburgh-St. Louis trains, although certainly the overnight *Metropolitan* and eastbound No. 6, *The Allegheny*, filled that role and many of the stops were made also by trains like *The American*. However, it did provide two Pittsburgh to Cincinnati trains, one a daylight run,

No. 205 westbound and No. 204, eastbound, which connected at Pittsburgh in both directions with *The Iron City Express,* and which handled coaches as well as through sleeping cars, which were operated as far as Cincinnati and then handed over to the Louisville and Nashville Railroad. Westbound No. 205 carried the through New York to Birmingham sleeping car and eastbound No. 204 carried both this Birmingham to New York car and the eastbound 10 roomette, 6 double bedroom car from Memphis to New York, which was handled westbound on *The Cincinnati Limited.* Night trains No. 202 and No. 203, eastbound and westbound respectively, not only provided patrons with reclining seat coaches but were the last main line trains to carry one of the prewar 18 roomette *City* series sleepers overnight between Pittsburgh and Cincinnati. In addition, eastbound No. 202 had a through New Orleans to Pittsburgh sleeper, as well as a Cincinnati to New York sleeper, that was handled east of Pittsburgh on *The St. Louisan.* Westbound No. 203 handled only the Pittsburgh to New Orleans heavyweight sleeper in addition to its 18 roomette car.

As can be seen, the Pennsylvania Railroad's main line trains, therefore, were not restricted to just the main body of through trains which the company ran, most of which were in the Blue Ribbon category. There was additional service, in

		Train No. 16				
Car Type	Description		From	To	Details	Car Des
1 MS-60	(X)		Cleveland	Washington	From 328 Pittsburgh, To 530 Harrisburg	
1 Express	X-29 DE Saturday, Sunday, Monday and Days after Holidays		Pittsburgh	Harrisburg		
1 Express	B-60 DE Sunday, Monday, Holiday and Days after Holidays		Indianapolis	New York	From 12 Pittsburgh	
1 MS-60	(X)		Pittsburgh	New York		
1 PB-70	Scheme 6		Pittsburgh	New York		
2 P-70GSR	Reclining Seats		%Pittsburgh	New York		
1 SL	10 Section, 1 DR, 2 Compartment		Birmingham	New York	From 204 Pittsburgh	L-3
1 SL	10 Roomette, 6 DBR		Memphis	New York	From 204 Pittsburgh	L-4
1 SL	21 Roomette		Pittsburgh	New York	LW	165
1 SL-Lounge	6 DBR, Buffet		Pittsburgh	New York		164
1 SL	12-1, DE Saturday		*Pittsburgh	New York		163
1 SL	12 Duplex SR, 4 DBR, Saturday		xPittsburgh	New York	LW	166
1 SL	21 Roomette, Saturday		xPittsburgh	New York	LW	167
1 SL	12 Duplex SR, 4 DBR		zPittsburgh	New York	LW	168
1 SL	8 Section, 1 DR, 2 Compt. DE Saturday		*Pittsburgh	Philadelphia	To 36 (86 November 27, Dec. 26) Harrisburg	169
1 MS-60			Pittsburgh	Harrisburg		
1 Express	X-29, Sunday		Pittsburgh	Altoona		

* Will NOT operate November 27, 28, December 25, 26, 31, January 1, 2
x Will ALSO operate November 27, 28, December 25, 26, 31, January 1, 2
z Will ALSO operate November 28, December 26, 31, January 2

fact quite a bit of service, between New York and Pittsburgh in both directions, with more trains being operated eastbound than westbound, there were both overnight trains between Pittsburgh and Chicago and Pittsburgh and Cincinnati with the addition of the Pittsburgh-Detroit night service that supplemented the work of *The Red Arrow*. In the fall of 1952, people heading for Pittsburgh or terminating there, had a number of trains to choose from in their travel plans.

No. 16 and No. 37
THE IRON CITY EXPRESS

In the fall of 1952, the Pennsylvania Railroad was still operating a second overnight New York to Pittsburgh train in addition to the Blue Ribbon all Pullman *Pittsburgher*. This was the old *Iron City Express*, which departed New York about an hour before *The Pittsburgher* at 11:00 p.m. and arrived in Pittsburgh at 7:50 a.m., while eastbound No. 16 departed Pittsburgh at 10:15 and arrived in New York at 7:15 a.m. Eastbound, *The Iron City Express*, as can be imagined, carried a substantial amount of headend traffic plus a combine and two modernized heavyweight reclining seat coaches. The sleeping cars were a mixture of heavyweight and lightweight equipment, with a 21 roomette

Inn series sleeper on the train, along with a 10 roomette, 6 double bedroom sleeper which was the through car from Memphis to New York brought into Pittsburgh from Cincinnati on No. 204. The train also carried a lightweight 12 duplex single room, 4 double bedroom sleeping car from the *Creek* series, and on Saturday nights, when *The Pittsburgher* did not operate, it carried an additional *Creek* series and *Inn* series sleeping car that handled Saturday night traffic between Pittsburgh and New York. As well as these cars, the train had two heavyweight sleepers, a standard 12 section, 1 drawing room Pittsburgh to New York car and a 10 section, 2 compartment, 1 drawing room car, which was a through sleeper between Birmingham and New York which the train received from No. 204 at Pittsburgh. In addition to the coaches and sleeping cars already mentioned, the eastbound train carried a Pittsburgh to Philadelphia 8 section, 2 compartment, 1 drawing room car which was handed over to *The Philadelphia Night Express* at Harrisburg. This car seems to have been operated for the purpose of providing an earlier departure from Pittsburgh for Philadelphia patrons. Lounge service was provided by a *Colonial* series 6 double bedroom, buffet-lounge car, which provided light snacks and a few sandwich entrees and

Car Type	Description	From	To	Details	Car Des
1 B-60	Papers Saturday	New York	Harrisburg		
1 B-60	Papers Saturday	New York	Pittsburgh		
1 Express	X-29, DE Saturday, Sunday & Holidays	New York	Pittsburgh		
2 P-70	Sunday	New York	Pittsburgh		
1 B-60	Saturday	New York	Pittsburgh		
1 PB-70	Scheme 6	New York	Pittsburgh		
2 P-70GSR	Reclining Seats	%New York	Pittsburgh		
1 SL	21 Roomette	New York	Pittsburgh	LW	370
1 SL-Lounge	6 DBR, Buffet	New York	Pittsburgh		371
1 SL	12-1, DE Saturday	*New York	Pittsburgh		372
1 SL	12-1, DE Saturday	*New York	Pittsburgh		373
1 SL	12 Duplex SR, 4 DBR	xNew York	Pittsburgh	LW	375
1 SL	21 Roomette, Saturday	xNew York	Pittsburgh	LW	376
1 SL	10 Section, 1 DR, 2 Compartment	New York	Birmingham	To 205 Pittsburgh	K374
1 Diner		New York	Columbus	To 205 Pittsburgh	
1 SL	12 Roomette, 2 SBR, 3 DBR	Boston	Pittsburgh	From 189 New York	377
1 SL	12-1, DE Saturday	zBoston	Pittsburgh	From 189 New York	378
1 SL-Lounge	8 Section, Buffet DE Saturday	zSpringfield	Pittsburgh	From 189 New York	379
1 PB-70	Papers, Saturday and Sunday	Philadelphia	Altoona	From 35 Harrisburg	
1 Express	B-60, DE Sunday and Holidays	Harrisburg	Altoona	To 14 Altoona	

* Will NOT operate November 27, 28, December 25, 26, 31, January 1, 2.
x Will ALSO operate November 27, 28, December 25, 26, 31, January 1, 2.
z Will NOT operate November 27, 28, December 25, 26, 31.

William F. Howes, Jr.

The Pennsylvania Railroad's premier overnight New York to Pittsburgh train was, of course, the all Pullman *Pittsburgher*, but it was preceded in both directions by the other overnight train on the New York-Pittsburgh route, No. 16 eastbound and No. 37 westbound, *The Iron City Express*. This train carried coaches as well as a variety of sleepers. While *The Pittsburgher* was an all room train, *The Iron City Express* carried a combination of lightweight and heavyweight cars and westbound, particularly, it had no less than three 12 section, 1 drawing room sleepers. Two of these cars were from New York to Pittsburgh, while a third car came through from Boston to Pittsburgh and was delivered to No. 37 from New Haven No. 189 at New York's Pennsylvania Station. Eastbound, No. 16 only carried one 12 section, 1 drawing room sleeper, however. Typical of the type of 12 section, 1 drawing room cars that one could have found on *The Iron City Express* in the 1950s was a car like Pennsylvania Railroad *LaRue*, seen here in June, 1960 at New Haven, Connecticut while in service on the special camp trains to the New England mountains. Cars like *LaRue* were part of the large fleet of 12 section, 1 drawing room standard sleepers that the Pennsylvania Railroad still fielded in the early 1950s.

which offered the patrons of *The Iron City Express* an early morning basic juice, toast and coffee breakfast at its tables in the lounge section.

Westbound No. 37 carried the usual amount of headend, the combine and coaches, and sleeping cars which its eastbound counterpart carried, with

Harry Stegmaier

The Iron City Express carried a 21 roomette sleeper in each direction between New York and Pittsburgh, with an extra car of the same type on Saturday nights when *The Pittsburgher* did not operate. One of the cars regularly assigned to the train in the 1950s was *Braddock Inn*, a Pennsylvania Railroad Budd-built 21 roomette car that had been delivered to the company in the first half of 1949. In 1956, it was renamed *Peter Schoenberger*. In 1963, *Braddock Inn* was converted to a 64 seat coach with a 12-seat smoking section for corridor operations. As No. 1509, it served on the corridor through the 1960s into the Penn Central era and beyond, until it was sold to New Jersey Transit in 1976. New Jersey Transit, in turn, sold it to the Maryland Department of Transportation and, in 1994, the car was restored to first class service again. It had come full circle from its days when it was a first class car on the Pennsylvania Railroad. MARC converted *Braddock Inn* in the early spring of 1994 to a café-parlor car and put the Pennsylvania Railroad Keystone, as well as the car's original name, on the letterboard. This café-parlor car operated until 2001 on one of MARC's express commuter trains between Washington and Martinsburg and, according to all reports, the seats were usually filled. It was nice to see the car back in first class service after spending almost thirty years as a corridor coach and commuter coach after its days as a 21 roomette sleeper on *The Iron City Express*. The car is shown here the day it was delivered as a café-parlor car on a Saturday in April, 1994 at Brunswick, Maryland. On Monday, café-parlor car service began between Martinsburg and Washington and return, five days a week on MARC.

Harry Stegmaier

Each *Iron City Express* consist included a 6 double bedroom, buffet-lounge car drawn from the prewar *Falls* series of cars that were built by Pullman Standard and delivered to the Pennsylvania Railroad in September, 1940. These prewar cars provided the lounge car accommodations on *The Iron City Express* in both directions for sleeping car passengers, as well as extra double bedrooms for sale. In addition, these cars also provided and served a small selection of sandwiches, as well as various alcoholic and non-alcoholic beverages in the evenings and, in the morning, provided a light breakfast service into Pittsburgh and New York, respectively. However, from time to time, *The Iron City Express* westbound carried a dining-lounge car between New York and Pittsburgh that was handed over to Train No. 205 at Pittsburgh to serve as its food service car between Pittsburgh and Cincinnati. This dining-lounge car was sometimes in service, depending upon the year, and served a breakfast menu on the westbound *Iron City Express* into Pittsburgh. However, in most cases, the only breakfast served was provided in the 6 double bedroom, buffet-lounge car. In this photograph, prewar Pennsylvania Railroad's 6 double bedroom-lounge car *Juniper Falls*, is seen still in Tuscan Red with Pennsylvania and Pullman lettering on June 6, 1969 at Jamaica, New York. The car had been sold to the Long Island Railroad by this time and, on this Friday afternoon, is serving as a Parlor-Lounge car on the Long Island Railroad's *Cannonball* for eastern Long Island, with a terminus at Montauk. *Juniper Falls* continued to serve the Long Island Railroad until 1975 when it was sold for scrap after being renamed *Patchoque*. It was a regular car on *The Iron City Express* in the early 1950s.

Special Tray Breakfast

(To Expedite Breakfast Service to our Passengers, the following Tray Breakfast is offered for your convenience.)

Eighty Five Cents

Orange Juice   or   Chilled Tomato Juice

Toast (2 Slices)

Butter   Marmalade

    Tea (Pot)

Coffee (Pot)   Milk (Indv. Container)

THE PULLMAN COMPANY

TT139-3M-J52

William F. Howes, Jr.

This Pullman Company rider which was attached to the snack and drink menu from 1952 was used on *The Iron City Express*, as is proven by Pullman records in the author's possession. Pullman had their own coding system for menus and one had to see an assignment sheet of menus to know which trains they were used on. Luckily, these became available through a purchase of Pullman menus and accompanying documentation from the head of the Pullman Company's Commissary at Penn Station, New York. These records show that this menu was used on *The Iron City Express* and, in addition, the special tray breakfast menu shows the light breakfasts that cars like *Juniper Falls* served to *Iron City Express* patrons.

Harry Stegmaier Collection

The Statesman was assigned a prewar 10 roomette, 5 double bedroom Pullman sleeper from the *Cascade* series, which had been built by Pullman Standard for the Pennsylvania Railroad and delivered in the late summer of 1940. Regularly assigned to *The Statesman* between Washington and Pittsburgh in the early 1950s was *Cascade Knoll*, seen in this July 1964 photograph in special charter service. *Cascade Knoll*, with its 10 roomettes and 5 double bedrooms, served the Pennsylvania Railroad until 1967 when it was sold to the U.S. Army which, in turn, sold it to Amtrak in 1973. Amtrak had little use for these prewar lightweight cars and sold this one to the Golden Arrow line and, as far as is known, it is still is in existence today.

the exception that it had two 12 section, 1 drawing room sleepers instead of one and did not carry the New York to Memphis car westbound, this car being handled on *The Cincinnati Limited*. The dining car listed in the consist book for No. 37 was deadheading and not available for the patrons of *The Iron City Express*. In addition to these cars, *The Iron City Express* also carried the two Boston to Pittsburgh cars, as well as a Springfield to Pittsburgh 8 section, buffet-lounge of the heavyweight variety drawn from the *Club* series of cars, all handled eastbound by *The New Englander*. *The Iron City Express* was, by 1952, one of those trains which the company could dispense with since *The Pittsburgher*, as well as a number of long haul trains, served the overnight Pittsburgh market in both directions from and to New York. *The Iron City Express* was discontinued in the following year once some of the heavy traffic that the railroad had experienced as a result of the Korean War had disappeared.

No. 35 and No. 36
THE PHILADELPHIA and PITTSBURGH NIGHT EXPRESSES
No. 50 and No. 51
THE STATESMAN

In 1952, traffic still warranted the operation overnight, in addition to *The Iron City Express* and *The Pittsburgher*, of a strictly Philadelphia to Pittsburgh overnight train, No. 35 and No. 36, *The Pittsburgh* and *Philadelphia Night Expresses*, respectively, as well as their Washington to Harrisburg connections, *The Statesman*, No. 51 and No. 50. No. 35, the westbound *Pittsburgh Night Express*, carried a large amount of headend traffic, including the special milk tank cars between Philadelphia and Harrisburg, which were added there to mail train No. 13. These cars were operated by the Surplee Dairy Company of Philadelphia, Pennsylvania and operated to Huntingdon, Pennsylvania, with the second car going on via the Huntingdon and Broad Top Mountain Railroad to Bedford, Pennsylvania in order to bring the dairy product of the rich farmlands of Huntingdon and Bedford counties to the Philadelphia market. They were, therefore, carried westbound on No. 35, empty as far as Harrisburg. As well as these cars, one can see that there were a large number of headend cars on the train between Philadelphia and Pittsburgh, plus a combine and a reclining seat P70KR coach. No. 35 also carried a pair of lightweight Philadelphia to Pittsburgh sleeping cars, one a prewar *Brook* series, 12 duplex, single room, 5 double bedroom car and a postwar 21 roomette car, plus a 12 section, 1 drawing room heavyweight

Train 35

Car Type	Description	From	To	Details	Car Des
1 Milk	Tank DE Saturday	Philadelphia	Bedford	To 13 Harrisburg	
1 Milk	Tank DE Saturday	Philadelphia	Huntington	To 13 Harrisburg	
1 MS-60	DE Saturday, Sunday, and Holidays	Philadelphia	Harrisburg		
1 MS-60	DE Sunday, Monday and Days after Holidays	Philadelphia(Sears)	Pittsburgh	From 581 Harrisburg	
1 MS-60		Philadelphia	Pittsburgh	From 581 Harrisburg	
1 Express	B-60, Messenger, DE Sunday Gold Star	Philadelphia	Pittsburgh	From 581 Harrisburg	
1 Express	B-60, DE Saturday, Sunday and Holidays	Philadelphia	Pittsburgh		
1 Express	R-50, Saturday	Philadelphia	Pittsburgh		
1 Express	B-60, Saturday Messenger	Philadelphia	Pittsburgh	GOLD STAR	
1 MS-60	DE Sunday	Philadelphia	Pittsburgh	Preferential Mails	
1 PB-70	Scheme 6	Philadelphia	Pittsburgh		
1 P-70KR	Reclining Seats	%Philadelphia	Pittsburgh		
1 SL-Lounge	6 SBR, Buffet	Philadelphia	Pittsburgh		355
1 SL	12-1, DE Saturday	*Philadelphia	Pittsburgh		354
1 SL	12 Duplex SR, 1 DR, 2 Compt., DE Sat.	*Philadelphia	Pittsburgh		353
1 SL	21 Roomette	Philadelphia	Pittsburgh		352
1 SL	8 Section, 1 DR, 2 Compt., DE Saturday	*Philadelphia	Pittsburgh		351
1 PB-70	Papers, Friday and Saturday	Philadelphia	Altoona	To 37 Harrisburg	
1 P-70KR	Reclining Seats	%Washington	Pittsburgh	From 535 Harrisburg	
1 SL	10 Roomette, 5 DBR	Washington	Pittsburgh	LW From 535 Harrisburg	511
1 SL	8 Section, 1 DR, 2 Compt. DE Sunday	xWashington	Pittsburgh	From 535 Harrisburg	512
1 SL	8 Section, 5 DBR, DE Sunday	xWashington	Pittsburgh	From 535 Harrisburg	513

* Will NOT operate November 27, 28, December 25, 26, 31, January 1, 2
x Will NOT operate November 28, 29, December 26, 27, January 1, 2, 3

Train 36

Car Type	Description	From	To	Details	Car Des
1 MS-60	X-29 (X)	Cincinnati	Philadelphia	From 204 Pittsburgh	
1 Express	B-60, Messenger, Gold Star	Pittsburgh	Philadelphia		
1 PB-70	Scheme 6	Pittsburgh	Philadelphia		
1 P-70KR	Reclining Seats	%Pittsburgh	Philadelphia		
1 SL	21 Roomette	Pittsburgh	Philadelphia	LW	360
1 SL	12 Duplex SR, 5 DBR	Pittsburgh	Philadelphia	LW	361
1 SL	12-1	*Pittsburgh	Philadelphia		362
1 SL-Lounge	6 SBR, Buffet	Pittsburgh	Philadelphia		363
1 SL	12-1	*Pittsburgh	Harrisburg		369
1 SL	8 Section, 1 DR, 2 Compartment	vPittsburgh	Philadelphia	From 16 Harrisburg	169
1 P-70KR	Reclining Seats	%Erie	Philadelphia	From 580 Harrisburg	
1 PC-70		Erie	Philadelphia	From 580 Harrisburg	
1 SL	10 Section, 3 DBR	Erie	Philadelphia	From 580 Harrisburg	
1 SL	10 Roomette, 5 DBR	vxCleveland	Philadelphia	LW, From 38 Harrisburg	381
1 SL	6 Section, 6 DBR	xCleveland	Philadelphia	From 38 Harrisburg	380
1 SL	12-1	Buffalo	Philadelphia	From 574 Harrisburg	747
1 SL	10 Roomette, 5 DBR	vBuffalo	Philadelphia	LW, To 536 Harrisburg	746
1 P-70KR	Reclining Seats	%Pittsburgh	Washington	To 536 Harrisburg	
1 SL	8 Section, 5 DBR	*Pittsburgh	Washington	To 536 Harrisburg	501
1 SL	8 Section, 1 DR, 2 Compartment	*Pittsburgh	Washington	To 536 Harrisburg	502
1 SL	10 Roomette, 5 DBR	Pittsburgh	Washington	To 536 Harrisburg	503

* Will NOT operate November 27, 28, December 25, 26, 31, January 1, 2
v Will NOT operate November 28, 29, December 26, 27, January 2, 3
x Deadhead to New York in No. 206 for service in No. 39

The Pittsburgh Night Express and *The Philadelphia Night Express* each carried a 12 section, 1 drawing room sleeper between Philadelphia and Pittsburgh. General service cars like Pennsylvania Railroad Pullman car, *Dunning*, seen here in New Haven, Connecticut on June 25, 1960, were the type of standard 12-1 sleeping cars that one might have found on *The Pittsburgh* and *Philadelphia Night Expresses* in the early 1950s.

sleeper and an 8 section, 2 compartment, 1 drawing room heavyweight sleeper. Another heavyweight sleeper lounge car with 6 single bedrooms and a buffet provided evening snacks and beverages as well as a light breakfast into Pittsburgh for patrons of *The Pittsburgh Night Express*. At Harrisburg, four cars were added that arrived from Washington on connecting train No. 535. This

train, of course, also picked up traffic from Baltimore. These cars, which made up *The Statesman* portion of the train, were added to No. 35 at Harrisburg and included a reclining seat coach, a 10 roomette, 5 double bedroom prewar lightweight sleeper and two heavyweight sleepers, one containing 8 sections and 5 double bedrooms and another 8 sections, 2 compartments and a

Each consist of No. 35 and No. 36 contained a PB70 combination coach. Modernized cars like No. 5114, seen here in 1956, were indicative of the type of combines that one could probably have found on these trains. Pennsylvania Railroad's Altoona Shops had rebuilt them from older cars. Some had been modernized with wide windows but did not contain reclining seats. No. 5114 is a good example of a rebuilt, modernized combine.

The Philadelphia Night Express and *The Pittsburgh Night Express* were each assigned a prewar, 12 duplex single room, 5 double bedroom sleeper such as Marsh Brook, the type of car in that series. *Marsh Brook* had been built by the Pullman Company for the Pennsylvania Railroad before World War II and contained the unique duplex single rooms as well as 5 double bedrooms, placed at each end of the car. *Marsh Brook* had been delivered to the Pennsylvania Railroad in September, 1940 and served the company for over 25 years until it was finally retired in 1966 and sold to the ill-fated Hofheinz enterprise in Texas which scrapped the car after the venture collapsed.

drawing room. The heavy amount of section space was obviously a necessity since they were probably patronized by large numbers of U. S. government workers who were only reimbursed for the cost of lower berth space.

Eastbound No. 36, because of the necessity of carrying larger numbers of sleeping cars, carried only two regular headend cars and, as far as the Philadelphia 30th. Street Station cars were concerned, it was almost identical to its westbound counterpart, No. 35. The exceptions were a standard 12 section, 1 drawing room sleeper handled from Pittsburgh to the Pennsylvania state capital at Harrisburg and, a Pittsburgh to Philadelphia sleeper, which was handled on *The Iron City Express* from Pittsburgh to Harrisburg, but carried as a through car on *The Pittsburgh Night Express* in its westbound trek. In addition to these cars, of course, there were *The Statesman* cars bound for Baltimore and Washington on connecting train No. 536, which were detached from No. 36 at Harrisburg and made up *The Statesman* from Harrisburg to the nation's capital. Similarities end there since eastbound No. 36 carried a large number of sleeping cars for Philadelphia which its westbound counterpart did not have. The overnight *Philadelphia Night Express* was very convenient for Philadelphia passengers because, unlike the through trains, it operated right into 30th. Street Station in downtown Philadelphia rather than bypass this major city like other main-line trains. Once *The Statesman* cars were detached from the train at Harrisburg, it then picked up a large number of cars from varying points. Three cars came from Erie, Pennsylvania and were handled to Philadelphia beyond Harrisburg on No. 36, two coaches and a heavyweight 10 section, 3 double bedroom sleeper, brought in on Pennsylvania's *Southern Express*, as well as two sleeping cars, one a heavyweight and one a prewar lightweight, which arrived in Harrisburg on *The Dominion Express* from Buffalo and were then transferred to No. 36. In addition to these cars, No. 36 also received a lightweight, prewar 10 roomette, 5 double bedroom sleeper and a 6 section, 6 double bedroom sleeper from *The Clevelander* at Harrisburg. This was a long standing tradition since Philadelphia seems to have been the destination for a number of overnight travelers from Cleveland. Well into the 1950s, *The Clevelander* delivered a strictly Philadelphia car to one train or another at Harrisburg, Pennsylvania. If one counts the cars beyond Harrisburg, No. 36 is an impressive train with no less than nine sleeping cars into Philadelphia's 30th. Street Station, plus the heavyweight sleeper lounge car with its 6 single bedrooms and buffet. Eventually, by the mid 1950s, with the big cutbacks of that decade, many

Both the *Pittsburgh* and *Philadelphia Night Express* trains, as well as *The Statesman* between Washington and Pittsburgh, were regularly assigned an 8 section, 2 compartment, 1 drawing room, heavyweight Pullman sleeper. An example of such a car is *Centhill*, seen here in this photograph. These were older cars assigned to secondary trains by the 1950s and each consist west of Harrisburg of Nos. 35-51 and 36-50 contained two of these 8 section, 2 compartment, 1 drawing room cars, one assigned to the Philadelphia-Pittsburgh line and another to the Washington-Pittsburgh line.

of the cars that *The Pittsburgh* and *Philadelphia Night Express* trains carried were discontinued and, eventually, Philadelphia bound sleeping cars were handled on other through trains such as *The Manhattan Limited* westbound or a connecting train from Harrisburg into 30th. Street Station, which carried the Philadelphia cars. Thus, No.35 and No. 36 could be dispensed with. The same was true of *The Statesman*. It was in direct competition with a number of fine Baltimore & Ohio trains between Pittsburgh and Washington, namely No. 7, *The Shenandoah* westbound, as well as No. 18, *The Cleveland Night Express* and even No. 6, *The Capitol Limited*, eastbound. *The Philadelphia Night Express* and *The Statesman*, along with *The Pittsburgh Night Express*, all disappeared from the Pennsylvania Railroad timetables between 1956 to 1958 era.

No. 44 and No. 144

No. 44, and on Saturday night No. 144, literally had no strictly westbound counterpart. Departing from Chicago at 11:40 p.m., the train did not reach Pittsburgh until 12:15 the next day, except on Sundays when it arrived at 11:40 in the morning. Its departure was only ten minutes later than *The Gotham Limited* but it took over three

hours more time for No. 44 to reach Pittsburgh. Obviously, when one looks at the consist book, this was a mail and express train that also carried among its massive amounts of headend traffic, a working RPO car. Passenger accommodations were sparse with only a P70GR reclining seat coach and a standard heavyweight 12 section, 1 drawing room sleeper, with sleeping car space sold only as far as Canton, Ohio, the car being utilized for parlor car seating beyond Canton. It is certainly unlikely that many through travelers would have used this slow mail and express train for its passengers accommodations unless they were headed for intermediate points in Ohio. Sleeping car traffic to Ohio points west of Canton and Canton itself was no longer substantial. The train did provide a convenient early morning train into the Steel City for Ohio communities east of Crestline, many of which were bypassed by almost all of the other through trains. Obviously, trains like No. 44 and No. 144 could not survive long amidst the declining patronage of the early 1950s and these trains were soon removed from the Pennsylvania Railroad timetables. However, they continued to run well into the 1960s as mail and express trains for the Pennsylvania Railroad, although under other numbers, and provided, in this regard, an

Train No. 44
Daily—Chicago-Crestline, Daily, except Sunday, Crestline-Pittsburgh

Car Type	Description	From	To	Details	Car Des
1 MS-60	DE Monday	Crestline	Pittsburgh		
1 MS-60	X-29 (X)	Canton	Pittsburgh	Donner Press	
1 MS-60	X-29, DE Monday and Days after Holidays	xCanton	Pittsburgh		
1 Express	R-50	xChicago	New York	To 18 Pittsburgh	
1 Express	B-60, Messenger GOLD STAR	xChicago	Harrisburg	To 18 Pittsburgh	
1 Express	B-60	xChicago	Harrisburg	To 46 Pittsburgh	
1 B-60	Mail and Express	Chicago	Lima		
1 Express	X-29 or R-50, DE Saturday	Chicago	Pittsburgh		
1 MS-60	(X)	*Detroit	Philadelphia	From 106 Mansfield	
1 MS-60		*Detroit	Pittsburgh	From 106 Mansfield	
1 Express	B-60 Open	*Detroit	Pittsburgh	From 106 Mansfield	
1 Express	B-60 GOLD STAR	*Detroit	Pittsburgh	From 106 Mansfield	
1 B-60	Baggage-Mail	*Detroit	Pittsburgh	From 106 Mansfield	
1 MS-60	B-60, Messenger GOLD STAR	xChicago	Pittsburgh		
1 B-60	Baggage-Express	xChicago	Pittsburgh	30 foot baggage, 30 foot express	
1 MS-60	(X)	xChicago	Pittsburgh		
1 MS-60	Open	xChicago	Pittsburgh		
1 BM-70M	DE Saturday and Sunday	Chicago	Pittsburgh		
1 B-60	Mail and Express, DE Sunday and Monday	Grand Rapids	Pittsburgh	From 500 Fort Wayne	
1 MS-60	DE Monday and Days after Holidays	xFort Wayne	Pittsburgh		
1 P-70GR	Reclining Seats	%Chicago	Pittsburgh		
1 SL	12-1	zChicago	Canton		442
1 B-60	Mail and Express, DE Sunday	xChicago	Canton		
1 Express	X-29 or R-60, DE Sunday	Chicago	Fort Wayne		

x To 144 Crestline Sunday a.m.
* DE Sunday and November 28, December 26, January 2
z DE Saturday and November 27, 28, December 25, 26, January 1, 2; advertise and diagram car Chicago-Canton, Ohio and use for parlor car space Canton-Pittsburgh.

Harry Stegmaier

No. 44-144 was primarily a train of headend cars between Chicago and Pittsburgh. Included in this mix was a working BM70M RPO-Baggage car every day but Saturday and Sunday. Typical of the BM70M cars is No. 6575, seen here at Altoona, Pennsylvania in May, 1971. These cars served the Pennsylvania Railroad in head-end service for a long period of time until they were finally retired in the late 1960s and early 1970s.

Harry Stegmaier Collection

Each No. 44-144 was assigned one reclining seat coach, a P70GR car. However, when these cars were assigned to other, more important trains, No. 44-144 simply got whatever cars were available Consequently, it was not unusual to find cars like Pennsylvania Railroad No. 3826, a P70FR coach, on No. 44-144. The P70FR cars had been rebuilt by the Altoona Car Shops from older P70 coaches before World War II. They were high capacity cars and did not have reclining seats. While they were mainly intended for service on the New York-Washington corridor, the P70FRs could often be found on secondary trains on the mainline in the 1950s and, certainly, No. 44-144, the train number on Sunday, was a secondary train

eastbound counterpart between Chicago and Pittsburgh overnight for westbound mail and express train No. 99, a Pittsburgh-Chicago train which did not handle revenue passengers.

No. 46
THE NEW ENGLANDER

The New Englander primarily served two purposes for the Pennsylvania Railroad. Departing Pittsburgh at 4:00 p.m., it provided a convenient late afternoon departure from the Steel City for passengers bound for New York, although it is unlikely that few through passengers would have chosen this train for their trip because of its early morning arrival at 1:50 a.m. at Penn Station. The

other primary purpose of the train was to carry the Pittsburgh to New England sleeping cars which were handed over to the New Haven Railroad at New York for the rest of their journey. These included a heavyweight, rebuilt, 12 roomette, 2 single bedroom, 3 double bedroom Boston sleeper, often *Keystone Banks*, as well as a standard 12 section, 1 drawing room sleeper plus an 8 section, buffet lounge sleeper which operated from Pittsburgh to Springfield, being carried beyond New York on New Haven train No. 186. Along with the through sleeping cars, the train carried a substantial amount of headend including, a working RPO car, a combine and reclining seat coaches. A dining lounge car provided the evening meal

Train No. 46

Car Type	Description	From	To	Details	Car Des
1 Express	B-60	Chicago	Harrisburg	From 44 (144 Sunday) Pittsburgh	
1 MS-60	X-29 (X)	St. Louis	Philadelphia	From 6 Pittsburgh	
1 MS-60	(X)	St. Louis	New York	From 6 Pittsburgh	
1 MS-60	B-60	St. Louis	New York	From 6 Pittsburgh	
1 BM-70M	DE Sunday	Pittsburgh	New York	Letter End West	
1 PB-70	Scheme 6	Pittsburgh	New York		
1 P-70GSR	Reclining Seats, Friday and Sunday	%Pittsburgh	New York		
3 P-70GSR	Reclining Seats	%Pittsburgh	New York		
1 Diner-Lounge	Pittsburgh	New York			
1 SL	12 Roomette, 2 SBR, 3 DBR	Pittsburgh	Boston	To '86 New York	K95
1 SL	12-1, DE Saturday	*Pittsburgh	Boston	To 186 New York	K94
1 SL-Lounge	8 Sections, Buffet, DE Saturday	*Pittsburgh	Springfield	To 186 New York	K93
2 P-70	Sunday	Harrisburg	New York		

* Will NOT operate November 27, 28, December 25, 26, 31

William F. Howes, Jr.

Each night out of Chicago, No. 44, or No. 144 on Sundays, was assigned a 12 section, 1 drawing room sleeper as far as Canton, Ohio, after which the space in the car was sold as parlor car space until its arrival at Pittsburgh. A secondary train like No. 44-144 would proudly have received a car like Pennsylvania Railroad's *McClellanville*, which is seen here in July, 1960 in the New Haven Railroad yards in New Haven, Connecticut while in camp train service. It provided first-class overnight space, primarily for businessmen heading for Canton and other intermediate cities, as well as for those few people who might have cared to avail themselves of the parlor car seating between Canton and Pittsburgh. *McClellanville* is typical of the standard 12 section, 1 drawing room Pullman sleepers operated by the Pennsylvania Railroad in the 1950s.

Harry Stegmaier

Each No. 46 carried, every day except Sunday, a BM70M Railway Post Office-Baggage Car in its daily trek from Pittsburgh to New York. Typical of such cars was No. 6544, seen here as a working RPO car in August, 1966. They were typical of the massive numbers of Railway Post Office cars operated by the Pennsylvania Railroad in the 1950s when the mail still traveled by train and, it might be added, much more efficiently than today

Each *New Englander* was regularly assigned three P70GSR reclining seat coaches, with extra cars added on the weekend. When these cars were needed elsewhere, of course, it might have received lesser cars but normally at least one or two P70GSR coaches could be found in the consist. In this photograph, taken in 1959, one sees P70GSR coach No. 4214, which by that time had been retired and sold. P70GSR No. 4214 was among a group of fifty coaches rebuilt in the spring and summer of 1942 by the Altoona Car Shops for mainline train service. They were, of course, created out of older P70 coaches and were given wide windows, as well as reclining seats. The P70GSR's were primarily found on trains like *The Trail Blazer* and *The Jeffersonian* until those trains were reequipped after World War II. By the 1950s, they were being used on secondary trains and, as can be seen from this photograph, many of them had been retired by the latter part of the decade. These were the kind of cars that probably would have been found on *The New Englander* in 1952.

for the coach and sleeping car passengers that rode No. 46, *The New Englander*. No. 46 had no west-bound counterpart since the New England sleeping cars were carried beyond New York on Pennsylvania's *Iron City Express*, westbound. *The New Englander* operated until the mid-1950s after which the New England sleeping cars, or what remained of them, were switched to other through Pennsylvania Railroad trains between Pittsburgh and New York.

No. 52 and No. 53
THE FORT PITT

The Fort Pitt, in both directions, was Pennsylvania's daylight train between Pittsburgh and Chicago and, as such, it made most of the local stops between those two points in both directions, thus providing daylight local service on the western portion of the New York-Chicago main line. As can be seen from the consist, both east-bound and westbound trains carried substantial headend traffic, including a working Railway Post

		Train No. 52				
Car Type	Description	From	To	Details		Car Des
2 B-60	Papers Wednesday	Chicago	Pittsburgh	Sun-Telegraph		
I Express	R-50, DE Saturday and Sunday	Chicago	Pittsburgh			
I Express	B-60, Messenger. GOLD STAR	Chicago	Pittsburgh			
3 MS-60	(X)	Chicago	Pittsburgh			
I MS-60	Open	*Chicago	Pittsburgh			
I BM-70M	Letter End West	Chicago	Pittsburgh			
I BM-70	30 foot apartment, DE Sun. & Mon.	xChicago	Pittsburgh			
I PB-70	Sunday and Monday	vChicago	Pittsburgh			
3 P-70KR	Reclining Seats	%Chicago	Pittsburgh			
I PL-Cafe	8 Chair, 9 seat	Chicago	Pittsburgh	Cars 1104 and 1111		520

* Sunday	Works in western region at Chicago, Fort Wayne, Crestline only
Train Rider	Daily except Sunday - Chicago-Crestline, Daily - Crestline-Pittsburgh
v Handles Mail Sunday	
* use baggage apartment for baggage.	

Office car. Passengers were accommodated in rebuilt, heavyweight, reclining seat coaches as well as two unique parlor cafe cars, No. 1104 and No. 1111 which contained, among them, seating for 17 parlor car passengers plus a cafe section. These cars were Pullman operated but owned by the Pennsylvania Railroad in an arrangement that dated back to the 1930s. *The Fort Pitt* was a popular daylight run and carried, as well as through passengers, a good deal of local traffic. Eastbound No. 52 departed Chicago as the Pennsylvania Railroad's early morning train at 8:30 a.m. with an arrival in Pittsburgh at 7:15 in the evening while westbound No. 53 departed Pittsburgh at 11:00

a.m. and, was the last train west to Chicago until *The Golden Triangle* at 11:00 p.m. at night, with an 8:10 p.m. arrival in Chicago. These trains filled in the gap in both directions between Pennsylvania Railroad's other through trains and provided a valuable service in the Pittsburgh to Chicago market in competition with the Baltimore & Ohio. The eastbound *Fort Pitt* was discontinued much earlier than its westbound counterpart which lasted until Amtrak, as an unnamed local train with coaches only, until May, 1971 and served as a westbound counterpart to the eastbound only *Admiral*, which also survived until Amtrak.

Harry Stegmaier

Each consist of *The Fort Pitt*, which was a heavy carrier of headend traffic, had a working Railway Post Office car between Pittsburgh and Chicago, with eastbound No. 52 having a second car with a 30 ft. RPO apartment five days a week. Typical of the RPO cars used on a train like this would have been BM70M No. 6555, seen here in May, 1971 at Altoona, Pennsylvania after it was retired by the Pennsylvania Railroad. The car is typical of the Railway Post Office cars used heavily in railway mail service by the company in the early 1950s. Some of the BM70Ms lasted right down until Amtrak although RPO routes were few and far between after 1967.

	Train No. 53					
Car Type	Description	From	To	Details		Car Des
I Express	X-29, DE Sunday, Monday, Tuesday, and Days after Holidays	New York	Chicago	From 93 Pittsburgh		
I Express	B-60, Messenger GOLD STAR	Pittsburgh	Chicago			
I MS-60	Wednesday, GRIT	Pittsburgh	Chicago			
I BM-70M	Letter End East	Pittsburgh	Chicago			
I MS-60	Open, DE Sunday and Holidays	Pittsburgh	Chicago			
I B-60		Pittsburgh	Chicago			
2 P-70	Sunday	Pittsburgh	Chicago			
2 P-70KR	Reclining Seats	%Pittsburgh	Chicago			
I PL-Cafe	8 Chair, 9 Seat	Pittsburgh	Chicago	Cars 1104 and 1111		530
I Express	R-50, DE Sunday, Monday and Days after Holidays	Philadelphia	Chicago	From 11 Pittsburgh		
I MS-60	DE Monday and Days after Holidays	Philadelphia	Council Bluffs	From 11 Pittsburgh		
I MS-60	DE Monday and Days after Holidays	Philadelphia	Chicago	From 11 Pittsburgh		
2 MS-60		Pittsburgh	Chicago			
I Rider	(X)	Pittsburgh	Chicago			
I MS-60	X-29	Pittsburgh	Fort Wayne			

Each consist of *The Fort Pitt* received, in normal cases, P70KR coaches between Pittsburgh and Chicago, with three being assigned to eastbound No. 52 and two to No. 53. However, like the rest of the coaches on the Pennsylvania Railroad, the P70KR cars were sometimes not available and, thus, it was not unusual to find cars from the P70FAR coach class on No. 52 and No. 53. In this photograph, No. 3957, a P70FAR, is seen in 1958 on train No. 91. The P70FAR cars had been rebuilt by Altoona before World War II from older P70 cars. While these cars had wide windows, they were nevertheless high capacity coaches and seated 84 in walkover seats. Trains like *The Fort Pitt* might get P70FAR cars instead of its usually assigned reclining seat P70KR cars when they were not available or were needed for other trains.

No. 60 and No. 61
THE PITTSBURGHER

The Pittsburgher was the premier all Pullman overnight train. In 1952 Pennsylvania Railroad's all-Pullman *The Pittsburgher* was its "star" train in the critical New York-Pittsburgh market. The train was heavily patronized by Pittsburgh people making trips to New York, spending a day in the Big Apple, the nation's center of commerce at the time, and then returning overnight to the Steel City. Executives and even junior executives from the steel companies and the mining companies rode the fast Pennsylvania Railroad overnighter. In addition, many of the department store buyers road *The Pittsburgher* to New York to make purchases for their big downtown department stores in Pittsburgh. In fact, some companies such as U.S. Steel and Kaufmann's Department stores, for example, simply reserved certain space on the *Pittsburgher* every night of the week. All of these people as well as other western Pennsylvania businessmen and financiers chose *The Pittsburgher* for their trips to the east and return. For a train as popular as *The Pittsburgher*, the Pennsylvania

Car Type	Description	From	To	Details	Car Des
		Train No. 60			
		Blue Ribbon			
		The Pittsburgher			
1 PB-70		Pittsburgh	New York	SW	
1 SL	21 Roomette	Pittsburgh	New York	LW	P-1
1 SL	21 Roomette	Pittsburgh	New York	LW	P-2
1 SL	4 Compartment, 4 DBR, 2 DR	Pittsburgh	New York	LW	P-4
1 SL-Lounge	6 DBR, Bar	#Pittsburgh	New York	LW	P-5
1 Diner		Pittburgh	New York	LW	
1 SL	12 Duplex SR, 4 DBR	Pittsburgh	New York		P-7
1 SL	10 Roomette, 6 DBR	#Pittsburgh	New York	LW	P-8
1 SL	12 Duplex SR, 4 DBR	Pittsburgh	New York	LW	P-9
1 SL	21 Roomette	Pittsburgh	New York	LW	P-10
1 SL	12 Duplex SR, 4 DBR	Pittsburgh	New York	LW, From 638 Harrisburg	P-11
1 SL	10 Roomette, 6 DBR	Roanoke	New York	LW, From 638 Harrisburg	W-6
1 SL	10 Section, 1 Compartment, 1 DR	Roanoke	New York	SW, From 638 Harrisburg	RN1

NOTE: Sleepers and diner are NOT turned at Pittsburgh and will operate with reversed consist on alternate days.

Railroad had equipped it with the most modern equipment available after World War II. This was not just done out of economic concerns, but political reasons as well. Some Pittsburgh financiers and steel company chairmen were on the company's board of directors, and as such, expected the finest accommodations that the company could provide when they traveled. As such, it was sometimes very difficult to obtain space on *The Pittsburgher* in the early 1950s.

Departing both its terminal cities late at night, with an early morning arrival, at either New York or Pittsburgh, Nos. 60 and 61, zipped across Pennsylvania and New Jersey in their nightly treks, except on Saturday. The train therefore, carried very little head end except for mail storage cars on Tuesday and Wednesday. In addition, each train had a PB-70 combine coach which was primarily used for baggage and as a crew rider because no coach passengers were carried on *The Pittsburgher*. Each *Pittsburgher* carried in its consist three 21 roomette *Inn* series sleepers, a 4 double bedroom, 4 compartment, 2 drawing room *Imperial* car, as well as three eastbound and two westbound 12 duplex single room, 4 double bedroom *Creek* series sleepers, which provided the excellent one person accommodations for the traveling business people. In addition to these cars, as well as a 10 roomette, 6 double bedroom *Rapids* series car the train carried a post-war 6 double bedroom, bar-lounge and a full dining car. The diner provided full breakfast service for its elite clientele into both New York and Pittsburgh from an extensive menu. However, a little know fact is that while the diner did not serve dinner, it was nevertheless set up to provid passengers who boarded early with a selection of sandwiches and other late evening type meals, such as a grilled steak sandwich, before departure. In addition to its post-war streamlined lightweight cars, No. 60 handled a 10-6 sleeper and a heavyweight 10 section, 1 compartment, 1 drawing room sleeper from Harrisburg to New York. These two cars operated over the Norfolk and Western Shenandoah Valley route to Hagerstown and were then delivered to Harrisburg on Train No. 638. No. 61 did not handle these cars but did carry a heavyweight 10 section, 3 double bedroom sleeper as far as Harrisburg in its overnight journey to Williamsport, Pennsylvania.

The Pittsburgher was a fine way to travel for the business community of the Steel City and Manhattan. This poplar overnight train, geared to the business community, always remained all Pullman and even after the advent of the interstate highways and jet aircraft, and with much business done by the telephone and other electronic means, *The Pittsburgher* carried a substantial crowd throughout the 1950s. However by the 1960s the general pace of the entire nation speeded up and more and more businessmen began deserting the train and it became a possibility for discontinuance since passengers could be handled on other trains

Train No. 61
Blue Ribbon
The Pittsburger

Car Type Des	Description	From	To	Details	Car
1 MS-60	Tuesday	Stamford	Pittsburgh	SW From 183 New York	
2 MS-60	Wednesday	Stamford	Pittsburgh	SW From 183 New York	
1 PB-70		New York	Pittsburgh	SW	
1 SL	21 Roomette	New York	Pittsburgh	LW	P-1
1 SL	21 Roomette	New York	Pittsburgh	LW	P-2
1 SL	4 compartment, 4 DBR, 2 DR	New York	Pittsburgh	LW	P-4
1 SL-Lounge	6 DBR, Bar	#New York	Pittsburgh	LW	P-5
1 Diner		New York	Pittsburgh	LW	
1 SL	12 Duplex SR, 4 DBR	New York	Pittsburgh	LW	P-7
1 SL	10 Roomette, 6 DBR	#New York	Pittsburgh	LW	P-8
1 SL	12 Duplex SR, 4 DBR	New York	Pittsburgh	LW	P-9
1 SL	21 Roomette	New York	Pittsburgh	LW	P-10
1 SL	10 Section, 3 DBR	New York	Williamsport	SW To 577 Harrisburg	

NOTE: Sleepers and diner NOT turned at Pittsburgh and will operate with reversed consist on alternate days.

Harry Stegmaier Collection

The Pittsburgher was, of course, an all-Pullman overnight train, and the pride of the Pennsylvania Railroad between New York and Pittsburgh. Therefore, it was equipped entirely with all room postwar lightweight cars. The only exceptions to this were the heavyweight cars that it carried westbound as far as Harrisburg for the New York to Willamsport service and, eastbound, a heavyweight sleeper from Roanoke which it picked up at Harrisburg. Otherwise, it was an entirely light-weight train. Each consist of *The Pittsburgher* carried a 4 double bedroom, 4 compartment, 2 drawing room sleeper. These cars were drawn from the Pennsylvania Railroad's *Imperial* series, built by American Car & Foundry and delivered to the company between September and December 1948. One car assigned to The Pittsburgher in the early 1950s was *Imperial Loch*. This car, seen here in Chicago in June 1963, contained the postwar style 4 double bedrooms, as well as 4 compartments and 2 drawing rooms. It served the Pennsylvania Railroad throughout its career and then went on to the Penn Central, but, by that time, it was often being leased out to the Seaboard Coast Line for service on the Florida trains, especially *The Silver Star* and *The Florida Special*. *Imperial Loch* was retired in 1971 and was scrapped by the company when Amtrak took over passenger service.

Harry Stegmaier Collection

In 1956, the Pennsylvania Railroad renamed a whole series of sleepers and sleeper-lounge cars specifically for *The Pittsburgher*. These were all named after western Pennsylvania merchants and industrial leaders. One such car was *Richard Beatty Mellon*, a 4 double bedroom, 4 compartment, 2 drawing room postwar car, built by American Car & Foundry, as *Imperial Cliff*. Renamed in 1956 *Richard Beatty Mellon*, it was then assigned primarily to *The Pittsburgher*, briefly renamed *B. F. Jones* then quickly renamed *Richard Beatty Mellon*. *Richard Beatty Mellon*, like all of the *Imperial* cars, lasted until the end of Pennsylvania, and later Penn Central passenger service and could often be found in the late 1960s on *The Broadway Limited*, formerly *The General*, which succeeded that train. The car is seen here in Denver, Colorado in the early 1960s in special train service.

Harry Stegmaier

Another car assigned to *The Pittsburgher* was 12 duplex single room, 4 double bedroom postwar sleeper *Cliff Creek*. *Cliff Creek* was one of the postwar cars built by Pullman Standard for the Pennsylvania Railroad containing the unique duplex single rooms, probably the most comfortable and spacious single person accommodations created by Pullman. *Cliff Creek* was a regular on *The Pittsburgher* in the early 1950s, having been delivered to the railroad in early 1949 from Pullman. The car is seen here in Chicago, Illinois in June, 1968. However, like the *Richard Beatty Mellon*, the car now carries the name *Charles Lockhart*, having been renamed from *Cliff Creek* in August, 1956, for its specific service on *The Pittsburgher*. Each consist of No. 60 and No. 61 contained three of the *Creek* series duplex single room, 4 double bedroom cars westbound and two such cars eastbound. The car was finally retired in 1968, shortly after this photograph was taken, and lay on the Altoona scrap line until 1972 when it was sold to a private party.

Harry Stegmaier

Each consist of *The Pittsburgher* carried a full dining car to service the numerous Pullmans on the train. Often assigned to *The Pittsburgher* was Pennsylvania Railroad's heavyweight diner No. 4467, which rode on four-wheel trucks after its modernization by the car shops in Altoona. That facility had created No. 4467 from a dining car built in 1916. The car emerged from Altoona in March, 1952 as a D78fR dining-lounge car with a round roof, and seating 32 in the dining section and 10 in its "short lounge." Cars like No. 4467 provided a substantial breakfast menu for the Pullman patrons of *The Pittsburgher* in the morning but it is often forgotten that this car also served a light evening luncheon, which included such items as a steak sandwich and Welsh Rarebit on toast. Pullman passengers boarding in New York or Pittsburgh could, before retiring, go to the diner and have a late evening light meal if they cared to do so since the car was open as soon as passengers boarded.

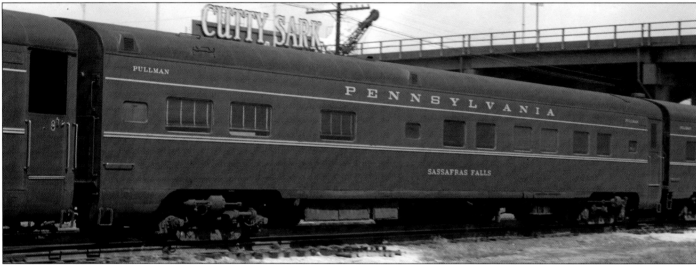

Harry Stegmaier Collection

Each consist of *The Pittsburgher* contained a 6 double bedroom bar-lounge car which was operated just ahead of the dining car on the train. *The Pittsburgher*, of course, provided evening bar service to Pullman patrons who wanted a nightcap before turning in. Regularly assigned to the train in the 1950s was 6 double bedroom, bar-lounge car *Sassafras Falls*. This was in the *Falls* series of cars which was delivered to the railroad from Pullman Standard in early 1949 and its 20-ft. lounge was undoubtedly usually well patronized on *The Pittsburgher*. The car lasted into the Penn Central era and was not retired until 1971 when it was scrapped. In 1956, a car from the same series as *Sassafras Falls*, *Linden Falls*, was renamed *Henry Phipps*, and was assigned to service on *The Pittsburgher*. The *Henry Phipps*, of course, contained 6 double bedrooms, a bar and 20-seat lounge. The *Henry Phipps* is seen here in August, 1966 in Denver, Colorado while in special train service. It was not retired until 1971, but by that time it was primarily in parlor room-buffet-lounge car service between New York and Philadelphia. *Henry Phipps* was retired in 1971 but survives today at the Altoona Railroad Museum.

overnight between New York and Pittsburgh such as No. 55 *The Pennsylvania Limited* and No. 22 *The Manhattan Limited*. However, discontinuing *The Pittsburgher* would have political consequences. Nevertheless whereas, the train had carried 145 people per trip in 1952, only 62 were riding it a decade later. Finally, after the approval of Richard King Mellon, the prominent Pittsburgh financier and a member of Pennsylvania Railroad's Board of Directors, and with the promise that additional sleepers would be added to other overnight tains between New York and Pittsburgh, the Pennsylvania Railroad discontinued the once elite overnighter on September 13, 1964. The last *Pittsburgher* was a sad ghost of its former self, with just one baggage car, three sleepers and a dining car. Nevertheless, this once great train remained all Pullman until the end and September 13, 1964 signaled the end of an era when businessmen rode overnight streamliners in the coarse of their financial transactions and other high profile endeavors.

Train No. 62
Blue Ribbon
The Golden Triangle

Car Type	Description	From	To	Details	Car Des
Express	Perishable (X)	Chicago	Harrisburg and Gateway	To 54 Pittsburgh	
Express	Perisahable (X)	Chicago	Hudson Cut-Off	To 54 Pittsburgh	
1 Express	R-50 or X-29, DE Sat.y, Sun., Holidays	Chicago	Pittsburgh		
1 MS-60	(X)	Chicago	Pittsburgh		
1 MS-60		Chicago	Pittsburgh		
1 BM-70	30 foot apartment, DE Sat. and Sun.	Chicago	Pittsburgh	Letter End West	
1 BM-60		Chicago	Pittsburgh	Letter End East	
1 PB-70	Sunday	Chicago	Pittsburgh		
2 P-70KR	Reclining Seats	%Chicago	Pittsburgh		
1 SL	12-1	¢Chicago	Pittsburgh	SW	626
1 SL	12 Duplex SR, 5 DBR	Chicago	Pittsburgh	LW	625
1 SL-Lounge	3 DBR, 1 DR, Buffet	#Chicago	Pittsburgh	LW	624
1 SL	10 Roomette, 6 DBR	#Chicago	Pittsburgh	LW	623
1 SL	4 Compartment, 4 DBR, 2 DR	Chicago	Pittsburgh	LW	622
1 SL	21 Roomette	Chicago	Pittsburgh	LW	621
1 SL	12 Duplex SR, 4 DBR	Chicago	Pittsburgh	LW	620
1 P-70GSR	Reclining Seats	*%Detroit	Pittsburgh	SW From 106 Mansfield	
1 SL	10 Roomette, 5 DBR	*Detroit	Pittsburgh	LW From 106 Mansfield	1061
1 SL	6 Section, 6 DBR	*Detroit	Pittsburgh	SW From 106 Mansfield	1060
1 BM-70	30 foot apartment, DE Sunday & Monday	*Detroit	Pittsburgh	SW From 106 Mansfield	

* Operate in No. 462, Mansfield-Pittsburgh, November 29, December 27, January 1, 3

No. 62-No. 63
THE GOLDEN TRIANGLE &
No. 105-No. 106

In the early 1950s, Pennsylvania Railroad's overnight *Golden Triangle* between Pittsburgh and Chicago was still a very popular Blue Ribbon train. Although not as prestigious as the all Pullman *Pittsburgher, The Golden Triangle* provided the overnight service for Pittsburgers to Chicago as well as Windy City residents heading for Pittsburgh. The eastbound train carried more headend traffic than the westbound, including a working Railway Post Office, as well as a second car, except on Sundays, that had a 30-foot RPO apartment. Passengers were accommodated in two rebuilt, heavyweight P70KR reclining seat coaches

Train No. 63
Blue Ribbon
The Golden Triangle
Daily except Sunday and November 27, 28, December 25, 26, 31, January 1, 2

Car Type	Description	From	To	Details	Car Des
Express	X-29, DE Saturday, Sunday & Holidays	Pittsburgh	Chicago		
1 MS-60	(X)	Pittsburgh	Chicago		
2 P-70KR	Reclining seats	%Pittsburgh	Chicago		
1 SL	12 Duplex SR, 4 DBR	Pittsburgh	Chicago	LW	630
1 SL	21 Roomette	Pittsburgh	Chicago	LW	631
1 SL	4 Compartment, 4 DBR, 2 DR	Pittsburgh	Chicago	LW	632
1 SL	10 Roomette, 6 DBR	#Pittsburgh	Chicago	LW	633
1 SL-Lounge	3 DBR, 1 DR, Buffet	#Pittsburgh	Chicago	LW	634
1 SL	12 Duplex SR, 5 DBR	Pittsburgh	Chicago	LW	635
1 SL	12-1	Washington	Chicago	SW From 33 Pittsburgh	50
1 P-70GSR	Reclining Seats	*%Pittsburgh	Detroit	SE To 105 Mansfield	
1 SL	10 Roomette, 5 DBR	*Pittsburgh	Detroit	LW To 105 Mansfield	106
1 SL	6 Section, 6 DBR	*Pittsburgh	Chicago	SW To 105 Mansfield	105
1 SL	6 Section, 6 DBR	Fort Wayne	Chicago	SW From 99 Fort Wayne	451
1 MS-60		Fort Wayne	Chicago	SW	
1 Express	R-50 or X-29, DE Sun., Mon., Tue.	Fort Wayne	Chicago	SW	

* Operate in No. 463, Pittsburgh-Mansfield, November 28, December 26, 31, January 2nd

Harry Stegmaier

The Golden Triangle was Pennsylvania Railroad's overnight Pittsburgh to Chicago train and, while not as prestigious as *The Pittsburgher*, nevertheless was equipped with mostly postwar lightweight sleeping cars. However, it also contained in its consist one heavyweight 12 section, 1 drawing room sleeper and carried coach passengers in a combine which operated only eastbound and two P70KR reclining seat coaches which operated in both directions. Nevertheless, it was primarily a Pullman train, popular with the overnight business traveler. Each consist of *The Golden Triangle* contained a 4 double bedroom, 4 compartment, 2 drawing room sleeping car. One such car assigned to *The Golden Triangle* on a regular basis was American Car & Foundry built *Imperial Ridge*, which the railroad had received in late 1948. *Imperial Ridge*, with its multi-person room configuration, like all of the *Imperial* cars, lasted until the Amtrak takeover of passenger service in May, 1971, although like the others it was usually by then on lease to the Seaboard Coast Line for its Florida trains, a long way from the days when it was a regular on the Pennsylvania's premier overnight Pittsburgh-Chicago train. The car is in special service in this photograph, which was taken in the mid-1960s.

David E. Staplin, Harry Stegmaier Collection

Each consist of overnight train No. 62 and No. 63 carried a 3 double bedroom, 1 drawing room, buffet-lounge sleeper. These cars were built by Pullman Standard and delivered to the Pennsylvania Railroad in May and June of 1949. Besides their 3 double bedrooms and drawing room, they had a buffet-lounge with 27 seats. Regularly assigned to *The Golden Triangle* on the Pittsburgh to Chicago overnight run to serve sandwiches and a light breakfast, as well as plenty of beverages for the Pullman passengers, was *Colonial Lanterns*, is seen here on January 28, 1970, long after it had been a major part of the Pennsylvania Railroad's Blue Ribbon fleet. By the time this photograph was taken in Philadelphia on January 28, 1970, the car had been demoted to parlor-buffet-lounge car service on the New York-Washington corridor and, by 1970, was pretty much restricted to New York-Philadelphia service. *Colonial Lanterns*, which had been placed in parlor car service as early as 1964, lasted through the Penn Central era, was retired in 1971, and was sold to a private party.

and, thus, *The Golden Triangle* was not in the all-Pullman category like *The Pittsburgher*. The eastbound and the westbound trains were nearly identical in their sleeping cars. Each train carried seven sleeping cars between Pittsburgh and Chicago, including a *Creek* series and a prewar *Brook* series car with duplex single rooms, and double bedrooms, a standard *Rapids* series 10 roomette, 6 double bedroom car, and an *Inn* series 21 roomette car plus a 4 double bedroom, 4 compartment, 2 drawing room *Imperial* car. A standard 12 section, 1 drawing room sleeper ran through from Washington and was handed over by a connecting

Harry Stegmaier

Lower Left: Each *Golden Triangle* consist also contained one 12 duplex single room, 4 double bedroom postwar Pullman built sleeper. The *Connoquenessing Creek* was regularly assigned to *The Golden Triangle* in the early 1950s. Its 12 duplex single rooms, as well as its 4 double bedrooms, were certainly popular with the overnight business travelers between Pittsburgh and Chicago. This car lasted longer than many of the other cars of the same type and survived through the Penn Central era until it was retired in May 1971 and was placed in work train service. The car is seen here in Chicago, Illinois in July, 1967 and was, by that late date, usually assigned to *The Broadway Limited* and, after that train's demise, to its successor, the former *General*.

train to *The Golden Triangle* at Pittsburgh, westbound, but operated only Chicago to Pittsburgh eastbound. In addition to these sleepers, the train also carried a *Colonial* series 3 double bedroom, 1 drawing room, buffet lounge car that provided evening beverages, snacks and a basic toast and beverage breakfast into both Chicago and Pittsburgh. In addition to these cars, No. 63 and No. 62, *The Golden Triangle*, carried the cars to and from Mansfield, Ohio which made up trains No. 105 and No. 106 to and from Detroit from that Ohio junction point. They provided Detroit with overnight coach and sleeping car service. In both directions, these included a rebuilt heavyweight reclining seat coach, a prewar lightweight 10 roomette, 5 double bedroom *Cascade* series sleeper and a 6 section-6 double bedroom heavyweight, modernized sleeper. In addition, the eastbound train also handled, on the rear, a Detroit to Pittsburgh RPO-baggage car from Mansfield to Pittsburgh.

Trains No. 105 and 106 were quite similar in

their makeup between Mansfield and Detroit. No. 105 arrived in Detroit at 7:40 a.m. only 25 minutes ahead of *The Red Arrow*, but eastbound No. 106 departed Detroit as a late night train at 11:40 p.m. with, of course, the morning arrival in Pittsburgh on *The Golden Triangle*. Both trains, No. 105 and No. 106, carried headend cars received from mail and express Train No. 99 westbound or delivered to Chicago-Pittsburgh overnight local No. 44 at Mansfield, with the exception of the RPO-baggage car which operated eastbound only. Besides the headend cars, there were only the coach and two sleeping cars that were received from or delivered to the *Golden Triangle* at Mansfield, Ohio. Both trains provided overnight service between Pittsburgh and Detroit. No. 106 was more heavily patronized because of it late night departure from Detroit at 11:40 p.m., provided excellent overnight service in a time slot that was not available otherwise. As with all trains of this nature, and with *The Red Arrow* still plying the rails to Toledo and Detroit, the Pennsylvania Railroad eventually eliminated No. 105 and No. 106 during the 1950s since they no longer served a public need in ever declining markets. The trains were losing money for the company. As for the headend traffic, it could simply be transferred to *The Red Arrow* as that train shrunk in size as the decade wore on, until its final discontinuance as a through Detroit train in 1959.

No. 72
THE JUNIATA

No. 72 departed Pittsburgh for New York City at 11:00 a.m. and was Pennsylvania Railroad's late morning train between the Steel City and Penn Station, New York where it arrived at 7:55 in the evening. Thus, *The Juniata* was a very popular daytime train and it would last until Amtrak in May, 1971 as one of the Penn Central's daylight Pittsburgh-New York runs. Although it was cut to coaches only at one point, it received a snack bar coach on and off in the Penn Central era. In 1952, however, *The Juniata* carried a heavy headend load, most of it brought in to Pittsburgh on No. 54, *The Gotham Limited*, from Chicago with one car coming in off *The St. Louisan* from St. Louis. In addition, it carried two Baggage-RPO cars, each with a 30-ft. RPO apartment between Pittsburgh and New York. As for its passenger accommodations, they were almost identical to the westbound *Metropolitan*, which the train seemed to mimic in its daylight schedule. These included four reclining seat coaches, a dining-lounge car to keep patrons fed, as well as a 28-seat 1 drawing room-parlor car for the first class passengers. In addition, it is interesting to note that the train picked up the two loaded milk cars at Huntingdon, Pennsylvania and carried them to Harrisburg, one from Bedford that arrived over the Huntingdon & Broad Top Mountain Railroad, while the other originated at

Car Type	Description	From	To	Details	Car Des
		Train No. 72			
1 MS-60	(X)	Pittsburgh	Harrisburg		
1 MS-60	(X)	Pittsburgh	Baltimore	To 570 Harrisburg	
1 MS-60	(X)	Pittsburgh	Philadelphia	To 602 Harrisburg	
Perishable Express	(X)	Chicago	Philadelphia	From 54 Pittsburgh, To 602 Harrisburg	
2 Express	X-29, Sunday, LIFE	Chicago	Philadelphia	From 54 Pittsburgh, To 602 Harrisburg	
1 Express	B-60	Chicago	Philadelphia	From 54 Pittsburgh, To 602 Harrisburg	
1 Express	B-60, Monday and Days after Holidays	Chicago	Boston	From 54 Pittsburgh, To 164 New York	
1 Express	B-60, Monday and Days after Holidays	St. Louis	Boston	From 32 Pittsburgh, To 164 New York	
1 Express	B-60, Monday and Days after Holidays	Pittsburgh	Boston	To 164 New York	
1 MS-60	(X)	Dayton	New York	From 202 Pittsburgh	
1 MS-60	(X)	Pittsburgh	New York		
2 BM-70	30 foot apartment, DE Sunday	*Pittsburgh	New York		
4 P-70KR	Reclining Seats	%Pittsburgh	New York		
1 Diner-Lounge	Pittsburgh	New York			
1 PL	28-1	Pittsburgh	New York		
1 Milk	Tank, Monday and day after Holidays	Bedford	Philadelphia	From H&BT Huntingdon, To 612 Harrisburg	
1 Milk	Tank, Monday and Day after Holidays	Huntingdon	Philadelphia	From H&BT Huntingdon, To 612 Harrisburg	

* RPO NOT in service North Philadelphia-New York.

Harry Stegmaier

Train No. 72, the Pennsylvania Railroad's *Juniata*, was really the carrier eastbound between Pittsburgh and New York of the cars handled westbound on No. 25, *The Metropolitan*. As such, No. 72 could usually be found with a fair amount of headend traffic attached as is clear from the consist, including two Railway Post Office cars. In this slide, one sees a good example of a Pennsylvania Railroad baggage car used in headend service. No. 9372, however, is a star car, obvious from the star on the side, which means it is equipped for baggage service and has basic accommodations for an on board luggage messenger.

Harry Stegmaier

Looking rather ragged is Pennsylvania Railroad's RPO-Baggage car No. 6571, which was sitting on the scrap line in Altoona as late as June, 1980, when this photograph was taken. It was typical of the types of Railway Post Office cars which the Pennsylvania Railroad used on *The Juniata*. Although only a 30-ft. RPO apartment was required, nevertheless, the railroad sometimes operated cars with much more space than was actually needed when other cars were not available. It would not have been unusual to see a car like No. 6571 gracing the headend consist of No. 72.

Train No. 75

Car Type	Description	From	To	Details	Car Des
1 Express	R-50, DE Sunday	Philadelphia	Pittsburgh	From 611 Harrisburg	
1 BM-70	30 foot apartment, DE Sunday	Philadelphia	Pittsburgh	From 611 Harrisburg	
1 MS-60		Harrisburg	Pittsburgh		
1 MS-60	(X)	New York	Pittsburgh		
1 MS-60		New York	Pittsburgh		
1 MS-60	DE Monday	Stamford	Pittsburgh	From 179 New York	
2 Express	X-29, DE Sunday, Monday and Days after Holidays	New York	Pittsburgh		
1 PB-70	Scheme 6	New York	Pittsburgh		
1 P-70GSR	Reclining Seats, Friday ad Sunday	New York	Pittsburgh		
4 P-70KR	Reclining Seats	%New York	Pittsburgh		
1 Coach-Lounge-Buffet		New York	Pittsburgh	Lounge End next to coaches	
1 Diner-Lounge		New York	Pittsburgh		
1 PL-Lounge	16 Chair, 16 Seat Bar	New York	Pittsburgh		
1 PL	28-1	New York	Pittsburgh		
1 P-70	Saturday	New York	Harrisburg		

The Juniata was usually assigned P70KR coaches but it was not unusual to find, running as extra cars or as replacements for the P70KRs, coaches like No. 1710, seen here in Washington, D. C. in March, 1967. No. 1710 is a P70FBR coach, rebuilt by the shops in Altoona from an older P70 in mid-1948. While these cars were primarily intended for service on the corridor trains between New York, Philadelphia and Washington, they were nevertheless often found on mainline trains when reclining seat coaches were not available. The P70FBR coaches sometimes were rebuilt with wide modern windows and, at other times, like No. 1710, still carried the smaller windows of an older era. The P70FBRs were air conditioned, of course, but seated 72 in non-reclining walkover seats. They certainly would not have been as comfortable as the regular reclining seat coaches that should have been on mainline trains. Nevertheless, these cars could be found on trains like No. 72 when extra cars were needed or the P70KR cars were not available.

Huntingdon, carrying the dairy products for the Surplee Dairy Company to the City of Brotherly Love. *The Juniata* was a convenient daylight train, and while its headend swelled enormously in the 1960s, it continued on until Amtrak in May, 1971. In fact, Amtrak continued a daylight train in its own schedules between Pittsburgh and New York in both directions in its first two years of operation.

No. 74 and No. 75
THE DUQUESNE

Another popular New York-Pittsburgh train was Pennsylvania Railroad's No. 74 and No. 75, *The Duquesne*. Both of these trains were very convenient daylight trains for the Pittsburgh market, with westbound No. 75 departing at 11:45 a.m. for the daylight run to Pittsburgh, which it reached at 8:15 p.m. Eastbound No. 74 departed the Steel City at 2:00 p.m. and arrived at New York's Penn Station at 10:35 in the evening. Both provided very convenient daylight schedules for the traveling public. The westbound train handled a good deal of headend traffic while the eastbound train had only one regularly assigned B60 baggage car for mail and express. Otherwise, the trains were

almost identical except for the fact that the westbound train carried a combine car from New York to Pittsburgh. Each train carried four reclining seat coaches in each direction with added cars on Friday and Sunday, heavy travel days. These were not limited to the one noted in the consist book. Several P70 coaches were sometimes added. The coach passengers were also served by a coach-buffet-lounge car, often one of the prewar Altoona built *Jeffersonian* or *Trail Blazer* observation-lounge-buffet cars, with diaphrams added and the observation end run next to the coaches, that contained a bar and served light meals. Following these cars was a regular dining-lounge car in both directions. First class passengers were accommodated westbound in a parlor-buffet-lounge car with its own kitchen, as well as a 28 seat, 1 drawing room-parlor car. These same cars operated eastbound. *The Duquesne*, with its parlor-buffet-lounge car, became one of the last trains in the country to have a daylight heavyweight parlor-buffet-lounge car in the consist, which it carried into the 1960s, first between New York and Pittsburgh and later between New York and Harrisburg with *Lions Club* and *Elks Club* usually holding down the assignment. The eastbound

David E. Staplin

The westbound *Duquesne* carried much more headend traffic than the eastbound train which only had one B60 baggage express car. Included in the westbound train, No. 75, was a working Railway Post Office car. While only a 30-ft. apartment was required, nevertheless the Pennsylvania Railroad often assigned cars like No. 6507, an RPO-Baggage car. The car is seen here on the Altoona scrap line on April 18, 1970, after it had been retired from service. Cars like No. 6507 did yeoman work fulfilling the Pennsylvania Railroad's RPO obligations throughout its career. It could either serve as a full RPO or as a partial RPO, depending upon the circumstances and, as well, could carry baggage.

Harry Stegmaier

Since *The Duquesne* was, in both directions, a popular daylight train between Pittsburgh and New York, it was usually assigned reclining seat coaches of the P70KR or P70GSR class. Nevertheless, it was not unusual to find the post-World War II Altoona rebuilds of the P70FBR class in the consist of the train. These were replacements for the regular cars and, because of the train's popularity, were often used as extra cars. Cars like No. 1664 are an example of the P70FBR class. These coaches could seat 72 people but did not have reclining seats. No. 1664 has had its clerestory roof replaced with a round roof during the rebuild program.

J. Williams and Big Four Graphics Collection

The Pennsylvania Railroad often assigned dining cars to *The Duquesne* to serve as its diner-lounge car. It seems, from movies taken during the 1950s, it was popular for the railroad to assign prewar ACF built dining cars to trains like *The Duquesne* between New York and Pittsburgh. No. 4510, delivered to the Pennsylvania Railroad from American Car & Foundry in August, 1939, as a full dining car, by the 1950s had been converted into a dining-lounge car with a few of the tables removed and lounge seats placed in one end for runs like *The Duquesne*. They, nevertheless, provided the train's patrons westbound between New York and Pittsburgh with both luncheon and dinner and eastbound served dinner. They were sufficient, however, for the clientele of the train, most of whom were economy minded.

train also carried two Washington coaches, which were dropped at Harrisburg. It picked up at that point a coach off of *The Buffalo Day Express* from Buffalo, which it carried on to Penn Station in New York. *The Duquesne*, as mentioned previously because of its schedule, was a popular daylight train. Thus it lasted as a daylight run into the Penn Central era and on down to Amtrak in May, 1971. By then it was often coaches only, although on and off, especially on weekends, the train did receive an infamous Penn Central Foodbar coach. Nevertheless, *The Duquesne* served a market that still provided a lot of revenue passengers. Even though it became a train of massive size because of its headend in the 1960's, it continued to serve that market, both east and westbound, until the coming of Amtrak.

No. 202 and No. 203

Pennsylvania Railroad Trains No. 202 and No. 203 were unnamed. They were the railroad's entry into the overnight Pittsburgh to Cincinnati market. No. 203 connected at Pittsburgh with *The St. Louisan*, which brought several of the cars in from the east which the train received. These cars were then switched into No. 203, which departed Pittsburgh at 10:40, with an early morning 6:40 a.m. arrival in Cincinnati. No. 203, the westbound train, carried a good deal of headend traffic, as well as a working RPO car, plus a combine for coach passengers and a reclining seat heavyweight, rebuilt coach. In addition, the train offered overnight Pittsburgh-Cincinnati travelers the choice of roomettes in a prewar *City* series car or more standard accommodations in a Pittsburgh to New Orleans, 10 section, 2 double bedroom, 1

No. 72 carried, in its consist, a parlor car with 28 seats and 1 drawing room between Pittsburgh and New York just like No. 25 did westbound. Cars like *Huey*, seen here in this photograph, at Sunnyside Yard, Long Island in early 1949, were typical of the parlor cars one could have found operating on trains like *The Juniata* in the early 1950s. These heavyweights were throwbacks to another era, but nevertheless provided comfortable first class accommodations on day trains like No. 72.

Train No. 74						
Car Type	Description	From	To	Details		Car Des
1 B-60		Pittsburgh	New York			
1 P-70GSR	Reclining Seats, Friday and Sunday	%Pittsburgh	New York			
4 P-70KR	Reclining Seats	%Pittsburgh	New York			
1 Coach-Buffet-Lounge		Pittsburgh	New York	Lounge End next to coaches		
1 Diner-Lounge	Pittsburgh	New York				
1 PL-Lounge	16 Chair, 16 Seat Bar	Pittsburgh	New York			74
1 PL	28-1	Pittsburgh	New York			73
1 P-70KR	Reclining Seats	%Pittsburgh	Washington	To 570 Harrisburg		
1 P-70GSR	Reclining Seats, Sunday	%Pittsburgh	Washington	To 570 Harrisburg		
1 P-70KR	Reclining Seats	%Buffalo	New York	From 570 Harrisburg		
1 P-70	Scheme 6, Sunday	Williamsport	New York	From 570 Harrisburg		

Parlor cars like *Dora*, seen here at North Philadelphia in September, 1948, would have been the kind of Pennsylvania Railroad Pullman operated parlor cars that would have graced *The Duquesne* and provided first class seating space for its daytime patrons in the early 1950s.

In addition to the parlor car, each consist of *The Duquesne* carried a Parlor-Buffet-Lounge car. Regularly assigned to the train were cars *Elks Club* and *Lions Club*. These cars lasted on the train until the early 1960s. In this photograph, *Lions Club* is seen in 1960 at Montauk, New York, while on lease briefly to the Long Island Railroad. *Lions Club* contained a parlor section as well as a dining section and an extensive buffet kitchen which could prepare meals served by the Pullman Company to the first class passengers on *The Duquesne* if they did not desire to partake of the Pennsylvania Railroad dining-lounge car service.

Harry Stegmaier Collection

Pennsylvania Railroad trains No. 202 and 203 were the overnight trains between Cincinnati and Pittsburgh, and carried a couple of very interesting sleeping cars in 1952 until their discontinuance early in 1953. One car was a 10 section, 1 drawing room, 2 double bedroom car that was operated on the through route between Pittsburgh and New Orleans in conjunction with the Louisville & Nashville. Since the Pennsylvania Railroad did not own any cars of this type, the Louisville & Nashville supplied the 10 section, 2 double bedroom, 1 drawing room cars from its sizeable group of that unusual type. One such car, *Andrew Pickens*, is seen here, in its traditional Louisville & Nashville blue colors. While in special charter service in 1965. It probably looks little different from the days when it held down the Pittsburgh-New Orleans sleeping car line on the through route shared by the Pennsylvania Railroad and the Louisville & Nashville and could have been found on Pennsylvania Railroad trains No. 202 and No. 203.

William F. Howes, Jr.
Another very interesting sleeper was the local Pittsburgh-Cincinnati sleeper in both directions on No. 202 and No. 203. These trains carried the last prewar 18 roomette cars assigned to any of the Pennsylvania's mainline intermediate or through trains. This *City* series, prewar lightweight cars built by Pullman Standard and

delivered in December, 1938, were by now on secondary runs like Nos. 202 and 203. Later they were put into charter service. In this photograph, *City of Trenton*, a prewar 18 roomette sleeper, is typical of the whole class of 18 roomette cars owned by the Pennsylvania Railroad. The car is seen in the New Haven Railroad passenger station yards in New Haven, Connecticut in September, 1960. Many of the 18 roomette cars went to Mexico and became the *Doctor* series of cars on the National Railways of Mexico. A few were scrapped in 1962, including *The City of Trenton*.

drawing room Louisville and Nashville car. In addition, the train carried a standard 12 section, 1 drawing room heavyweight sleeper from Pittsburgh to Columbus and thus served the market to Ohio's capital city. Eastbound No. 202 was very much like its counterpart in that it departed Cincinnati late at night at 11:20 p.m. and arrived in Pittsburgh the next morning at 7:00 a.m. The only difference in the trains really was an addition to the eastbound train of a 12 section, 1 drawing room standard heavyweight sleeper from Cincinnati, that went through to New York on No. 32, *The St. Louisan*. This car was handled westbound on *The Cincinnati Limited*. It might be added here that the through Pittsburgh to New Orleans sleeping car was handled beyond Cincinnati on Louisville and Nashville trains No. 99 southbound and No. 98 northbound, *The Pan American*, second only to *The Hummingbird* in

class on Louisville and Nashville's Cincinnati-New Orleans main line. This Pittsburgh to New Orleans sleeping car, however, was discontinued on March 16, 1953 and another heavyweight sleeper was added to the overnight train between Pittsburgh and Cincinnati, although it too was short lived. Like other trains, No. 202 and No. 203 were found dispensable by the mid-1950s. They were discontinued. Their headend traffic was simply transferred to *The Cincinnati Limited* or other mail trains. Coach and Pullman traffic could be handled by Pennsylvania's *Cincinnati Limited* as well.

No. 204 and No. 205

Unnamed trains No. 204 and No. 205 were Pennsylvania Railroad's daylight Pittsburgh to Cincinnati trains. As such, No. 205 departed Pittsburgh westbound at 10:15 in the morning and

Train No. 202					
Car Type	Description	From	To	Details	Car Des
1 MS-60	X-29 (X)	Dayton	New York	From 108 Columbus, To 72 Pittsburgh	
1 MS-60	X-29 (X)	Dayton	Pittsburgh	From 108 Columbus	
1 MS-60	X-29	Columbus	Pittsburgh		
1 MS-60	DE Monday and Days after Holidays	Columbus	Philadelphia	To 96 Pittsburgh	
1 Express	B-60, DE Sunday and Holiday	Cincinnati	Boston	To 96 Pittsburgh	
1 MS-60	X-29	Cincinnati	Pittsburgh		
1 BM-70M	Letter End East	Cincinnati	Pittsburgh		
1 PB-70		Cincinnati	Pittsburgh		
1 P-70GSR	Reclining Seats	%Cincinnati	Pittsburgh		
1 SL	18 Roomette	Cincinnati	Pittsburgh	LW	206
1 SL	10 Section, 1 DR, 2 DBR	New Orleans	Pittsburgh	From L&N 98, Cincinnati	L62
1 SL	12-1	Cincinnati	New York	To 32 Pittsburgh	202
1 SL	12-1, DE Sunday and Nov. 28, Dec. 26, Jan. 2	Columbus	Pittsburgh		204
1 B-60	Mail and Express	Cincinnati	Columbus		
1 X-29	Mail and Express, DE Sun. and Holidays	Steubanville	Pittsburgh		

Train No. 203					
Car Type	Description	From	To	Details	Car Des
1 MS-60	X-29 or R-50, DE Sun. & Mon.	Columbus	Cincinnati		
1 MS-60	(X)	Pittsburgh	Columbus		
1 Express	B-60, DE Saturday	Pittsburgh	Columbus		
1 Express	R-50, DE Sundays, Mondays, and Days after Holidays	New York	Columbus	From 95 Pittsburgh	
1 Express	X-29, DE Sunday, Monday and Days after Holidays	New York	Cincinnati	From 95 Pittsburgh	
1 Express	B-60, Messenger GOLD STAR	Pittsburgh	Cincinnati		
1 MS-60	(X)	New York	Cincinnati	From 25 Pittsburgh	
1 MS-60	(X)	Pittsburgh	Cincinnati		
1 MS-60	Semi-Open, DE Sunday and Monday	Pittsburgh	Cincinnati		
1 BM-70M		Pittsburgh	Cincinnati		
1 PB-70		Pittsburgh	Cincinnati		
1 P-70GSR	Reclining Seats	%Pittsburgh	Cincinnati		
1 SL	18 Roomette	Pittsburgh	Cincinnati	LW	203
1 SL	10 Section, 1 DR, 2 DBR	Pittsburgh	New Orleans	To L&N 99, Cincinnati	205
1 SL	12-1, DE Saturday and Nov. 27, Dec. 25 and Jan. 1	Pittsburgh	Columbus		201
1 X-29	Baggage-Mail-Express, DE Sundays and Holidays	Pittsburgh	Steubenville	8 foot Express	

arrived in Cincinnati at 5:40 p.m. while No. 204 departed at 1:00 p.m. and arrived in Pittsburgh at 8:30 in the evening. Both No. 205 and No. 204 connected with *The Iron City Express* at Pittsburgh. The trains were very similar in their makeup in both directions with a good deal of headend traffic including a working Baggage-RPO car with a 70-ft. apartment, two reclining seat coaches, a heavyweight 10 section, 1 drawing room, 2 compartment sleeping car which operated from New York to Birmingham, Alabama via Louisville and Nashville Trains No. 1 southbound and No. 4 northbound, *The Azalean*. This was a train mostly of headend equipment, even in 1952 but with coaches and dining car service and the through sleeping car. This through sleeping car line would not last for a very long period and, in fact, would be discontinued on February 2, 1953 about a month and a half before the Pittsburgh-New Orleans car was also discontinued. Heavyweight sleeping car routes such as these did

not attract many patrons especially when they had to travel on slow trains like Nos. 204 and 205 or Louisville and Nashville's *Azalean*. In addition to the heavyweight sleeper, No. 204 handled the through Memphis to New York sleeping car which was operated westbound on *The Cincinnati Limited* in conjunction with the Louisville and Nashville. The only other difference in the train was that No. 205 carried deadhead a 10 roomette, 6 double bedroom sleeper between Columbus and Cincinnati. Like No. 202 and No. 203, trains No. 204 and 205 were found expendable in the cutbacks of the 1950s and their cars were moved to other trains so that the daylight runs between Pittsburgh and Cincinnati could be discontinued. The heavy amount of headend traffic could be easily be accommodated on a mail and express train. Revenue passengers on trains like these were declining rapidly. Daylight trains like these only had a few more years to live on most railroads.

Train No. 204

Car Type	Description	From	To	Details	Car Des
1 MS-60	X-29 (X)	*Cincinnati	New York	To 22 Pittsburgh	
1 MS-60	X-29, DE Sunday and Monday	*Cincinnati	Nw York	To 22 Pittsburgh	
1 MS-60	X-29 (X)	Cincinnati	Philadelphia	To 36 Pittsburgh	
1 B-60	Baggage-Express, Sunday	Cincinnati	Pittsburgh	Messenger, GOLD STAR	
1 Express	B-60, DE Sunday	Cincinnati	Pittsburgh	Messenger, GOLD STAR	
1 BM-70M	DE Sunday	Cincinnati	Pittsburgh	Letter End West	
1 MS-60	Semi-Open	Cincinnati	Pittsburgh		
2 P-70GSR	Reclining Seats	%Cincinnati	Pittsburgh		
1 SL	10 Section, 1 DR, 2 Compartment	Birmingham	New York	From L&N 4, Cincinnati, To 16 Pittsburgh L-3	
1 SL	10 Roomette, 6 DBR	Memphis	New York	LW From L&N 4, Cincinnati, To 16, Pittsburgh	
1 MS-60	X-29, Sunday	Columbus	Cincinnati		
1 Diner-Lounge	Columbus		Pittsburgh		

*May move in No. 14 from Pittsburgh

Train No. 205

Car Type	Description	From	To	Details	Car Des
1 MS-60	(X)	Pittsburgh	Columbus		
1 Express	B-60, Messenger, DE Sun., Mon., and Days after Holidays	New York	Dayton	From 93 Pittsburgh, To 33 Columbus	
1 M-70	Sunday	Pittsburgh	Cincinnati	From 11 Columbus	
1 Express	R-50, DE Sunday, Monday and Days after Holidays	New York	Birmingham	To L&N 1, Cincinnati	
1 Express	R-50, DE Sunday, Monday and Days after Holidays	New York	Cincinnati	From 93 Pittsburgh	
1 Express	B-60, Messenger, GOLD STAR, Daily except Sunday	Pittsburgh	Cincinnati		
1 MS-60	(X)	Pittsburgh	Cincinnati		
1 BM-70M	DE Sunday and Monday	Pittsburgh	Cincinnati	Letter End West	
1 B-60		Pittsburgh	Cincinnati		
2 P-70GSR	Reclining Seats	%Pittsburgh	Cincinnati		
1 SL	10 Section, 1 DR, 2 Compartment	New York	Birmingham	From 37 Pittsburgh, To L&N 1, Cincinnati K374	
1 Diner-Lounge		New York	Columbus	From 37 Pittsburgh	
1 SL	10 Roomette, 6 DBR	*Columbus	Cincinnati		

* Car off No. 3 for No. 201 Cincinnati. Car off No. 200 fills Columbus Line 403 train No. 40.

As well as the through passenger trains which the Pennsylvania Railroad operated on its main lines between New York, Pittsburgh, Chicago and St. Louis, the company also originated a large number of mail and express trains. Only a few of them carried revenue passengers. The railroad was the prime carrier of both express and US mail in both directions between the east coast and the midwest, with much more traffic than either the New York Central or the Baltimore & Ohio Railroads. The latter, of course, ran a large mail and express business between the nation's capital and St. Louis, with lesser amounts to Chicago, but it could not compete with the Pennsylvania in direct mail and express traffic. These mail and express trains were shown in the consist books.

This chapter deviates somewhat from the format of previous chapters by simply discussing the mail and express trains as a group.

Pennsylvania Railroad Trains No. 11 and 12 were Pittsburgh to St. Louis mail trains, with No. 11 receiving much of its traffic at Pittsburgh from Pennsylvania Railroad Train No. 93, an overnight run from New York to that city, delivering its cars in Pittsburgh to trains that departed in the morning. This included mail train No. 11, with cars destined not just for St. Louis but for faraway points such as Memphis, New Orleans, Oklahoma City and other southwestern terminals. As can be seen from the consist, No. 11 carried massive amounts of headend in X-29, R-50, and B-60 headend cars, with a single PB-70 combine on the rear as a rider

				M	T	W	Th	F	SA	SU	Connection
R-50 or X-29	Express	*New York	St. Louis	l	--	--	--	--	--	2	
B-60	Express Messenger	New York	St. Louis	l	--	--	--	--	--	l	GOLD STAR
R-50	Express	x*New York	Memphis	--	--	l	l	l	l	--	93 Pittsburgh
B-60	Express	x*New York	New Orleans	--	l	l	l	l	l	--	93 Pittsburgh
B-60	Express GOLD STAR	*New York	St. Louis	--	l	l	l	l	l	--	93 Pittsburgh
MS-60		*Philadelphia	St. Louis	--	l	l	l	l	l	l	
MS-60		v*Philadelphia	Kansas City	--	l	l	l	l	l	l	
MS-60	(X)	v*Philadelphia	Los Angeles								
X-29	Papers	Wilkes Barre	St. Louis	--	--	--	--	--	2	--	
MS-60		vNew York	Kansas City	l	l	l	l	l	l	l	
MS-60		vNew York	Texarkana	--	l	l	l	l	l	l	
MS-60		vNew York	Los Angeles	--	l	l	l	l	l	l	
MS-60	Mexican	New York	St. Louis	--	l	l	l	l	l	l	
MS-60	Open	New York	St. Louis	--	l	l	l	l	l	l	
M-70	L.E. East	Pittsburgh	Cincinnati	---	---	---	---	---	--	l	205 Columbus
M-70	L.E. East	Pittsburgh	St. Louis	l	l	l	l	l	l	--	
MS-60	(X)	*Pittsburgh	St. Louis	--	l	l	l	l	l	--	
PB-70	Papers	New York	St. Louis	--	--	--	--	--	--	l	
P-70	Scheme 6	Pittsburgh	St. Louis	l	l	l	l	l	l	l	
MS-60	(X)	*Pittsburgh	St. Louis	--	l	l	l	l	l	--	
X-29	Express	*New York	St. Louis	--	2	2	2	2	2	--	93 Pittsburgh
R-50	Express	@ *New York	Oklahoma City	--	--	l	l	l	l	--	93 Pittsburgh
R-50	Express	v*New York	Dallas	--	l	l	l	l	l	--	93 Pittsburgh
R-50	Express	v*New York	Houston	--	l	l	l	l	l	--	93 Pittsburgh
R-50	Express	v*New York	San Antonio	--	l	l	l	l	l	--	93 Pittsburgh
PB-70	NAG Express	*New York	St. Louis	--	l	l	l	l	l	--	93 Pittsburgh
X-29	Express	*New York	Indianapolis	--	l	l	l	l	l	--	93 Pittsburgh
MS-60	(X)	Pittsburgh	Indianapolis	--	l	l	l	l	l	--	

Train No. 11

* Do NOT operate days after Holidays
x To IC St. Louis
v To MP St. Louis
@ To Wabash 17 St. Louis
z Also Days after Holidays

Pennsylvania Railroad Mail and Express trains often substituted some of their special horse express cars, as well as their baggage and mail cars that were equipped for carrying theatrical scenery, for regular headend cars. In this slide, No. 6096, *Edwin Forrest*, is a baggage car which was equipped to handle theatrical scenery. Cars like these were often found on the mail and express trains of the company, substituting for regular cars, and in fact, by the 1950s, were often used to handle mail and express on a regular basis.

A good example of a horse express car is seen here in No. 5826, once named *Empire City Racing Association*. These triple-door horse express cars, of course, had end doors for handling horses, but, by the 1950s were simply being used to handle headend traffic on the Pennsylvania Railroad's mail and express trains.

Train No. 12

Daily——St. Louis-Columbus

Daily except Sunday——Columbus-Pittsburgh

Car Type	Description	From	To	Details	Car Des
Deadhead Baggage		*St. Louis	Pittsburgh		
I MS-60	(X)	St. Louis	Pittsburgh		
I Express	B-60, Messenger,	*St. Louis	Pittsburgh		
I MS-60	Open	*St. Louis	Pittsburgh	GOLD STAR	
I Express	B-60, DE Sunday, Monday and Days after Holidays	Indianapolis	New York	To 16 Pittsburgh	
I MS-60		*Louisville	Pittsburgh	From 305 Indianapolis	
I MS-60	Open	Indianapolis	Columbus		
I Express	R-50 or X-29 DE Sunday	St. Louis	Columbus		
I B-60	Baggage-Mail-Express	St. Louis	Columbus		
I Express	B-60, Messenger, DE Sat., Sun., Tue.	Columbus	Pittsburgh		
I B-60	Baggage-Express	Columbus	Pittsburgh	Contains 30 foot express Saturday, Sunday, Tuesday	
I MS-60	Open	*St. Louis	Pittsburgh		
I P-70	Scheme 6	*St. Louis	Pittsburgh		
I X-29	Mail-Express	Indianapolis	Richmond		
I MS-60	(X)	Dayton	Pittsburgh		

* To 212 Columbus Sunday.

for the crew and any deadheading employees who wished to use the mail train. This car came all the way through from New York on mail train No. 93 as a rider. The train departed Pittsburgh in the morning and arrived in St. Louis late at night or early the following morning. Its eastbound counterpart, No. 12, again was a non-revenue passenger mail and express train and was lighter on headend traffic than its westbound counterpart. This is easily explainable since eastbound headend traffic never matched the westbound mail and express traffic which Pennsylvania Railroad had. This was the case as well with railroads like the New York Central and B&O. Mail train No. 12 departed St. Louis very late at night or early in the morning with an arrival in Pittsburgh the next evening and carried a good number of headend cars plus one P-70 coach as a rider for the mail and express train crew.

No. 13 and 14 proved the exception to most

Harry Stegmaier

Typical of the B60 baggage and express cars that one could find on the headend of the mail and express trains is a class B60B car, No. 9055, which is seen here in May, 1971 on the scrap line at Altoona. These were probably the most common of all of the Pennsylvania Railroad's headend cars for mail, express and baggage and could be found in large numbers on Pennsylvania's mail and express trains.

Train No. 13
Daily Except Sunday

Car Type	Description	From	To	Details	Car Des
1 Milk	Tank	Philadelphia	Bedford	From 35 Harrisburg	
				From H&BT Huntingdon	
1 Milk	Tank	Philadelphia	Huntingdon	From 35 Harrisburg	
				To H&BT Huntingdon	
1 MS-60	DE Sunday and Monday	New York	Harrisburg		
1 MS-60	(X)	New Haven	Pittsburgh	From 183 New York	
1 MS-60	(X)	Meriden	Pittsburgh	From 183 New York	
1 MS-60	X-29, DE Sunday and Monday	Newark, N.J.	Pittsburgh		
1 MS-60		New York	Pittsburgh		
1 BM-70	30 foot apartment	New York	Pittsburgh	Letter End East	
1 MS-60	Open	Harrisburg	Pittsburgh		
1 MS-60	Open Monday	Harrisburg	Pittsburgh		
1 MS-60	Open, DE Sunday, Monday and Days after Holidays	Philadelphia	Pittsburgh	From 613 Harrisburg	
1 Express	B-60, Messenger, DE Sunday, Monday, and Days after Holidays	Philadelphia	Pittsburgh	From 613 Harrisburg	
1 Express	B-60, Messenger, DE Sunday, Monday, and Days after Holidays	Philadelphia	Pittsburgh	GOLD STAR, From 613 Harrisburg	
1 Express	B-60, DE Monday, and Days after Holidays, Messenger	Harrisburg	Pittsburgh		
1 B-60		New York	Pittsburgh		
3 P-70GSR	Reclining Seats	%New York	Pittsburgh		
1 MS-60		Harrisburg	Johnstown		
1 B-60	Papers, Thursday	Philadelphia	Altoona	From 613 Harrisburg	
1 MS-60	X-29, DE Sunday and Monday	Philadelphia (Sears)	Dayton	From 613 Harrisburg	

David E. Staplin

The Pennsylvania Railroad had converted a large number of box cars into mail and express train service, such as No. 9682, seen here on the Altoona scrap line on April 18, 1970. These box cars handled mail and express on a regular basis for the Pennsylvania Railroad in the 1950s and 1960s and were equipped with special high speed trucks for passenger train service. No. 9682 is a good example of this type of box car used in mail and express service by the Pennsylvania Railroad.

Train No 14
Daily Except Sunday

Car Type	Description	From	To	Details	Car Des
1 Express	X-29, DE Sunday and Monday	Pittsburgh	Harrisburg		
1 MS-60	(X)	Pittsburgh	Harrisburg		
1 MS-60	DE Sunday, Monday and Holidays	Pittsburgh	Harrisburg		
1 MS-60		Pittsburgh	Baltimore	To 554 Harrisburg	
1 MS-60	DE Sunday, Monday,Tuesday & Days after Holidays	Pittsburgh	Philadelphia	To 602 Harrisburg	
Express	(X)	Various	Hudson Cut-Off	From 70 and 2 Harrisburg	
1 MS-60		Harrisburg	New York		
2 MS-60		Pittsburgh	New York		
1 MS-60	Open	Pittsburgh	New York		
1 M-70	Letter End West	Pittsburgh	New York		
1 B-60	Baggage-Mail Open	Pittsburgh	New York		
1 Express	B-60, Monday Messenger	Pittsburgh	New York		
1 Express	B-60, Messenger GOLD STAR	Pittsburgh	New York		
1 Express	B-60, DE Sunday, Mon, and Holidays	Pittsburgh	Altoona	Messenger	
1 P-70		Pittsburgh	New York		
1 P-70		Harrisburg	New York		
1 B-60	Mail and Express Solid	Pittsburgh	Johnstown		
1 Express	B-60, Messenger, DE Sun. & Holidays	Altoona	Harrisburg	From 37 Altoona	

Pennsylvania Railroad mail and express trains. No. 13 and No. 14 were New York to Pittsburgh trains and Pittsburgh to New York trains, respectively, and both carried revenue passengers. No. 13 departed New York at 3:45 a.m. with an arrival in Pittsburgh at 5:15 p.m. the next afternoon, except on Sundays when it made the run quicker and arrived at 2:35 p.m. Both No. 13 and its Sunday counterpart, No. 85, made lots of local stops between Philadelphia and Pittsburgh and thus was the recipient of a number of local revenue passengers as well as plenty of deadheading crewmen. Between Harrisburg and Huntington, this train carried the two milk cars for Huntington, one of which went to Bedford over the Huntington & Broad Top Mountain Railroad. In addition, carried a large amount of headend traffic and a working RPO car with a 30-ft. RPO apartment. It also carried three reclining seat coaches to handle local traffic and deadheading crewmen. Eastbound No.

Harry Stegmaier Collection

Mail and express trains carried P70 coaches as riders for the crew as well as for passengers on those trains which handled revenue customers. Typical of the kind of car one might have found on these mail and express trains is P70 coach No. 940, seen here in Chicago to Valpariso commuter service in June, 1963. These cars did not have reclining seats and had not been rebuilt in any of the railroad's upgrading programs. They provided very basic coach accommodations for revenue paying passengers on those mail and express trains which carried them. On non-revenue passenger carrying trains, they acted as riders for the train crew and deadheading railroaders.

Train No. 18

Car Type	Description	From	To	Details	Car Des
Express	(X)	Various	Hudson Cut-Off		
B-60	Deadhead (X)	Johnstown	New York		
I Express	R-50	Chicago	New York	From 44 (144 Sunday) Pittsburgh	
I Express	B-60, GOLD STAR	Chicago	New York	From 44 (144 Sunday) Pittsburgh	
I Express	B-60, DE Sunday, Monday and Holidays	Pittsburgh	New York		
I Express	B-60	St. Louis	New York	From 6 Pittsburgh	
I Express	B-60, DE Sunday and Monday	St. Louis	Harrisburg	From 6 Pittsburgh	
I Express	B-60	St. Louis	Philadelphia	From 6 Pittsburgh	
				To 604 (86 Sun. and Holidays) Harrisburg	
I MS-60	(X)	Cleveland	Philadelphia	From 318 Pittsburgh	
				To 604 (86 Sun. and Holidays) Harrisburg	
I MS-60	(X)	Detroit	Philadelphia	From 44 (462 Holidays) Pittsburgh	
				To 604 (86 Sun. and Holidays) Harrisburg	
I Express	X-29, DE Sunday, Monday and Days after Holidays	Harrisburg	New York		
I MS-60	DE Monday	Harrisburg	New York		
I MS-60	Open	Pittsburgh	Harrisburg		
I MS-60	Open Saturday and Sunday	Pittsburgh	Harrisburg		
I BM-70M	Letter End East	Pittsburgh	New York		
I M-70	DE Saturday and Sunday	Pittsburgh	New York	Letter End East	
I MS-60		Pittsburgh	New York		
I PB-70		Pittsburgh	New York		
I P-70GSR	Reclining Seats	%Pittsburgh	New York		
I MS-60	X-29	Harrisburg	Lancaster		

14, which operated every day except Sunday, was very much like No. 13 in that it carried a large amount of headend traffic from Pittsburgh to New York with some cars destined for other intermediate points. It departed Pittsburgh at 3:45 a.m. and made a number of local stops, especially east of Johnstown, thus providing a local service for revenue passengers. Its final arrival at 3:25 p.m. at Penn Station, New York, meant that it took almost twelve hours to cover the route between its originating point at Pittsburgh and New York City. Few through passengers would have ridden a slow train like this but there were, of course, the local passengers and the deadheading crewmen that populated its one straight P-70 coach, with an additional P-70 coach added to handle additional

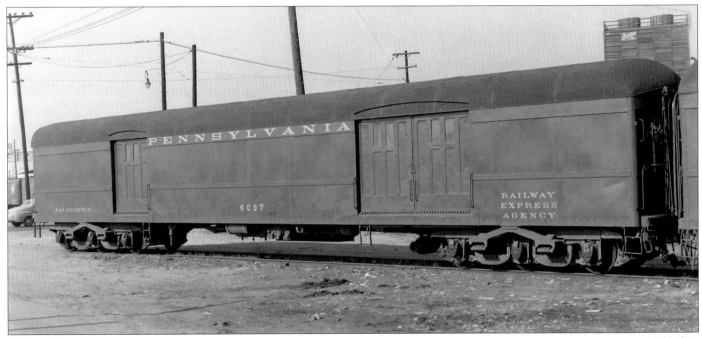

Bob's Photo

In this photograph is another of the Pennsylvania Railroad's baggage cars that were equipped for handling theatrical scenery. No. 6097 is named *Nat Goodwin*. These cars often served on the mail and express trains as regular cars for express, mail and baggage in the 1950s and 1960s. *Nat Goodwin* was photographed in November, 1954 in San Diego, California.

traffic between Harrisburg and New York. This train did not carry a working RPO car, just mail and express cars on the headend. Photographs from the period show both No. 13 and No. 14 as very long trains, sometimes almost 30 cars long, especially westbound No. 13. These trains were dropped from the timetable as passenger trains later in the 1950s but continued on as mail and express trains well into the 1960s. Pennsylvania Railroad Train No. 18 between Pittsburgh and New York also carried revenue passengers although few through passengers would have ridden this train which took over twelve hours to reach its destination. No. 18 departed Pittsburgh at 4:50 p.m. in the afternoon and did not arrive at New York's Penn Station until 4:55 a.m. the next morning, again making plenty of local stops along the way including such places as Torrance, Cresson, and Tyrone. No. 18 was primarily, of course, a mail and express train with plenty of headend equipment, much of it received from Chicago to Pittsburgh mail and express train No. 44, which also carried passengers, and from No. 6, *The Allegheny*, at Pittsburgh. Local passengers, as well as deadheading crewmen, were accommodated in its PB-70 combine as well as its one reclining seat coach, which also served the crew of No.

18. Like Nos. 13 and 14, this train would be dropped from the public timetables as a passenger carrying train in the mid 1950s but continued operating as a mail and express train, although under another number well into the 1960s.

The Pennsylvania Railroad operated two strictly New York to Pittsburgh mail and express trains. No 93 operated every day but Sunday and Monday, and was primarily an overnight mail and express train from Manhattan to the Steel City, with a large number of through cars which were handed over at Pittsburgh to trains like No. 205 for Cincinnati, *The Fort Pitt* for Chicago and No. 11 to St. Louis, with some cars terminating in Pittsburgh itself. Crew and deadhead riders were accommodated in a combine car that was carried on the rear of the train, with only one headend car behind it. This combine, plus much of the headend on the rear of the train, was blocked in such a fashion that it could be easily detached and make up the rear of No. 11, already mentioned, the St. Louis mail train, which departed Pittsburgh in the morning. Mail and express Train No. 95 also operated every day but Sunday and Monday and was primarily an early morning train from New York City with an afternoon arrival in Pittsburgh where much of its massive headend traffic was handled

Bob's Photo

The Pennsylvania Railroad operated a significant batch of refrigerated express cars, such as the one seen in this photograph. These R50B class milk Express refrigerator cars could be found in large numbers on Pennsylvania Railroad's mail and express trains in the 1950s and 1960s.

Train No. 93

Daily Except Sunday and Monday

Will NOT Operate November 28, December 24, 25, 26, 27, Janaury 2, Febraury 24

Car Type	Description	From	To	Details	Car Des
1 X-29	Papers Tuesday	*Wilkes-Barre	Youngstown	To 329 Pittsburgh	
1 X-29	Papers Wednesday	*Wilkes-Barre	Akron	To 323 Pittsburgh	
1 X-29	Papers Thursday	*Wilkes-Barre	Toledo	To 99 Pittsburgh	
1 X-29	Papers Thursday or Friday	*Wilkes-Barre	Dayton	To 27 Pittsburgh	
1 X-29	Papers Thursday	*Sunbury	Pittsburgh		
1 Express	X-29	Harrisburg	Pittsburgh		
1 MS-60		Baltimore	Pittsburgh	From 535 Harrisburg	
1 Express	B-60	Baltimore	Pittsburgh	From 535 Harrisburg	
1 Milk	R-50 (X)	Sunnyside	Salamnca	To 527 Harrisburg	
1 Express	R-50 or X-29, DE Sunday, Monday, Tuesday	New York	York	To 530 Harrisburg	
1 Express	B-60	New York	Pittsburgh Div.	To 13 Harrisburg	
1 Express	B-60 Tuesday	New York	Harrisburg		
1 Express	X-29, DE Sunday, Monday, Tuesday	New York	Harrisburg		
1 Express	B-60	New York	Dayton	To 205 Pittsburgh	
1 Express	R-50	New York	Birmingham	To 205 Pittsburgh	
1 Express	R-50	New York	Cincinnati	To 205 Pittsburgh	
1 Express	X-29, DE Sunday, Monday, Tuesday	New York	Chicago	To 53 Pittsburgh	
1 Express	B-60	New York	Chicago	To 53 Pittsburgh	
1 Express	B-60	New York	Akron	To 323 Pittsburgh	
1 Express	B-60, Messenger, GOLD STAR	New York	Pittsburgh		
1 Express	X-29, DE Sunday, Monday, Tuesday	New York	Pittsburgh		
1 Express	R-50, DE Sunday, Monday, Tuesday	New York	Memphis	To 11 Pittsburgh	
1 Express	B-60	@New York	New Orleans	To 11 Pittsburgh	
1 Express	B-60, Messenger GOLD STAR	New York	St. Louis	To 11 Pittsburgh	
2 Express	X-29	New York	St. Louis	To 11 Pittsburgh	
1 Express	R-50, DE Sunday, Monday, Tuesday	New York	Oklahoma City	To 11 Pittsburgh	
1 Express	R-50	New York	Dallas	To 11 Pittsburgh	
1 Express	B-60	New York	Houston	To 11 Pittsburgh	
1 Express	B-60	New York	San Antonio	To 11 Pittsburgh	
1 PB-70	Rider	New York	St. Louis	To 11 Pittsburgh	
1 Express	X-29	New York	Indianapolis	To 11 Pittsburgh	

* From 578 Harrisburg
@ Must be B-60

over to No. 99, a Pittsburgh-Chicago mail train, to No. 27, *The Metropolitan*, and to Pennsylvania Railroad's Cincinnati night train, No. 203. It carried a huge amount of headend, as is obvious from the consists, but no RPO car, and was laden, to a large extent, with much headend traffic that originated in the New England states at such places as Providence, Boston, Bridgeport and other locales. Crew accommodations were a Pennsylvania cabin car on the rear for the crew between New York and Pittsburgh. Passengers were not carried on this train. The eastbound counterpart of No. 95 was Pittsburgh to New York mail and express train No. 96, which was very much like its westbound counterpart. It carried a large amount of headend traffic, much of it destined for New England points, and with the crew carried in a cabin car on the rear.

This train did not have a working RPO car either but did carry two deadhead RPO cars from Pittsburgh to Philadelphia, and New York, respectively. It received headend traffic at Pittsburgh from No. 54, *The Gotham Limited*, the overnight train from Cincinnati, and from *The St. Louisan*.

The last of the mail and express trains which appears in the consist book, is Pittsburgh to Chicago overnight mail and express train No. 99. This train's eastbound counterpart was really No. 44, or on Sundays No. 144, which did carry passengers from Chicago to Pittsburgh. No. 99 left Pittsburgh in the evening and arrived at Chicago the next morning, picking up much of its headend traffic from the east from No. 95 as well as a few other trains. In addition to the Chicago-bound traffic, it also carried Toledo and Detroit headend

Train No. 95

Daily Except Sunday and Monday

Will NOT Operate November 28, December 25, 26, January 2, February 24

Car Type	Description	From	To	Details	Car Des
Milk	R-50 (X) Cans	South Edmenston	Berns or Kendalsville	To 99 or 71 Pittsburgh	
1 Express	X-29	New York	Harrisburg		
1 Express	B-60	New York	Chicago	To 99 Pittsburgh	
1 Express	R-50	New York	Columbus	To 203 Pittsburgh	
1 Express	X-29	New York	Cincinnati	To 203 Pittsburgh	
1 Express	X-29	New York	Indianapolis	To 27 Pittsburgh	
1 Express	B-60	Boston	Indianapolis	To 27 Pittsburgh	
1 Express	R-50	Hartford	St. Louis	To 27 Pittsburgh	
1 Express	B-60 Messenger	Providence	St. Louis	To 27 Pittsburgh	
1 Express	B-60	South Norwalk	St. Louis	To 27 Pittsburgh	
1 Express	B-60	Reading	St. Louis	From Reading Harrisburg, To 27 Pittsburgh	
1 Express	R-50	Delmar	St. Louis	From 601 Harrisburg, To 27 Pittsburgh	
1 Express	B-60	Philadelphia	St. Louis	From 601 Harrisburg, To 27 Pittsburgh	
1 Express	R-50	Philadelphia	Indianapolis	From 601 Harrisburg, To 27 Pittsburgh	
1 Express	B-60	Philadelphia	St. Paul	From 601 Harrisburg, To 99 Pittsburgh	
1 Express	R-50	Philadelphia	Chicago	From 601 Harrisburg, To 99 Pittsburgh	
1 Express	B-60	Harrisburg	Chicago	To 99 Pittsburgh	
1 Express	R-50, Tuesday, Wednesday, Thursday, Saturday	South Norwalk	Chicago	To 99 Pittsburgh	
1 Express	B-60, Messenger	Providence	Chicago	To 99 Pittsburgh	
1 MS-60		Providence	Chicago	To 99 Pittsburgh	
1 Express	B-60	Boston	Chicago	To 99 Pittsburgh	
1 Express	B-60	Hartford	Chicago	To 99 Pittsburgh	
1 Express	B-60	Bridgeport	Chicago	To 99 Pittsburgh	
1 Express	X-29	Bridgeport	Pittsburgh		
1 Express	X-29	Hartford	Pittsburgh		
1 MS-60		New Haven	Pittsburgh		
2 MS-60		Providence	Pittsburgh		
1 Express	B-60	Boston	Pittsburgh		
1 Express	R-50	Boston	Pittsburgh		
1 Express	R-50 or X-29	Boston	Harrisburg		
1 Express	B-60	Philadalphia	Pittsburgh	From 601 Harrisburg	
1 Cabin					

Another example of the baggage cars that were equipped to handle theatrical scenery is No. 6061, *Romeo*, which is seen in this photograph. Again, it is being used as regular headend car. One can see from this photograph that they had special doors on the end for the unloading for theatrical scenery when they were used for that purpose.

Train No. 96

DE Monday and Days After Holidays

Car Type	Description	From	To	Details	Car Des
I MS-60	DE Monday and Tuesday	Pittsburgh	Reading	To Reading Harrisburg	
I MS-60		Pittsburgh	Harrisburg	Buffalo-Washington North Mails	
I MS-60	(X)	Pittsburgh	Philadelphia	To 612 (646 Sunday) Harrisburg	
I MS-60	X-29	Columbus	Philadelphia	From 202 Pittsburgh, To 612 (646 Sunday) Harrisburg	
I Express	X-29 (X)	Pittsburgh	Philadelphia	To 612 (646 Sunday) Harrisburg	
I Express	X-29 Sunday	Pittsburgh	Harrisburg		
I BM-70	Deadhead	Pittsburgh	Philadelphia	To 612 (646 Sunday) Harrisburg	
I BM-70	Deadhead	Pittsburgh	New York		
Baggage	New Haven or Boston and Maine Deadhead (X)	Pittsburgh	Stamford and New Haven		
X-29 or R-50	Deadhead	Pittsburgh	New Haven		
I Express	B-60, DE Sun., Mon., Tues. & Days after Holidays	Chicago	Hartford	From 54 Pittsburgh	
I Express	X-29 Wednesday LIFE	Chicago	New London	From 54 Pittsburgh	
I Express	B-60	Chicago	Boston	From 54 Pittsburgh	
I Express	B-60, Tuesday	Berwick	Boston	From 526 Harrisburg	
2 B-60	P.R.R. Deadhead	Pittsburgh	Boston		
I Express	B-60 Messenger	St. Louis	Boston	From 32 Pittsburgh	
I Express	B-60	Cincinnati	Boston	From 202 Pittsburgh	
I Express	B-60 Messenger	Pittsburch	Boston		
I Express	B-60, DE Sun., Mon., Tues. & Days after Holidays	Pittsburgh	Springfield		
I Rider	Cabin P.R.R	Pittsburgh	New Haven		
I or 2 Express	Perishable (X)	Various	Hudson Cut-Off		
I Milk	R-50 (X)	xKendallville	South Edmeston	From 54 Pittsburgh	
I Milk	R-50 (X)	xBerne	South Edmeston	From 54 Pittsburgh	
I Milk	Tank DE Sat., Mon., and Days after Holidays	Bedford	Philadelphia	From HB&T Huntingdon To 612 (646 Sunday) Harrisburg	
I Milk	Tank DE Sat., Mon., and Days after Holidays	Bedford	Philadelphia	From HB&T Huntingdon To 612 (646 Sunday) Harrisburg	

x Cut off Hudson for DL&W I5

Often the crew of a mail and express train was accommodated in one of the Pennsylvania Railroad's non-rebuilt, regular combination coaches such as No. 5159, seen here in Pittsburgh. No. 5159 did not have reclining seats but did provide crew accommodations on mail and express trains plus coach space on those trains which would handle revenue passengers. They were a very common sight on Pennsylvania Railroad mail and express trains in the 1950s.

Train No. 99

Car Type	Description	From	To	Details	Car Des
1 MS-60	X-29 (X)	Canton	Chicago	Danner Press	
1 B-60	Mail and Express DE Sunday and Holidays	Canton	Chicago		
1 X-29	Papers Thursday	xWiles-Barre	Toledo	To 105 Mansfield	
1 Express	B-60 Messenger, DE Saturday	xPittsburgh	Toledo	To 105 Mansfield	
1 MS-60	DE Saturday	xPittsburgh	Detroit	To 105 Mansfield	
1 B-60	Baggage-Mail DE Saturday	xPittsburgh	Detroit	To 105 Mansfield	
1 SL	6 Section, 6 DBR	Pittsburgh	Chicago	To 63 (23 Sunday and November 28, 29, December 26, 27, January 1, 2, 3)	451
1 P-70GSR	Reclining Seats	%Pittsburgh	Chicago		
1 MS-60	Open	Pittsburgh	Chicago		
1 BM-70M	DE Sunday	Pittsburgh	Chicago	Letter End West	
1 BM-70M		Pittsburgh	Chicago		
1 Express	B-60 Messenger, GOLD STAR	Pittsburgh	Chicago		
1 Express	B-60, DE Monday and days after Holidays	New York	Chicago	From 95 (85 Sunday) Pittsburgh	
1 Express	B-60	*Philadelphia	St. Paul	From 95 Pittsburgh, To Milwaukee 57 Chicago	
2 Express	R-50	*Philadlephia	Chicago	From 95 Pittsburgh	
1 Express	B-60	*Harrisburg	Chiacgo	From 95 Pittsburgh	
1 Express	R-50, Tuesday, Wednesday, Thursday, Saturday	South Norwalk	Chicago	From 95 Pittsburgh	
1 Express	B-60 Messenger	*Providence	Chicago	From 95 Pittsburgh	
1 MS-60		*Providence	Chicago	From 95 Pittsburgh	
1 Express	B-60	*Boston	Chicago	From 95 Pittsburgh	
1 Express	B-60	*Hartford	Chicago	From 95 Pittsburgh	
1 Express	B-60	*Bridgeport	Chicago	From 95 Pittsburgh	
1 Express	B-60, Sunday, Monday and Days after Holidays	Boston	Chicago	From 25 Pittsburgh	
1 MS-60	(X)	Providence	Chicago	From 13 (85 Sunday), Pittsburgh	
1 MS-60	(X)	Pittsburgh	Chicago		
1 P-70	Rider	Pittsburgh	Chicago		
1 MS-60	X-29	Pittsburgh	Canton		
1 MS-60	X-29 Sacks Monday	Pittsburgh	Canton		

x Will NOT operate November 27, December 25, Janaury 1
* Daily except Sunday, Monday and Days after Holiday

traffic which it dropped at Mansfield, Ohio for Mansfield to Detroit Train No. 105. It is interesting to note that Train No. 99 carried a 6 section, 6 double bedroom sleeper and a reclining seat coach, although it is not in the public timetables. These cars were primarily in the train for deadheading crewmen and for Pennsylvania Railroad's supervisory personnel between Pittsburgh and Chicago. No. 99 carried two working Railway Post Office cars as well and, on the rear of the train, a P-70 coach served as a rider for the crew between Pittsburgh and Chicago. As a general rule, however, No. 99 did not carry revenue passengers, only pass riders, deadheading crewmen and the crew, although it is interesting to note that in one or two issues of the public timetable in the 1950s, the 6 section, 6 double bedroom sleeper somehow appeared under *The Golden Triangle* as being received from No. 99 at Fort Wayne. However, through revenue passengers did not ride on No. 99, nor was it in the public timetable.

As one can see, besides the headend traffic carried on regular passenger trains, the Pennsylvania Railroad operated quite a few through mail and express trains, a few of which, as noted, carried revenue passengers. To count them up, there was one through Pittsburgh to St. Louis mail train in both directions, three New York to Pittsburgh mail and express trains, if one includes revenue passenger carrying No. 13, and three Pittsburgh to New York mail and express trains, with two of them, No. 14 and No. 18, carrying revenue passengers. Between Pittsburgh and Chicago, there was overnight mail train No. 99, although its eastbound counterpart was No. 44, another overnight mail train which did carry revenue passengers and is treated in Chapter 3 of this book. A look at the consist book shows that the

Pennsylvania Railroad certainly had a large amount of mail and express traffic on its mainline routes, carried in a variety of cars, with the crew accommodated in regular passenger cars or, in some cases, simply a Pennsylvania Railroad cabin car. Most of these mail and express trains not only continued until the late 1960s, when the Postal Service, as well as the Railway Express Company, switched to trucks, but they actually grew in number and swelled in their consists, sometimes to 40 cars. As the 1960s wore on, mail and express traffic made a good deal of revenue for the Pennsylvania Railroad. In fact, the Pittsburgh to St. Louis mail train actually began carrying passengers in the 1960s between Pittsburgh and St. Louis on its trek from the Steel City to the Mississippi River. Mail and express trains made up a large and very important portion of the Pennsylvania Railroad's service in the 1950s. This mail and express traffic would actually continue to grow over the next fifteen years. Solid mail and express trains were a common site on the Pennsylvania Railroad in the 1960s before the trucks received that business, thanks to the stupid decisions made by the U. S. Postal Service and the Railway Express Agency.

ISSUED JANUARY 25, 1953

ISSUED JANUARY 25, 1953

PENNSYLVANIA RAILROAD

PENNSYLVANIA RAILROAD

K.L. Miller Collection
From Timetable Form 1, Janaury 25, 1953

Harry Stegmaier Collection

Two Pennsylvania Railroad E units lead Pennsylvania train No. 55, *The Gotham Limited*, westbound at Plymouth, Indiana in 1953. On this day, the train has 16 cars in its consist including, if one looks carefully, two railway post office cars, as well as coaches, a diner and first class sleepers on the rear. By 1953, trains like No. 55, *The Gotham Limited*, were to a large extent, being laden down with heavy headend traffic, which brought in most of the revenue, rather than the passengers aboard.

Harry Stegmaier Collection

Backlit by the setting sun, a trio of Alco units in an A-B-A set, lead Pennsylvania Railroad's train No. 70, *The Admiral*, in the summer of June, 1953, at Plymouth, Indiana. The train has left Chicago two hours earlier and will make a stop at Plymouth at 8:03 daylight savings time, but 7:03 standard time. One can see in the train, if one looks carefully at the consist of No. 70 containing headend, including a working RPO car, a baggage car, a dormitory car, two of the P85BR coaches, another coach, a diner and then a sleeper-lounge and three sleepers on the rear, including the through sleeper from San Francisco.

For Distinctive Travel Comfort

Broadway Limited

ALL-PRIVATE-ROOM FLEET LEADER
CHICAGO · PHILADELPHIA · NEW YORK

This outstanding streamliner—leader of Pennsylvania Railroad's passenger fleet— has earned an enviable reputation over the years for train service superb in every respect. The magnificent *Broadway Limited* offers the finest in luxury travel available on the rails today.

You choose from six types of private rooms ranging from the cozy Roomette to luxurious Master Room with private bath and shower. Observation-Lounge and Club-Lounge Cars are restfully appointed with easy chairs, game tables, magazine libraries and refreshment buffets . . . for complete leisure and enjoyment en route. And the beautiful Master Dining Car is a most gracious setting for the enjoyment of delicious food, skillfully prepared in gleaming kitchens, and courteously served in the traditional *Broadway Limited* manner. Ride this great train on your next trip.

EASTBOUND
Lv. Chicago (Union Station) . . . 4:30 P.M.
Ar. Philadelphia (N. Phila. Station) 8:00 A.M.
Ar. New York (Penna. Station) . . 9:30 A.M.

WESTBOUND
Lv. New York (Penna. Station) . . 6:00 P.M.
Lv. Philadelphia (N. Phila. Station) 7:21 P.M.
Ar. Chicago (Union Station) . . . 9:00 A.M.
For Schedules Consult Tables 1 and 2

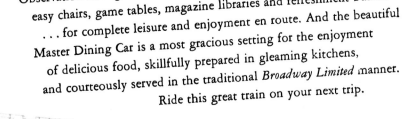

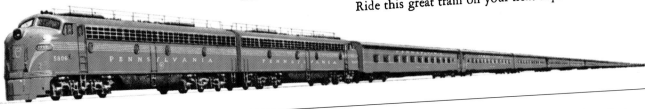

K.L. Miller Collection
From Timetable Form 1, January 25, 1953.

Harry Stegmaier Collection

A Pennsylvania Railroad classic K4 Pacific, No. 5054, leads *The Gotham Limited* around Horseshoe Curve toward Altoona in 1948. The train was still steam powered in those days, but would be dieselized shortly after this photograph was taken. From the look of the photograph, it is probable, that on this day, *The Gotham Limited*, usually heavy on headend, is in two sections with a separate mail and express section of the train being operated, as was common in the 1940s after World War II.

Harry Stegmaier Collection

Rolling up No. 4 track on Horseshoe Curve in 1948, we see a helper locomotive assisting *The Metropolitan's* T-1 as it rounds the curve. Again, on this day as in the previous photo, the train is probably being run in two sections, one for headend traffic, while the passenger section of No. 25 contains only two headend cars, followed by a combine, four coaches, a dining car and what appears to be two parlor cars and a coach on the rear. The coach is probably the Washington to Pittsburgh car handled on the rear of that train west of Harrisburg. This photo shows a classic, daylight Pennsylvania Railroad passenger train on the main line in the heyday of passenger service after World War II.

New York, Philadelphia, Washington and Baltimore to Pittsburgh—(Continued on Page 13)

Table 1

For additional stops and local service consult local time tables
For Sleeping, Parlor, Dining Cars and Coaches, see pages 4 and 5

(Eastern Standard Time)

Miles	Station	85 Mail and Express Sunday only	13 Mail and Express Except Sunday	25 The Metropolitan Daily	75 The Duquesne Daily	33 The St. Louisan Daily	23 Manhattan Limited Daily	77 The Trail Blazer Daily Dec.12 to Jan.20 incl.	49 The General Daily Except Dec.25	49 The Trail Blazer Daily Except Dec.12 to Jan.20 incl.	59 Liberty Limited Daily	69 The Red Arrow Daily	41 Cincinnati Limited Daily
		AM	AM	AM	AM	PM	PM	PM	PM	PM		PM	PM
.0	Lv New York, N.Y. (Penna. Sta.)	3.45	3.45	8.05	v11.45	v12.55	v2.50	z4.40	z5.00	z5.00	----	v5.10	h5.25
	Lv New York, N.Y. (Hudson Term.)	3.20	3.20	7.45	v11.24	v12.36	v2.36	z4.24	z4.40	z4.40	----	v5.00	h5.08
	" Jersey City, N.J. (Exchange Pl.)(u)	3.23	3.23	7.48	v11.27	v12.39	v2.39	z4.27	z4.43	z4.43	----	v5.20	h5.28
	Ar Newark, N.J.	3.40	3.40	8.05	v11.44	v12.56	v2.56	z4.44	z5.00	z5.00	----	v5.25	h5.40
10.0	Lv Newark, N.J.	4.00	4.00	8.20	v11.59	v1.10	v3.05	z4.55	z5.14	z5.14	----	c6.38	h6.27
58.1	" Trenton, N.J.	----	m4.47	9.05	c1.13	c2.24	c4.20	z5.39	z5.57	z5.57	----	7.06	h6.56
85.9	Philadelphia, Pa. North Philadelphia Station	5.23	5.23	9.38	1.41	2.53	4.48	----	----	----	----	7.06	h7.23
	" Pennsylvania Station (30th St.)	----	----	10.07	----	----	5.06	----	----	----	----	----	----
111.4	" Paoli, Pa.	----	----	10.21	1.58	----	----	----	----	----	----	----	----
124.0	" Downingtown, Pa.	----	----	10.29	----	----	----	----	----	----	----	----	----
130.0	" Coatesville, Pa.	----	----	10.59	2.27	3.37	5.35	----	----	----	----	----	----
135.7	" Parkesburg, Pa.	6.45	6.47	----	----	----	----	----	----	----	----	----	h8.06
159.3	" Lancaster, Pa.	7.00	7.04	----	----	----	----	----	----	----	----	7.50	h8.40
170.8	" Mount Joy, Pa.	7.10	7.19	----	----	----	----	----	----	----	----	----	----
177.6	" Elizabethtown, Pa.	7.20	7.31	----	----	4.10	6.08	----	----	----	----	8.27	----
185.1	" Middletown, Pa.	7.32	7.45	11.32	3.01	----	----	----	----	----	----	----	----
194.6	Ar Harrisburg, Pa.	----	----	----	3.01	4.10	6.08	7.58	8.09	8.09	----	8.27	h8.40
.0	Lv Washington, D.C. (Penna. Sta.)	----	----	8.10	----	----	1.10	----	----	----	----	----	----
40.1	" Baltimore, Md. (Penna. Sta.)	----	----	9.03	----	----	1.56	----	----	----	----	----	----
96.3	" York, Pa.	----	----	10.37	----	----	3.25	----	----	----	----	----	----
		----	----	11.20	----	----	4.05	----	----	----	----	----	----
123.4	Ar Harrisburg, Pa.	----	----	11.47	3.01	4.22	6.08	7.58	8.09	8.09	8.25	8.27	h8.40
194.6	Lv Harrisburg, Pa.	7.50	8.15	----	----	----	----	----	----	----	----	----	9.50
209.4	" Duncannon, Pa.	8.13	8.38	----	----	----	----	----	----	----	----	----	----
222.0	" Newport, Pa.	8.27	8.53	12.50	----	----	----	----	----	----	----	----	----
243.6	" Mifflin, Pa.	8.53	9.20	----	----	----	7.22	----	----	----	----	----	----
255.2	" Lewistown, Pa.	9.13	9.40	----	----	----	7.49	----	10.30	10.30	10.30	10.48	t11.11
279.7	" Mount Union, Pa.	9.48	10.15	1.51	5.10	5.35	8.03	10.20	10.20	----	----	10.48	t11.11
291.6	" Huntingdon, Pa.	10.15	10.41	2.16	5.35	5.35	8.30	10.20	10.20	----	----	10.56	----
311.2	" Tyrone, Pa.	10.50	11.30	2.16	----	----	8.56	----	----	----	----	11.57	----
325.4	Ar Altoona, Pa.	11.25	12.10	----	----	----	9.59	----	----	----	----	----	----
325.4	Lv Altoona, Pa.	11.45	12.30	2.16	3.18	6.35	----	----	----	----	----	----	----
339.9	" Cresson, Pa.	12.18	1.07	2.52	----	----	----	----	----	----	----	----	----
362.9	" Johnstown, Pa.	12.50	2.07	----	----	----	10.40	----	----	----	----	----	----
387.0	" Torrance, Pa.	----	2.52	----	----	----	10.55	----	----	----	----	----	----
394.3	" Derry, Pa.	1.33	3.20	4.07	----	7.14	----	----	----	----	----	----	----
399.2	" Latrobe, Pa.	1.50	4.00	4.07	----	7.28	----	----	----	----	----	----	----
408.5	" Greensburg, Pa.	----	----	----	----	----	----	----	----	----	----	----	----
412.6	" Jeannette, Pa.	----	----	----	----	----	----	----	----	----	----	----	----
417.9	" Irwin, Pa.	----	----	----	----	----	----	----	----	----	----	----	----
425.5	" Wilmerding, Pa.	----	----	----	----	----	11.32	----	----	----	----	----	----
427.1	" East Pittsburgh, Pa.	----	----	----	----	----	11.43	----	----	----	----	----	----
429.2	" Braddock, Pa.	----	----	4.43	8.04	----	----	12.49	12.59	12.59	12.59	1.17	1.42
432.7	" Wilkinsburg, Pa.	2.26	5.02	4.55	8.15	9.10	----	----	----	----	----	----	----
434.7	" East Liberty, Pa.	2.35	5.15	----	----	----	----	----	----	----	----	1.30	----
439.3	Ar Pittsburgh, Pa.	----	----	----	----	----	11.43	11.32	12.49	12.59	12.59	1.17	1.42
		PM	PM	PM	PM	PM	PM	AM	AM	AM	AM	AM	AM

Column notes (printed vertically): Train 77 and the 49 Trail Blazer — "For Special Service Charge See Page 39 / Reserved Seat Coaches." Train 49 (The General) — "Sleeping Cars." Liberty Limited (59) — "Sleeping Cars and Reserved Seat Coaches."

Boston to New York—N.Y., N.H. & H.R.R.

EASTERN STANDARD TIME	AM	AM *8.30	AM *11.00	PM *3.00	PM *6.00	PM *11.00	PM *11.50
Lv Boston, Mass. (South Sta.)	-----	8.30	11.00	3.00	6.00	11.00	11.50
Lv Providence, R.I.	*6.20	9.25	11.48	3.50	6.48	12.05	1.10
Lv New Haven, Conn.	7.55	11.42	1.49	5.55	8.56	2.20	3.25
Ar New York, N.Y. (Penna. Sta.)	AM	1.15	3.20	7.20	10.25	3.50	5.15
		PM	PM	PM	PM	AM	AM

REFERENCE MARKS

* Daily.

⊕ Carries only coaches for passengers; no dining car or Pullman service.

c Stops only to receive passengers.

g Stops only to receive passengers for York and points beyond.

h Stops only to receive passengers for Lewistown and points west of Pittsburgh.

m Mondays only.

t Stops only to receive passengers for points west of Pittsburgh.

u Hudson & Manhattan R.R. Station.

v Stops only to receive passengers for points west of Philadelphia.

z Stops only to receive passengers for Lancaster and points beyond.

COACHES ON ALL TRAINS EXCEPT Nos. 29 AND 31

New York, Philadelphia, Washington and Baltimore to Pittsburgh—(Continued)

Table 1 (Continued)

For additional stops and local service consult local time tables
For Sleeping, Parlor, Dining Cars and Coaches, see pages 4 and 5

(Eastern Standard Time)

Miles	Station	Broadway Limited 29 Daily	"Spirit of St. Louis" 31 Daily Except Dec. 24, 25, 26 & 31	The Jeffersonian All-Coach Streamliner 65 Daily	Pennsylvania Limited 1 Daily	The Penn Texas 3 Daily	The Admiral / The Akronite 71 Daily	The Clevelander 39 Daily	Pittsburgh Night Express / The Statesman 35 Daily	The American 67 Daily	Iron City Express 37 Daily	Gotham Limited 55 Daily	The Pittsburgher 61 Ex. Sat. Nights & Dec. 25, 26, 31, Jan. 1 & 2
		PM	PM	PM	PM	PM	PM	PM	PM	PM	PM	PM	PM
.0	Lv New York, N. Y. (Penna. Sta.)	t 6.00	v 6.10	o 6.15	v 6.45	t 7.35	v 8.00	o 8.40					
----	Lv New York, N. Y. (Hudson Term.)	t 5.48	v 5.56	o 6.00	v 6.30	t 7.20	v 7.42	o 8.24		v10.25	v11.00	v11.35	v11.59
----	" Jersey City, N. J. (Exchange Pl.)(u)	t 5.51	v 5.59	o 6.03	v 6.33	t 7.23	v 7.45	o 8.27		v10.12	v10.45	v11.15	v11.45
----	Ar Newark, N. J.	t 6.08	v 6.16	o 6.20	v 6.50	t 7.40	v 8.02	o 8.44		v10.15	v10.48	v11.18	v11.48
10.0	Lv Newark, N. J.	t 6.14	v 6.24	o 6.29	v 7.00	t 7.50	v 8.15	o 8.55		v10.32	v11.05	v11.35	v12.05
58.1	" Trenton, N. J.				v 7.44	t 8.35	v 9.00	o 9.39		v10.40	v11.15	v11.50	v12.20
85.9	Philadelphia, Pa. — North Philadelphia Station												
	Pennsylvania Station (30th St.)	t 7.21	c 7.40	o 7.46	c 8.14	t 9.06	c 9.31	o10.13		c11.54	c12.30	c 1.09	c 1.37
111.4	" Paoli, Pa.	t 7.46	8.05	o 8.11									
124.0	" Downingtown, Pa.				8.42				11.20		12.20		
130.0	" Coatesville, Pa.					t 9.35	9.58	o10.39	11.50				
135.7	" Parkesburg, Pa.								12.04				
159.3	" Lancaster, Pa.								12.15				
170.8	" Mount Joy, Pa.		8.48		9.27								
177.6	" Elizabethtown, Pa.			r 8.55				r11.23	12.48		1.41		
185.1	" Middletown, Pa.												
194.6	Ar Harrisburg, Pa.	t 9.01	9.22	q 9.30	10.02	t10.53	11.16	t11.59	1.27	1.37	2.15	2.54	3.30
.0	Lv Washington, D. C. (Penna. Sta.)		6.15	q 6.15	6.15	t 7.45	7.45	t 8.50	10.30				
40.1	" Baltimore, Md. (Penna. Sta.)		7.02	q 7.02	7.02	8.32	8.32	t 9.37	11.22				
96.3	" York, Pa.		8.31	q 8.31	8.31	10.01	10.01	t11.06	12.54				
123.4	Ar Harrisburg, Pa.		9.20	q 9.20	9.20	10.45	10.45	t11.50	1.35				
194.6	Lv Harrisburg, Pa.	t 9.01	9.22	q 9.42	10.17	t10.53	11.28	t12.12	1.55	1.47	2.25	2.54	3.30
209.4	" Duncannon, Pa.												
222.0	" Newport, Pa.												
243.6	" Mifflin, Pa.												
255.2	" Lewistown, Pa.												
279.7	" Mount Union, Pa.												
291.6	" Huntingdon, Pa.												
311.2	" Tyrone, Pa.												
325.4	Ar Altoona, Pa.	t11.24	11.50	q12.00	12.36	t 1.29	1.06						
325.4	Lv Altoona, Pa.	t11.24	11.50	q12.04	12.36	t 1.29	1.31	t 2.33					
339.9	" Cresson, Pa.						2.01	t 2.33	4.20	4.06	4.43	5.20	d 6.07
362.9	" Johnstown, Pa.						2.01		4.20	4.06	4.43	5.20	d 6.07
387.0	" Torrance, Pa.					§ 3.01							
394.3	" Derry, Pa.								5.26				
399.2	" Latrobe, Pa.								5.54	5.50	6.20	6.20	
408.5	" Greensburg, Pa.									g 6.19			
412.6	" Jeannette, Pa.								6.11				
417.9	" Irwin, Pa.												d 7.59
425.5	" Wilmerding, Pa.								6.27		6.38		
427.1	" East Pittsburgh, Pa.										6.53		
429.2	" Braddock, Pa.												
432.7	" Wilkinsburg, Pa.										b 7.21		
434.7	" East Liberty, Pa.								7.10		7.35		d 8.49
439.3	Ar Pittsburgh, Pa.	1.52	2.19	2.28	3.05	4.00	4.30	5.12	7.35	6.40	7.50	7.55	9.00
		AM	AM	AM	AM	AM	AM	AM	AM	AM	AM	AM	AM

Column notes: No. 29 and No. 31 — "No Coaches or Checked Baggage." No. 65 — "All Seats Reserved. For Special Service Charge See Page 39." No. 61 — "No Coaches."

REFERENCE MARKS

§ Sundays only.

b Stops only on notice to conductor to discharge passengers.

c Stops only to receive passengers.

d Stops only to discharge passengers.

g Stops Saturdays only to discharge passengers.

o Stops only to receive passengers for Lancaster, Pittsburgh and points west.

q Stops only to receive passengers for Pittsburgh and points west.

r Stops to discharge passengers and to receive passengers for Pittsburgh and points west.

t Stops only to receive passengers for points west of Pittsburgh.

u Hudson & Manhattan R. R. Station.

v Stops only to receive passengers for points west of Philadelphia.

COACHES ON ALL TRAINS EXCEPT No. 61.

Pennsylvania Railroad E-7 units, led by No. 5845, head up Pennsylvania Railroad's train No. 71, *The Admiral*, at the Pennsylvania Railroad diamond at Fort Wayne, Indiana in 1956. By this time, *The Admiral* was heavy in headend traffic, having inherited some of that from the now discontinued *Gotham Limited*. Behind the two E-7's are nine headend cars, followed by three coaches, a dining car, a sleeper-lounge and three sleeping cars, making a 17-car train, which was probably no problem for the two E-7's on the flatlands of Indiana as they rolled No. 71 towards Chicago.

In this photograph, one sees a massively long Pennsylvania Railroad *Penn Texas* as it heads east out of St. Louis. The consist is filled with passenger cars from as far away as El Paso, San Antonio and Houston, including two cars in *Eagle* colors with Missouri Pacific 14 roomette, 4 double bedroom Pullman *Eagle Bay* on the rear of the train. *The Penn Texas* could become very long at times, and it is seen here in this photograph in the 1950s while still a major player in Pennsylvania's St. Louis to New York service.

Mark Hildebrandt

The successor to *The Broadway Limited* was *The General*, although it had been renamed *The Broadway Limited* in the Penn Central era. This photograph, taken in 1969, shows *The Broadway Limited* was still a fairly good looking train as it paused at Crestline, Ohio eastbound in May, 1969. The car in the foreground of the picture is a 12 duplex single room, 4 double bedroom sleeper, *Club Creek*, and although the cars are now PC, they are still in the Tuscan Red that one would have expected.

Harry Stegmaier Collection

In the fall of 1953, Pennsylvania Railroad E-8 5893 leads No. 30, *The St. Louisan*, a train by that time heavy on headend traffic, past signals guarding the interlocking at Spruce Creek, Pennsylvania. The train is about to enter eastbound into Spruce Creek Tunnel on No. 1 track.

An E-7A and E-7B lead train No. 74, Pennsylvania Railroad's popular Pittsburgh to New York *Duquesne* around Horseshoe Curve in the summer of 1948. The Brunswick Green unit with the five stripes certainly looks handsome in this photograph, handling Pennsylvania Railroad's daylight run.

In the fall of 1953, E8A 5837 leads a long mail and express train No. 14 into the early morning sunlight as it approaches the tunnel at Spruce Creek, Pennsylvania. As is obvious, the train is loaded with mail and express but it does carry passengers who care to ride it in its single P70 coach in the consist, which is out of sight around the curve.

Pittsburgh to Baltimore, Washington, Philadelphia and New York—(Continued on Page 15)

Table 2

For additional stops and local service consult local time tables

For Sleeping, Parlor, Dining Cars and Coaches, see pages 6 and 7

(Eastern Standard Time)

Miles	Station	The Admiral 70 Daily	Pennsylvania Limited 2 Daily	⊕ Mail and Express 14 Except Sunday	The St. Louisan 32 Daily	Gotham Limited 54 Daily	The Juniata 72 Daily	The Duquesne 74 Daily	The New Englander 46 Daily	⊕ Mail and Express 18 Daily	Manhattan Limited 22 Daily	The American 66 Daily	Iron City Express 16 Daily	Philadelphia Express 16-36 Ex. Sat. Nights & Dec. 24, 25, 26, 31, Jan. 1 & 2	Philadelphia Express 16-86 Dec. 24 only
		AM	AM	AM	AM	AM	AM	PM	PM	PM	PM	PM	PM	PM	PM
.0	Lv Pittsburgh, Pa.	3.13	3.30	3.45	8.00	9.10	11.00	2.00	4.00	4.50	10.00	10.02	10.15	10.15	10.15
4.6	" East Liberty, Pa.	------	------	------	------	------	11.11	2.11	c4.11	5.02	------	------	c10.26	c10.26	c10.26
6.6	" Wilkinsburg, Pa.	------	------	------	------	------	------	------	------	------	------	------	------	------	------
10.1	" Braddock, Pa.	------	------	------	------	------	------	------	------	------	------	------	------	------	------
12.2	" East Pittsburgh, Pa.	------	------	------	------	------	------	------	------	5.14	------	------	------	------	------
13.8	" Wilmerding, Pa.	------	------	------	------	------	------	------	------	------	------	------	------	------	------
21.4	" Irwin, Pa.	------	------	------	------	------	------	------	------	------	------	------	------	------	------
26.7	" Jeannette, Pa.	------	------	------	------	------	------	------	------	------	------	------	------	------	------
30.8	" Greensburg, Pa.	§ 4.08	------	5.00	------	------	11.43	2.44	4.48	5.48	------	------	11.01	11.01	11.01
40.1	" Latrobe, Pa.	------	------	5.21	------	p 9.59	11.55	2.58	5.03	6.09	------	------	11.16	11.16	11.16
45.0	" Derry, Pa.	------	------	------	------	------	------	------	------	------	------	------	------	------	------
52.3	" Torrance, Pa.	------	------	------	------	------	------	------	5.18	6.36	------	------	------	------	------
76.4	" Johnstown, Pa.	§ 4.55	------	6.17	9.30	10.37	12.37	3.40	5.49	7.40	------	------	11.59	11.59	11.59
99.4	" Cresson, Pa.	------	------	7.06	------	------	------	------	------	8.40	------	------	------	------	------
113.9	Ar Altoona, Pa.	5.58	6.05	7.40	10.37	11.40	1.40	4.45	6.57	9.17	12.35	12.45	1.05	1.05	1.05
113.9	Lv Altoona, Pa.	5.58	6.05	7.52	10.37	11.40	1.40	4.45	6.57	9.29	12.35	12.45	1.05	1.05	1.05
128.1	" Tyrone, Pa.	------	------	8.17	------	------	1.59	------	7.19	9.46	------	------	1.26	1.26	1.26
147.7	" Huntingdon, Pa.	------	6.48	8.50	------	------	2.24	------	7.44	10.14	------	------	1.51	1.51	1.51
159.6	" Mount Union, Pa.	------	------	9.07	------	------	------	------	7.58	------	------	------	------	------	------
184.1	" Lewistown, Pa.	------	7.25	9.42	------	12.55	3.00	6.00	8.28	10.56	------	------	2.28	2.28	2.28
195.7	" Mifflin, Pa.	------	------	------	------	------	------	------	8.46	------	------	------	------	------	------
217.3	" Newport, Pa.	------	------	------	------	------	------	------	------	------	------	------	------	------	------
229.9	" Duncannon, Pa.	------	------	------	------	------	------	------	------	------	------	------	------	------	------
244.7	Ar Harrisburg, Pa.	8.20	8.39	11.15	1.00	2.04	4.18	7.10	9.47	12.19	2.58	3.07	3.49	3.49	3.49
244.7	Lv Harrisburg, Pa.	------	8.50	------	2.15	2.15	------	7.19	------	No Checked Baggage	4.15	4.15	------	------	------
271.8	Ar York, Pa.	------	9.27	------	2.57	2.57	------	7.57	------		4.52	4.52	------	------	------
328.0	" Baltimore, Md. (Penna. Sta.)	------	11.17	------	4.33	4.33	------	9.35	------		6.40	6.40	------	------	------
368.1	Ar Washington, D. C.	------	12.10	------	5.20	5.20	------	10.30	------		7.35	7.35	------	------	------
244.7	Lv Harrisburg, Pa.	8.27	8.46	11.40	1.10	2.12	4.28	7.20	10.00	12.44	2.58	3.07	3.49	5.35	6.30
254.2	" Middletown, Pa.	------	------	------	------	------	------	------	------	------	------	------	------	------	6.41
261.7	" Elizabethtown, Pa.	------	------	------	------	------	------	------	------	------	------	------	------	------	6.50
268.5	" Mount Joy, Pa.	------	------	------	------	------	------	------	------	------	------	------	------	------	6.59
280.0	" Lancaster, Pa.	9.02	9.19	12.15	1.44	2.45	5.01	7.53	10.37	1.26	------	------	------	6.12	7.12
303.6	" Parkesburg, Pa.	------	------	------	------	------	------	------	------	------	------	------	------	------	7.53
309.3	" Coatesville, Pa.	9.32	------	------	------	3.16	5.33	------	11.12	1.57	------	------	------	------	8.01
315.3	" Downingtown, Pa.	------	------	------	------	------	------	------	------	------	------	------	------	------	8.09
327.0	" Paoli, Pa.	d 9.51	d10.05	1.05	2.30	3.34	5.53	8.40	11.35	------	d 4.25	q 4.38	d 5.17	d 7.05	8.22
	Ar Philadelphia, Pa.														
	" Pennsylvania Station (30th St.)	------	------	------	------	------	------	------	------	------	------	------	------	7.35	8.50
353.4	" North Philadelphia Station	d10.16	d10.30	d 1.32	d 2.59	4.00	6.20	9.06	12.02	2.47	d 4.52	d 5.06	5.45	------	------
381.2	" Trenton, N. J.	v10.46	------	------	3.29	------	------	d 9.35	------	d 3.35	d 5.35	------	6.15	------	------
429.3	Ar Newark, N. J.	d11.30	d11.44	d 3.00	4.15	d 5.17	7.40	10.20	1.34	4.32	d 6.25	6.28	7.00	------	------
------	Lv Newark, N. J.	11.42	11.54	3.06	4.18	5.29	7.49	10.30	1.50	4.50	6.31	6.41	7.06	------	------
------	Ar Jersey City, N. J. (Exchange Pl.)(u)	11.59	12.11	3.23	4.38	5.46	8.06	10.47	2.07	5.07	6.48	6.58	7.28	------	------
------	" New York, N. Y. (Hudson Term.)	12.02	12.14	3.26	4.41	5.49	8.09	10.50	2.10	5.10	6.51	7.01	7.31	------	------
439.3	Ar New York, N. Y. (Penna. Sta.)	11.45	11.59	3.25	4.30	5.50	7.55	10.35	1.50	4.55	6.40	6.45	7.15	------	------
		AM	AM	PM	PM	PM	PM	PM	AM	AM	AM	AM	AM	AM	AM

No Checked Baggage on Sundays. (No. 72)

New York to Boston—N. Y., N. H. & H. R. R.

EASTERN STANDARD TIME							
	AM	AM	AM	PM	PM	PM	PM
Lv New York, N. Y. (Penna. Sta.)	* 2.20	* 3.10	*11.00	* 2.00	* 4.00	* 7.00	* 8.25
Ar New Haven, Conn.	3.55	4.40	12.33	3.32	5.30	8.28	9.59
Ar Providence, R. I.	6.32	7.05	2.53	5.52	7.37	10.35	------
Ar Boston, Mass. (South Sta.)	7.45	8.10	3.45	6.45	8.25	11.25	------
	AM	AM	PM	PM	PM	PM	PM

REFERENCE MARKS

* Daily.
§ Sundays only.
⊕ Carries only coaches for passengers; no dining car or Pullman service.
c Stops only to receive passengers.
d Stops only to discharge passengers.
p Stops only on signal to discharge passengers from Ft. Wayne and beyond.
q Stops only to discharge passengers from Pittsburgh and points west.
u Hudson & Manhattan R. R. Station.
v Stops only to discharge passengers from points west of Philadelphia.

COACHES ON ALL TRAINS

Pittsburgh to Baltimore, Washington, Philadelphia and New York—(Continued)

Table 2 (Continued)

For additional stops and local service consult local time tables

For Sleeping, Parlor, Dining Cars and Coaches, see pages 6 and 7

(Eastern Standard Time)

Miles	Station	The Penn Texas 4 Daily	The Pittsburgher 60 Ex. Sat. Nights & Dec. 25, 26, 31, Jan. 1 & 2	Philadelphia Night Express / The Statesman 36 Ex. Sat. Nights & Dec. 24 & 31	Philadelphia Night Express / The Statesman 86 Sat. Nights & Dec. 24 & 31	The Clevelander / The Akronite 38 Daily	Cincinnati Limited 40 Daily	The Red Arrow 68 Daily	The General 48 Daily Except Dec. 26	The Trail Blazer 48 Daily	Liberty Limited 58 Daily	Broadway Limited 28 Daily	"Spirit of St. Louis" 30 Daily Except Dec. 25, 26, 27 & Jan. 1	The Jeffersonian All-Coach Streamliner 64 Daily
		PM	PM	PM	PM	PM	PM	PM	AM	AM	AM	AM	AM	AM
.0	Lv Pittsburgh, Pa.	d10.47	11.00	11.10	11.10	11.35	11.45	11.56	12.13	12.13	12.41	1.22	1.25	1.40
4.6	" East Liberty, Pa.	------	c11.14	c11.21	c11.21	------	------	------	------	------	------	------	------	------
6.6	" Wilkinsburg, Pa.	------	No Coaches	------	------	------	------	------	------	For Special Service Charge See Page 39.	------	No Coaches or Checked Baggage.	No Coaches or Checked Baggage.	For Special Service Charge See Page 39.
10.1	" Braddock, Pa.	------		------	------	------	------	------	------	------	------			
12.2	" East Pittsburgh, Pa.	------		------	------	------	------	------	------	------	------			
13.8	" Wilmerding, Pa.	------		------	------	------	------	------	------	------	------			
21.4	" Irwin, Pa.	------		------	------	------	------	------	------	------	------			
26.7	" Jeannette, Pa.	------		------	------	------	------	------	------	------	------			
30.8	" Greensburg, Pa.	------		11.55	11.55	------	------	------	------	------	------			
40.1	" Latrobe, Pa.	------	c12.00	12.09	12.09	------	------	------	------	------	------			
45.0	" Derry, Pa.	------	------	------	------	------	------	------	------	------	------			
52.3	" Torrance, Pa.	------	------	------	------	------	------	------	------	------	------			
76.4	" Johnstown, Pa.	------	------	12.51	12.51	------	------	------	------	------	------			
99.4	" Cresson, Pa.	------	------	------	------	------	------	------	------	------	------	------	------	------
113.9	Ar Altoona, Pa.	d 1.33	1.45	1.55	1.55	2.07	2.28	2.38	d 2.48	d 2.48	3.10	d 3.52	3.59	4.17
113.9	Lv Altoona, Pa.	d 1.33	1.45	1.55	1.55	2.07	2.28	2.38	d 2.48	d 2.48	3.10	d 3.52	3.59	4.17
128.1	" Tyrone, Pa.	------	------	------	------	------	------	------	------	------	------	------	------	All Seats Reserved
147.7	" Huntingdon, Pa.	------	------	------	------	------	------	------	------	------	------	------	------	
159.6	" Mount Union, Pa.	------	------	------	------	------	------	------	------	------	------	------	------	
184.1	" Lewistown, Pa.	------	------	------	------	------	------	------	------	------	------	------	------	
195.7	" Mifflin, Pa.	------	------	------	------	------	------	------	------	------	------	------	------	
217.3	" Newport, Pa.	------	------	------	------	------	------	------	------	------	------	------	------	
229.9	" Duncannon, Pa.	------	------	------	------	------	------	------	------	------	------	------	------	
244.7	Ar Harrisburg, Pa.	d 3.59	4.10	4.20	4.20	4.30	4.50	5.00	d 5.09	d 5.09	5.31	d 6.13	6.20	d 6.39
244.7	Lv Harrisburg, Pa.	d 4.15	------	4.50	4.50	4.50	------	5.15	Sleeping Cars	Reserved Seat Coaches.	5.31	------	6.49	6.49
271.8	Ar York, Pa.	d 4.52	------	5.27	5.27	5.27	------	5.52		------	6.12	------	7.26	7.26
328.0	" Baltimore, Md. (Penna. Sta.)	d 6.40	------	7.00	7.00	7.00	------	7.38		------	d 7.47	------	d 8.59	d 8.59
368.1	Ar Washington, D. C.	d 7.35	------	7.50	7.50	7.50	------	8.25		------	8.35	------	9.50	9.50
244.7	Lv Harrisburg, Pa.	d 3.59	4.10	5.35	6.30	4.30	4.50	5.30	d 5.09	d 5.09	Sleeping Cars and Reserved Seat Coaches.	d 6.13	6.20	d 6.39
254.2	" Middletown, Pa.	------	------	------	6.41	------	------	------	------	------		------	------	------
261.7	" Elizabethtown, Pa.	------	------	------	6.50	------	------	------	------	------		------	------	------
268.5	" Mount Joy, Pa.	------	------	------	6.59	------	------	------	------	------		------	------	------
280.0	" Lancaster, Pa.	------	------	6.12	7.12	------	------	6.04	------	------		------	6.59	7.24
303.6	" Parkesburg, Pa.	------	------	------	7.53	------	------	------	------	------		------	------	------
309.3	" Coatesville, Pa.	------	------	------	8.01	------	------	------	------	------		------	------	------
315.3	" Downingtown, Pa.	------	------	------	8.09	------	------	------	------	------		------	------	------
327.9	" Paoli, Pa.	------	d 5.50	d 7.05	8.22	d 6.02	d 6.15	d 6.55	q 6.29	q 6.29		y 7.35	q 7.45	q 8.07
	Ar Philadelphia, Pa.													
------	" Pennsylvania Station (30th St.)	------	------	7.35	8.50	------	------	------	------	------		------	------	------
353.4	" North Philadelphia Station	d 5.55	d 6.17	------	------	d 6.29	d 6.39	d 7.20	d 6.54	d 6.54		d 8.00	d 8.11	d 8.31
381.2	" Trenton, N. J.	d 6.24	d 6.48	------	------	7.00	d 7.14	7.50	d 7.22	d 7.22		------	------	v 9.04
429.3	Ar Newark, N. J.	d 7.10	d 7.42	------	------	d 7.54	d 8.03	8.40	d 8.09	d 8.09		d 9.10	d 9.20	v 9.50
------	Lv Newark, N. J.	7.15	7.49	------	------	8.05	8.13	8.45	8.18	8.18	------	9.17	9.25	9.54
------	Ar Jersey City, N. J. (Exchange Pl.)(u)	7.38	8.06	------	------	8.22	8.30	9.02	8.38	8.38	------	9.34	9.42	10.11
------	" New York, N. Y. (Hudson Term.)	7.41	8.09	------	------	8.25	8.33	9.05	8.41	8.41	------	9.37	9.45	10.14
439.3	Ar New York, N. Y. (Penna. Sta.)	7.20	8.00	------	------	8.10	8.20	8.55	8.25	8.25	------	9.30	9.35	10.05
		AM	AM	AM	AM	AM	AM	AM	AM	AM	AM	AM	AM	AM

REFERENCE MARKS

c Stops only to receive passengers.
d Stops only to discharge passengers.
q Stops only to discharge passengers from Pittsburgh and points west.
u Hudson & Manhattan R. R. Station.
v Stops only to discharge passengers from points west of Philadelphia.
y Stops only on notice to conductor to discharge passengers from points west of Pittsburgh.

COACHES ON ALL TRAINS EXCEPT Nos. 28, 30 and 60.

New York, Philadelphia, Washington and Baltimore to Chicago

Table 3

For Sleeping, Parlor, Dining Cars and Coaches, see pages 4 and 5

Miles	Station (Eastern Standard Time / C.S.T.)	The St. Louisan / The Golden Triangle 33-63 Except Sat. & Dec. 25, 26, 31, Jan. 1 & 2	Manhattan Limited 23 Daily	The Trail Blazer 77 Daily Dec. 12 to Jan. 20 incl.	The General 49 Daily Except Dec. 25	The Trail Blazer 49 Daily Except Dec. 12 to Jan. 20 incl.	Liberty Limited 59 Daily	Broadway Limited 29 Daily	Pennsylvania Limited 1 Daily	The Admiral 71 Daily	Gotham Limited 55 Daily	The Fort Pitt 53 Daily
		PM	PM	PM	PM	PM	PM	PM	PM	PM	PM	AM
.0	Lv New York, N. Y. (Penna. Sta.)	------	v 2.50	z 4.40	z 5.00	z 5.00	------	t 6.00	v 6.45	v 8.00	v11.35	------
------	Lv New York, N. Y. (Hudson Terminal)	------	v 2.36	z 4.24	z 4.40	z 4.40	------	t 5.48	v 6.30	v 7.42	v11.15	------
------	" Jersey City, N. J. (Exchange Place) (u)	------	v 2.39	z 4.27	z 4.43	z 4.43	------	t 5.51	v 6.33	v 7.45	v11.18	------
------	Ar Newark, N. J.	------	v 2.56	z 4.44	z 5.00	z 5.00	------	t 6.08	v 6.50	v 8.02	v11.35	------
10.0	Lv Newark, N. J.	------	v 3.05	z 4.55	z 5.14	z 5.14	------	t 6.14	v 7.00	v 8.15	v11.50	------
58.1	" Trenton, N. J.	------	v 3.50	z 5.39	z 5.57	z 5.57	------	------	v 7.44	v 9.00	------	------
	Philadelphia, Pa.											
85.9	" North Philadelphia Station	------	c 4.20	z 6.10	z 6.26	z 6.26	------	t 7.21	c 8.14	c 9.31	c 1.09	------
111.4	" Paoli, Pa.	------	4.48	z 6.36	z 6.52	z 6.52	------	t 7.46	8.42	9.58	------	------
159.3	" Lancaster, Pa.	------	5.35	7.22	7.34	7.34	------	------	9.27	------	------	------
194.6	Ar Harrisburg, Pa.	------	6.08	7.58	8.09	8.09	------	t 9.01	10.02	11.16	2.54	------
.0	Lv Washington, D. C.	1.10	e 1.10	------	Sleeping Cars	------	g 5.30	------	6.15	7.45	10.30	------
40.1	" Baltimore, Md. (Pennsylvania Sta.)	1.56	e 1.56	------		------	g 6.15	------	7.02	8.32	11.22	------
96.3	" York, Pa.	3.25	e 3.25	------		------	7.44	------	8.31	10.01	12.54	------
123.4	Ar Harrisburg, Pa.	4.05	e 4.05	------		------	8.25	------	9.20	10.45	1.35	------
194.6	Lv Harrisburg, Pa.	4.22	6.08	7.58	8.09	8.09	8.25	t 9.01	10.17	11.28	2.54	------
325.4	" Altoona, Pa.	6.40	8.56	10.20	10.30	10.30	10.48	t11.24	12.36	2.01	5.20	------
362.9	" Johnstown, Pa.	------	9.59	------	------	------	------	------	------	§ 3.01	6.20	------
439.3	Ar Pittsburgh, Pa.	9.10	11.43	12.49	12.59	12.59	1.17	1.52	3.05	4.30	7.55	------
439.3	Lv Pittsburgh, Pa.	11.00	11.43	12.49	12.59	12.59	1.17	1.52	3.05	4.50	8.10	11.00
508.9	Ar Salem, O.	12.30	------	------	------	------	------	------	------	------	------	12.29
522.3	" Alliance, O.	12.48	------	------	------	------	------	------	------	6.22	------	12.49
541.0	" Canton, O.	1.14	------	------	------	------	------	------	------	6.51	10.04	1.21
548.8	" Massillon, O.	------	------	------	------	------	------	------	------	r 7.04	------	1.36
563.3	" Orrville, O.	------	------	------	------	------	------	------	------	p 7.20	------	1.56
574.4	" Wooster, O.	------	------	------	------	------	------	------	------	7.37	------	2.12
614.6	" Mansfield, O.	2.47	------	4.04	4.14	4.14	------	------	------	8.29	11.30	3.15
628.1	" Crestline, O.	d 3.10	d 3.35	4.21	4.31	4.31	d 4.48	d 5.24	6.39	8.49	11.53	3.35
640.5	" Bucyrus, O.	------	------	------	------	------	------	------	------	9.12	------	------
657.3	" Upper Sandusky, O.	------	------	------	------	------	------	------	------	------	------	4.17
700.2	" Lima, O.	------	------	5.37	5.48	5.48	------	------	7.55	10.22	1.08	5.05
727.3	" Van Wert, O.	------	------	------	------	------	------	------	8.22	------	------	5.38
759.7	" Ft. Wayne, Ind.	4.20	4.43	5.33	5.44	5.44	5.56	d 6.32	7.53	10.20	1.05	6.15
799.0	" Warsaw, Ind.	------	------	------	------	------	------	------	8.35	------	1.48	6.03
823.9	" Plymouth, Ind.	------	o 5.45	q 6.35	q 6.46	q 6.46	6.58	------	9.02	11.26	------	6.33
864.1	" Valparaiso, Ind.	------	§ 6.20	------	------	------	------	------	------	12.06	------	7.13
882.7	" Gary, Ind.	y 6.30	d 6.40	d 7.30	d 7.41	d 7.41	h 7.55	------	9.54	12.33	------	7.33
900.7	" Englewood, Ill.	d 6.53	d 7.02	d 7.55	d 8.05	d 8.05	d 8.15	d 8.45	d10.20	d 1.00	d 3.25	d 7.55
907.7	Ar Chicago, Ill. (Union Station)	7.10	7.20	8.10	8.20	8.20	8.30	9.00	10.35	1.15	3.40	8.10
		AM	AM	AM	AM	AM	AM	AM	AM	PM	PM	PM

No. 33-63: No Checked Baggage Pittsburgh to Chicago. Nos. 77 and 49 (The Trail Blazer): Reserved Seat Coaches. For Special Service Charge See Page 39. No. 59: Sleeping Cars and Reserved Seat Coaches. No. 29: No Coaches or Checked Baggage.

Boston to New York—N. Y., N. H. & H. R. R.

EASTERN STANDARD TIME							
	AM	AM	AM	PM	PM	PM	PM
Lv Boston, Mass. (South Sta.)	------	* 8.30	*11.00	* 3.00	* 6.00	*11.00	*11.50
Lv Providence, R. I.	------	9.25	11.48	3.50	6.48	12.05	1.10
Lv New Haven, Conn.	* 6.20	11.42	1.49	5.55	8.56	2.20	3.25
Ar New York, N.Y. (Penna. Sta.)	7.55	1.15	3.20	7.20	10.25	3.50	5.15
	AM	PM	PM	PM	PM	AM	AM

REFERENCE MARKS FOR TABLE 3

* Daily.
§ Sundays only.
C.S.T. Central Standard Time.
c Stops only to receive passengers.
d Stops only to discharge passengers.
e No. 33 arriving Pittsburgh 9.10 p. m. Saturdays and Dec. 25, 26, 31, Jan. 1 and 2.
g Stops only to receive passengers for York and points beyond.
h Stops only on notice to conductor to discharge passengers from points south of Harrisburg.
o Stops only on notice to conductor to discharge passengers from Pittsburgh and points east.
p Stops only on notice to conductor to discharge passengers from Harrisburg and points beyond or on signal or notice to agent to receive passengers for Fort Wayne and beyond.
q Stops only on notice to conductor to discharge passengers from points east of Harrisburg.
r Stops only on notice to conductor to discharge passengers from Pittsburgh and points east and on signal or notice to agent to receive passengers for points west of Mansfield.
t Stops only to receive passengers for points west of Pittsburgh.
u Hudson & Manhattan Railroad Station.
v Stops only to receive passengers for points west of Philadelphia.
y Stops only on notice to conductor to discharge passengers from points beyond Fort Wayne.
z Stops only to receive passengers for Lancaster and points beyond.

COACHES ON ALL TRAINS EXCEPT No. 29

Bob's Photo

By 1965, Pennsylvania Railroad train No. 30, *The Spirit of St. Louis*, was no longer the all-Pullman train it had been in 1952. Instead, as one can see, the train is at St. Louis Union Depot and is headed by an E-8 and two E-7's and has become primarily a mail and express train with a few passenger cars to accommodate the coach and sleeping car passengers that were still riding the rails in 1965.

Chicago to Baltimore, Washington, Philadelphia and New York

		The Fort Pitt	Manhattan Limited	The General	The Trail Blazer	Liberty Limited	Broadway Limited	The Admiral	Pennsylvania Limited	The Golden Triangle	Gotham Limited		
Table 4										62 Ex. Sat. Nights & Dec. 25, 26, 31, Jan. 1 & 2			
For Sleeping, Parlor, Dining Cars and Coaches, see pages 6 and 7		52 Daily	22 Daily	48 Daily Except Dec. 25	48 Daily	58 Daily	28 Daily	70 Daily	2 Daily	54 Daily	44-144 -74	44-74
Miles													
		AM	PM	PM	PM	PM	PM	PM	PM	PM	PM	PM	PM
.0	Lv Chicago, Ill. (Union Sta.)	8.30	12.01	12.01			4.30		5.30	6.30	10.15	11.30	11.45	k11.40	k11.55
7.0	Englewood, Ill.	8.46	12.15				4.48		5.50	6.45	10.30	11.51	12.06		
25.0	Gary, Ind.	9.07	c12.38	c 3.15			5.10		6.05	7.05	10.51			2.30	2.30
43.6	Valparaiso, Ind.	9.28		c 3.47		3.37			6.26	7.30	d11.51				
83.8	Plymouth, Ind.	10.05		4.30					6.51	8.13					
108.7	Warsaw, Ind.	10.30	i 1.53	5.27	5.27	5.10								
148.0	Ft. Wayne, Ind.	11.07	2.30	4.09	7.26	5.27	6.07			10.12		12.42	1.54	2.30
180.4	Van Wert, O.	12.44	4.09	4.42		7.26	8.06			10.53				4.55
207.5	Lima, O.	1.17	4.42					9.57		11.30	11.59	2.49	4.00	5.10
250.4	Upper Sandusky, O.	2.22	5.53	8.37	8.37	9.16			11.55		4.35		6.30	7.00
267.2	Bucyrus, O.	2.40	5.53	9.02	9.02							6.55	7.47	8.00
279.6	Crestline, O.	3.10	6.57					12.51				7.08	8.08	8.42
293.1	Mansfield, O.	3.52										8.32	8.54	9.10
333.3	Wooster, O.	4.09						1.21		6.05	6.53		9.25	9.46
344.4	Orrville, O.	4.28	7.26	10.20	10.20					6.31	7.15	7.30	9.45	10.15
358.9	Massillon, O.	4.47	7.41					3.30			7.30	8.55	d11.40	d12.15
366.7	Canton, O.	5.12		12.13	12.13	12.41				8.20				
385.4	Alliance, O.	5.30									9.10	2.00		
398.8	Salem, O.	5.38	9.40	12.13	12.13	12.41		1.22		3.13	3.30	10.37	3.40	4.00
468.4	Ar Pittsburgh, Pa.	7.15										11.40	4.45	4.45
			10.00					1.22		3.13	3.30	2.04	7.10	7.10
468.4	Lv Pittsburgh, Pa.		12.35											
544.8	Johnstown, Pa.		2.58	d 2.48	d 2.48	3.10		3.52		3.13	3.30		2.00	
582.3	Ar Altoona, Pa.			d 5.09	d 5.09	5.31		4.55		4.55	5.58	2.15	7.19	7.19
713.1	Ar Harrisburg, Pa.		4.15					6.13		6.05	6.39	2.27	9.23	9.35
			4.52			5.31				8.50		2.35	9.30	10.30
713.1	Lv Harrisburg, Pa.		6.40			6.12				9.27		2.55		
740.2	Ar York, Pa.		7.35			7.47				11.17				
796.4	" Baltimore, Md. (Penna. Sta.)					8.35		6.13		8.46		2.12	7.20	7.20
836.1	Ar Washington, D. C.		2.58	d 5.09	d 5.09			y 7.35		9.02	9.19	2.58	8.10	8.10
										10.05		3.40	8.40	8.40
713.1	Lv Harrisburg, Pa.		d 4.25	q 6.29	q 6.29			d 8.00		d10.15	d10.30	4.00	9.06	9.06
748.4	Ar Lancaster, Pa.									d10.46	d10.46	d 5.17	9.35	9.35
796.3	" Paoli, Pa.		d 4.52	d 6.54	d 6.54			d 9.10		d11.30	d11.44		9.38	9.38
	" Philadelphia, Pa.		d 5.35	d 7.22	d 7.22							5.29	10.30	10.30
	" North Phila. Station		d 6.35	d 8.09	d 8.09					11.42	11.54	5.49	10.47	10.47
821.8	" Trenton, N. J.			8.18	8.18	8.18		9.17	11.59	12.11		10.50	10.50
849.6	Ar Newark, N. J.		6.31	8.38	8.38	8.38		9.34	12.02	12.14			
897.7	Lv Newark, N. J.		6.48	8.41	8.41	8.41		9.37					
	Ar Jersey City, N. J. (Ex. Place) (u)		6.51								5.58	*10.35	*10.35
	" New York, N. Y. (Hud. Term.)			8.25	8.25	8.25		9.30	11.45	11.59			
907.7	Ar New York, N. Y. (Penna. Sta.)		6.40										
		PM	AM	AM	AM	AM		AM	AM	AM	PM	AM	AM

New York to Boston—N. Y., N. H. & H. R. R.

EASTERN STANDARD TIME	AM	AM	AM	PM	PM	PM	PM	PM
Lv New York, N. Y. (Penna. Sta.)	2.20	3.10	*11.00	2.00	4.00	7.00	8.25	9.59
Ar New Haven, Conn.	3.55	4.40	12.35	3.35	5.32	8.32	10.05	
Ar Providence R. I.	6.32	7.05	2.45	5.45	7.45	10.35	11.25	
Ar Boston, Mass. (South Sta.)	7.45	8.10	3.45	6.45	8.25	11.25		PM
	PM	AM	AM	AM	PM	PM		

REFERENCE MARKS FOR TABLE 4

• Daily.
‡ Sundays only.
† Daily except Sundays.
‡ Daily except Saturdays.
C.S.T. Central Standard Time.
c Stops only to receive passengers.
d Stops only to discharge passengers.

e Stops only on notice to conductor to discharge passengers from Fort Wayne and beyond.
f Stops only on signal or notice to agent or conductor to receive or discharge passengers.
k Saturdays only.
p Stops daily except Sundays on signal or notice to agent to receive passengers for Pittsburgh and points east. Regular stop Sundays only.

q Stops only to discharge passengers from Pittsburgh and points west.
r Stops only on signal or notice to agent to receive passengers for points south of Harrisburg.
t Stops only on notice to conductor to discharge revenue passengers from Englewood or Chicago.
u Hudson & Manhattan Railroad Station.
v Stops only to discharge passengers from points west of Philadelphia.
y Stops only on notice to conductor to discharge passengers from points west of Pittsburgh.
z Stops daily except Sundays to receive passengers. Regular stop Sundays only.

COACHES ON ALL TRAINS EXCEPT No. 28.

New York, Philadelphia, Washington and Baltimore to Indianapolis, Louisville and St. Louis

		The Metropolitan	The St. Louisan	"Spirit of St. Louis"	The Jeffersonian All-Coach Streamliner	The Penn Texas	The American
Table 5							
For complete service between Pittsburgh and Columbus consult page 20		25-27 Daily	33 Daily	31 Daily Except Dec. 24,25, 26 & 31	65 Daily	3 Daily	67 Daily
For Sleeping, Parlor, Dining Cars and Coaches, see pages 4 and 5							
Miles		AM	PM	PM	PM	PM	PM
.0	Lv New York, N. Y. (Pa. Sta.)	8.05	v12.55	v 6.10	z 6.15	t 7.35	v10.25
	Lv New York, N. Y. (Hudson Terminal)	7.45	v12.35	v 5.56	z 6.00	t 7.23	v10.12
	" Jersey City, N. J. (Ex. Pl.) (H.&M.R.R.)	7.48	v12.39	v 5.59	z 6.03	t 7.26	v10.15
	Ar Newark, N. J.	8.05	v12.56	v 6.16	z 6.20	t 7.40	v10.32
10.0	Lv Newark, N. J.	8.20	v 1.10	v 6.24	z 6.29	t 7.50	v10.40
58.1	" Trenton, N. J.	9.05				t 8.35	
85.9	Philadelphia, Pa.	9.38	c 2.24	v 7.40	z 7.46	t 9.06	d11.54
111.4	North Philadelphia Station	10.07	3.37	8.48	z 8.01	t 9.23	12.20
159.3	Paoli, Pa.	10.59		9.00	z 8.31	t 9.55	
194.6	Lancaster, Pa.	11.32		9.30	z 9.30		
	Ar Harrisburg, Pa.		8.10	1.10	6.15	t 7.45	10.30
.0	Lv Washington, D. C.		9.03	1.56	7.02	t 8.02	11.15
40.1	" Baltimore, Md. (Penna. Station)		10.37	4.05	7.20	t10.45	12.35
96.3	" York, Pa.						
123.4	Ar Harrisburg, Pa.		11.20				1.37
194.6	Lv Harrisburg, Pa.	11.47	4.22			t10.53	1.47
325.1	" Altoona, Pa.	2.16	2.40	11.50	z 9.42	t11.29	1.35
362.9	" Johnstown, Pa.	3.18			z12.04		
439.3	Ar Pittsburgh, Pa.	4.55	9.10	2.19	2.28	4.00	4.06
439.3	Lv Pittsburgh, Pa.		9.23	2.19	2.28	4.00	6.40
482.5	Ar Steubenville, O.	6.55	d10.31				
529.8	" Dennison, O. (Uhrichsville) ■	7.33			4.48		7.00
547.4	" Newcomerstown, O.	8.47					8.16
561.7	" Coshocton, O.	9.08					8.31
575.4	" Trinway, O. (Zanesville)	9.29					f 9.31
597.1	" Newark, O. (Granville)	9.45					9.49
630.2	Ar Columbus, O.	10.15			5.58	7.16	10.00
630.2	Lv Columbus, O.	11.30	1.15	6.15	6.43	8.00	10.31
684.9	Ar Xenia, O.		1.15	6.15	6.43		11.15
700.9	" Dayton, O.	12.50	2.42	7.41	8.10	7.16	12.42
742.4	Lv Dayton, O.	1.10	2.42	7.41	8.15	9.27	12.53
742.4	Ar Richmond, Ind.	1.05	2.40	7.31	8.05	9.18	12.59
810.6	" Richmond, Ind.	1.15	2.40	7.31	8.07	9.18	12.53
	Ar Indianapolis, Ind.	2.25	3.58	8.45	9.23	10.32	2.00
810.6	Lv Indianapolis, Ind.	3.40	5.50			t 1.55	
921.7	Ar Louisville, Ky. ⊠	6.30	8.15			t 4.30	
810.6	Lv Indianapolis, Ind.	2.50	3.58	8.45	9.23	10.32	2.00
849.5	Ar Greencastle, Ind.					t11.17	
882.6	" Terre Haute, Ind.	4.07			10.43	f11.52	
950.5	" Effingham, Ill.		6.30	f10.10	11.55	b 1.25	b 4.02
1047.3	" East St. Louis, Ill.		8.05	b12.52	1.35		6.02
1050.6	Ar St. Louis, Mo.	8.10	8.20	b12.10	1.40	1.40	6.20
		AM	PM	PM	PM	PM	PM

Boston to New York—N. Y., N. H. & H. R. R.

EASTERN STANDARD TIME	AM	AM	AM	PM	PM	PM	PM
Lv Boston, Mass. (South Sta.)		8.30	*11.00	3.00	6.00	*11.00	11.00
Lv Providence, R. I.		9.25	11.48	4.08	6.48	12.05	11.50
Lv New Haven, Conn.	6.20	11.42	1.48	6.03	8.48	2.20	1.10
Ar New York, N. Y. (Penna. Sta.)	7.55	1.15	3.20	7.20	9.35	3.50	5.15
	AM	PM	PM	PM	PM	AM	PM

REFERENCE MARKS FOR TABLE 5

C.S.T. Central Standard Time.

• Daily.
‡ Sundays only.
⊠ For Louisville service via Cincinnati, see page 20.
■ Taxicab service is available in both directions between Dennison and New Philadelphia-Dover when applied for locally by passenger.

b Stops only on notice to conductor to discharge passengers.
c Stops only to receive passengers.
f Stops only on signal or notice to agent or conductor to receive or discharge passengers.

g Stops to discharge passengers from points east of Pittsburgh and to receive passengers.
q Stops only to receive passengers for Pittsburgh and points west.
r Stops to discharge passengers and to receive passengers for Pittsburgh and points west.
t Stops only to receive passengers for points west of Pittsburgh.
v Stops only to receive passengers for points west of Philadelphia.
z Stops only to receive passengers for Lancaster, Pittsburgh and points west.

COACHES ON ALL TRAINS EXCEPT No. 31.

St. Louis, Louisville and Indianapolis to Baltimore, Washington, Philadelphia and New York

Table 6

For complete service between Columbus and Pittsburgh consult page 21

For Sleeping, Parlor, Dining Cars and Coaches, see pages 6 and 7

Miles		The American 66 Daily	The Penn Texas 4 Daily	"Spirit of St. Louis" 30 Daily Except Dec.24,25, 26 & 31	The Jeffersonian All-Coach Streamliner 64 Daily	The St. Louisan 32 Daily	The Allegheny 6-74 Daily
		A.M.	A.M.	P.M.	P.M.	P.M.	P.M.
.0	Lv St. Louis, Mo.	9.00	10.15	12.40	1.00	6.30	11.05
3.3	" East St. Louis, Ill.	a 9.14		a12.54	a 1.14	a 6.44	a11.19
100.1	" Effingham, Ill.	10.40	ⱡ11.55	y 2.20	2.40	9.15	1.50
168.0	" Terre Haute, Ind.	11.45	1.45	3.25	3.45		3.10
201.1	" Greencastle, Ind.		2.25				
240.0	Ar Indianapolis, Ind.	1.10		4.50	5.05	10.35	11.30
		8.00		2.00		7.40	1.50
		10.10		4.20	4.20	10.10	
.0	Lv Louisville, Ky.						3.10
111.1	Ar Indianapolis, Ind.						4.27
240.0	Lv Indianapolis, Ind.	1.10	2.25	5.00	6.00	10.50	6.27
308.2	Ar Richmond, Ind.	2.21	3.36	6.11	6.19	11.56	6.20
308.2	Lv Richmond, Ind.	4.09	3.33	6.11	6.19	1.44	6.30
317.3	Ar Dayton, O.	4.17		8.05	8.10	2.00	6.53
349.7	Lv Dayton, O.	q 4.41	6.53		9.37		7.55
365.7	" Xenia, O.	5.45	6.53		10.25	3.25	8.48
420.4	Ar Columbus, O.	5.45		9.28		4.20	
453.5	Lv Columbus, O.	t 6.59		10.16	k11.02		9.26
475.2	" Newark, O. (Granville)	7.15					
488.9	" Trinway, O. (Zanesville)						10.07
503.2	" Coshocton, O.	7.52		1.25	z12.31	6.25	11.07
520.8	" Newcomerstown, O.	8.48			1.40	7.40	12.15
568.1	" Dennison, O. (Uhrichsville) (▪)	10.02	d10.47				
611.3	" Steubenville, O.			1.25	1.40	8.00	3.40
	Ar Pittsburgh, Pa.	10.02	d10.47			9.30	4.45
					4.17	10.37	4.45
611.3	Lv Pittsburgh, Pa.	12.45	d 1.33	1.59	d 6.39	1.00	7.10
687.7	" Johnstown, Pa.	3.07	d 3.59	6.20			
725.2	" Altoona, Pa.			6.49		2.15	7.19
856.0	Ar Harrisburg, Pa.	4.15	d 4.15	7.26	7.26	4.25	7.57
		4.52	d 4.52	8.59	8.59	5.20	9.35
856.0	Lv Harrisburg, Pa.	6.40	d 6.40	9.50	9.50		10.30
883.1	" York, Pa.	7.35	d 7.35				
939.3	Ar Baltimore, Md. (Pennsylvania Station)			6.20	6.39	1.10	7.20
979.4	Ar Washington, D. C.	3.07	d 3.59	6.59	7.24	1.44	7.53
				7.45	8.07	2.30	8.40
856.0	Lv Harrisburg, Pa.	d 4.38		8.11	d 8.31	d 3.59	9.06
891.3	Ar Lancaster, Pa.				9.04	4.15	9.35
	" Paoli, Pa.	d 5.06	d 5.55		9.50	4.15	10.20
932.2	Ar Philadelphia, Pa.		d 6.24	d 9.20			
	North Philadelphia Station	6.28	d 6.24				10.30
964.7	" Trenton, N. J.		d 7.10		9.54	4.18	10.30
992.5	Ar Newark, N. J.	6.41	7.15	9.25	10.11	4.38	10.50
1040.6		6.58	7.38	9.42	10.14	4.41	
	Lv Newark, N. J.	7.01	7.41	9.45			
	Ar Jersey City, N. J. (Exchange Place) (H. & M. R. R.)				10.05	4.30	10.35
	Ar New York, N. Y. (Hudson Terminal)	6.45	7.25	9.35			
1050.6	Ar New York, N. Y. (Penna. Sta.)	A.M.	A.M.	A.M.	A.M.	P.M.	P.M.

New York to Boston—N. Y., N. H. & H. R. R.

EASTERN STANDARD TIME	A.M.	A.M.	A.M.	P.M.	P.M.	P.M.	P.M.	P.M.
Lv New York, N. Y. (Penna. Sta.)	● 2.20	● 3.10	●11.00	● 2.00	● 4.00	● 7.00	8.25	9.59
Ar New Haven, Conn.	3.55	4.40	12.33	3.35	5.35	8.35	10.35	
Ar Providence, R. I.	6.32	7.05	2.35	5.35	8.45	11.25		
Ar Boston, Mass. (South Sta.)	7.45	8.10	3.45					

REFERENCE MARKS FOR TABLE 6

- ● Daily.
- § Sundays only.
- ⊠ For Louisville service via Cincinnati, see page 21.
- ▪ Taxicab service is available in both directions between Dennison and New Philadelphia-Dover when applied for locally by passenger.
- C.S.T. Central Standard Time.
- a Stops only on signal or notice to agent to receive passengers.
- d Stops only to discharge passengers.
- f Stops only on signal or notice to agent or conductor to receive or discharge passengers.
- g Stops on notice to conductor to discharge passengers from St. Louis and beyond and on signal or notice to agent to receive passengers for points beyond.
- k Stops Saturdays only.
- q Stops only to discharge passengers from Pittsburgh and points west.
- v Stops only to discharge passengers from points west of Philadelphia.
- y Stops only on signal or notice to agent to receive passengers for points east and south of Harrisburg.

COACHES ON ALL TRAINS EXCE

New York, Philadelphia, Washington and Baltimore to Columbus, Cincinnati and Louisville

Table 7

For Sleeping, Parlor, Dining Cars and Coaches, see pages 4 and 5

Miles		The Metropolitan 25-27 Daily	The St. Louisan 53 Daily	The St. Louisan 32-203 Daily	Cincinnati Limited 41 Daily	"Spirit of St. Louis" 31 Daily Except Dec.24,25, 26 & 31	The Jeffersonian All-Coach Streamliner 65 Daily	The Penn Texas 3 Daily	The American 67 Daily	Iron City Express 37-205 Daily
		A.M.	P.M.	P.M.	P.M.	P.M.	P.M.	P.M.	P.M.	P.M.
.0	Lv New York, N. Y. (Penna. Station)	8.05	v12.55	v12.55	h 5.25	v 6.10	o 6.15	t 7.35	v10.45	v11.00
	Lv New York, N. Y. (Hudson Terminal)	7.45	v12.36	v12.36	h 5.08	v 5.56	o 6.00	t 7.20	v10.12	v10.45
	Ar Jersey City, N. J. (Exch. Pl.) (H. & M.)	7.48	v12.33	v12.39	h 5.11	v 5.59	o 6.03	t 7.23	v10.45	v10.48
	Ar Newark, N. J.	8.05	v12.56	v12.56	h 5.21	v 6.16	o 6.06	t 7.40	v10.32	v11.05
10.0	Lv Newark, N. J.	8.20	v 1.10	v 1.10	h 5.40	v 6.24	o 6.29	t 7.50	v10.40	v11.15
58.1	" Trenton, N. J.	9.05			h 6.27			t 8.33		v11.59
85.9	Philadelphia, Pa.	9.38	c 2.24	c 2.24	h 6.56	v 7.40	o 7.46	t 9.06	c11.54	c12.30
111.4	North Philadelphia Station	10.07	2.52	2.52	h 7.00	8.05	8.22	t 9.35	12.20	
150.3	Paoli, Pa.	10.59	3.37	3.37	h 8.06	8.48	8.48			
194.6	Ar Harrisburg, Pa.	11.32	4.10	4.10	h 8.40	9.22	9.20			
40.1	Lv Washington, D. C.	8.10	1.10	1.10	h 5.05	6.15	o 7.45	t 9.45	10.30	1.41
96.3	Baltimore, Md. (Penna. Station)	9.03	1.55	1.55	h 5.45	8.01	8.32	t 9.02	11.10	2.15
123.4	York, Pa.	10.37	3.06	3.06		8.31	9.00	t10.02	12.54	
	Ar Harrisburg, Pa.	11.20	4.06	4.06		9.20	9.20	t10.45	1.35	
194.6	Lv Harrisburg, Pa.	11.47	4.22		1.42	9.22	9.42	t10.53	1.47	2.25
325.4	" Altoona, Pa.	2.16	6.40	6.40		11.50	q12.04	t11.29	4.06	4.43
362.9	" Johnstown, Pa.	3.28		7.40					4.58	5.07
439.3	Ar Pittsburgh, Pa.	4.55			t11.11					7.50
439.3	Lv Pittsburgh, Pa.	6.29	9.10	9.10	1.42	2.19	2.28	4.00	6.40	
482.5	Ar Steubenville, O.	7.33		9.23	1.42	2.19	2.28	4.00	7.00	10.15
529.8	" Dennison, O. (Uhrichsville) (▪)	8.47	g10.31	10.40	1.06				8.17	11.30
547.4	" Newcomerstown, O.	9.08		11.59			4.48		9.31	12.35
561.7	" Coshocton, O.									1.25
575.4	" Trinway, O. (Zanesville)			1.44					9.47	
597.1	" Newark, O. (Granville)	§ 9.45							10.03	1.39
630.2	Ar Columbus, O.	10.15	1.15	2.30		5.44	5.58	7.16	10.15	
630.2	Lv Columbus, O.	11.00	1.15	2.30		5.44	5.58	7.16	11.15	
684.9	Ar Xenia, O.			3.15	5.44	6.15	6.43			
745.9	" Norwood (Cincinnati), O.			4.45	v 6.49					
750.4	" Winton Place, O.			d 6.18	8.10					
755.1	Ar Cincinnati, O. (Union Terminal)			6.28	8.19					
				6.45	8.30					
755.1	Lv Cincinnati, O. (Union Ter.) (L. & N.)			9.00	9.00					
869.1	Ar Louisville, Ky.			11.10	11.10					
982.7	" Bowling Green, Ky.			1.35	1.35					
1249.3	Ar Memphis, Tenn.			8.40	8.40					
1055.6	Ar Nashville, Tenn.			3.20	3.20					7.50
1261.0	" Birmingham, Ala.			7.55	7.55					z 2.10
1676.8	" New Orleans, La.			7.10	7.10					7.30
		P.M.	A.M.	A.M.	P.M.	P.M.	P.M.	P.M.	A.M.	P.M.

Boston to New York—N. Y., N. H. & H. R. R.

EASTERN STANDARD TIME	A.M.	A.M.	A.M.	P.M.	P.M.	P.M.	P.M.
Lv Boston, Mass. (South Sta.)		8.30	●11.00	● 3.00	● 6.00	●11.00	●11.50
Lv Providence, R. I.	● 6.20	9.48	11.48	4.05	6.45	12.05	1.10
Lv New Haven, Conn.	7.55	11.42	1.49	5.56	9.00	2.20	3.25
Ar New York, N. Y. (Penna. Sta.)		1.15	3.20	7.20	10.40	3.50	5.15
	A.M.					A.M.	A.M.

REFERENCE MARKS FOR TABLE 7

- ● Daily.
- § Sundays only.
- ⊠ For Louisville service via Indianapolis, see page 18.
- ▪ Taxicab service is available in both directions between Dennison and New Philadelphia-Dover when applied for locally by passenger.
- Additional train leaves Cincinnati 8.00 p. m., arrives New Orleans 3.10 a. m.
- C.S.T. Central Standard Time.
- c Stops only to receive passengers.
- d Stops only to discharge passengers.
- f Stops only on signal or notice to agent or conductor to receive or discharge passengers.
- g Stops to discharge passengers from points east of Pittsburgh and to receive passengers for points west of Pittsburgh.
- h Stops only to receive passengers for Lewistown and points west of Pittsburgh.
- o Stops only to receive passengers for Lancaster, Pittsburgh and points west.
- q Regular stop daily except Sundays; signal stop Sundays.
- s Stops only to receive passengers for Pittsburgh and points west.
- t Stops to discharge passengers and to receive passengers for Pittsburgh and points west.
- t Stops only to receive passengers for points west of Pittsburgh.
- v Stops only to receive passengers for points west of Philadelphia.
- z Passengers may use local sleeping car leaving Cincinnati 10.50 p. m., arriving Nashville 8.05 a. m.

COACHES ON ALL TRAINS EXCEPT No. 31

Thomas W. Dixon Jr. Collection
What better to represent the "Standard Railroad of the World" than this wonderful publicity photo depicting Brunswick Green E Units powering a passenger train across one of the numerous stone viaducts in the heart of Pennsylvania?

Table 7

For Sleeping, Parlor, Dining Cars and Coaches, see pages 4 and 5

Miles		The Metro-politan 25-27 Daily	The St. Louisan 33 Daily	The St. Louisan 32-203 Daily	Cincinnati Limited 41 Daily	"Spirit of St. Louis" 31 Daily Except Dec.24,25, 26 & 31	The Jeffersonian All-Coach Streamliner 65 Daily	The Penn Texas 3 Daily	The American 67 Daily	Iron City Express 37-205 Daily
		AM	PM	PM	PM	PM	PM	PM	PM	PM
.0	Lv New York, N. Y. (Penna. Station)	8.05	v12.55	v12.55	h 5.25	v 6.10	o 6.15	t 7.35	v10.25	v11.00
	Lv New York, N. Y. (Hudson Terminal)	7.45	v12.36	v12.36	h 5.08	v 5.56	o 6.03	t 7.20	v10.12	v10.45
	Jersey City, N. J. (Exch. Pl.) (H. & M.)	7.48	v12.33	v12.39	h 5.11	v 5.59	o 6.03	t 7.23	v10.15	v10.45
	Ar Newark, N. J.	8.05	v12.56	v12.56	h 5.25	v 6.16	o 6.20	t 7.50	v10.32	v11.15
10.0	Lv Newark, N. J.	8.20	v 1.10	v 1.10	h 5.40	v 6.24	o 6.29	t 8.35	v10.40	v11.59
58.1	Trenton, N. J.	9.05			h 6.27					c12.30
85.9	Philadelphia, Pa.	9.38	c 2.24	c 2.24	h 6.56	8.06	o 7.46	t 9.06	e11.54	1.41
	North Philadelphia Station	10.07	2.53	2.53	h 7.23	8.48	r 8.55	t 9.35	12.20	2.15
111.4	Paoli, Pa.	10.59	3.37	3.37	h 8.06	9.22	q 9.30		t 1.37	
159.3	Lancaster, Pa.	11.32	4.10	4.10	h 8.40			t10.53		
194.6	Ar Harrisburg, Pa.					6.15	q 7.45	t10.30	10.30	
			1.10	1.10		7.02	r 7.02	t11.22	11.22	
.0	Lv Washington, D. C. (Penna. Station)	8.10	1.56	1.56		8.10	q 8.31	t110.01	12.54	
40.1	Baltimore, Md. (Penna. Station)	9.03	3.25	3.25		9.20	q 9.20	t 1.35	1.35	
96.3	York, Pa.	10.37	4.06	4.06						2.25
123.4	Ar Harrisburg, Pa.	11.20				9.22	q 9.42	t10.53	1.47	4.43
		11.47	4.22	4.22	h 8.40	11.50	q12.04	t 1.29	4.06	5.50
194.6	Lv Harrisburg, Pa.	2.16	6.40	6.40	t11.11				6.40	7.50
325.4	Altoona, Pa.	3.18			1.42	2.19	2.28	4.00		10.15
362.9	Johnstown, Pa.	4.55	9.10	9.10			2.28	4.00	7.00	11.30
439.3	Ar Pittsburgh, Pa.	6.20	9.23	10.40	1.42				8.17	12.26
		7.35	d10.31	11.59			4.48		9.11	12.56
439.3	Lv Pittsburgh, Pa.	8.10		1.06					f 9.31	1.12
482.5	Ar Steubenville, O.	8.47			1.44				9.47	1.13
529.8	Dennison, O. (Uhrichsville) (*)	9.08					5.58	7.16	10.03	1.49
547.4	Newcomerstown, O.	9.29					6.43	8.00	10.31	2.45
561.7	Coshocton, O.	9.45			2.30	5.44			11.15	2.46
575.4	Trinway, O. (Zanesville)	10.15			3.15	5.44				3.40
597.1	Newark, O. (Granville)	11.00	1.15		3.15	6.49	6.15		d 5.20	5.10
630.2	Ar Columbus, O.				4.45	p 6.49			d 5.20	5.40
630.2	Lv Columbus, O.				6.18	d 8.10				
684.9	Ar Xenia, O.				6.28	d 8.19				
745.9	Norwood (Cincinnati), O.				6.45	8.30			d 7.05	
750.4	Winton Place, O.								d 9.25	
755.1	Ar Cincinnati, O. (Union Terminal)								11.59	
755.1	Lv Cincinnati, O. (Union Ter.) (L. & N.)		9.00	9.00					7.50	
869.1	Ar Louisville, Ky.		11.10	11.10						
982.7	Bowling Green, Ky.		1.35	1.35				z 2.10		
1249.3	Ar Memphis, Tenn.		8.40	8.40				x 7.30		
1055.6	Ar Nashville, Tenn.		3.20	3.20						
1261.0	Birmingham, Ala.		7.55	7.55						
1678.8	Ar New Orleans, La.		7.10	7.10						
			AM	AM	AM	AM	AM	AM	AM	PM

Boston to New York—N. Y., N. H. & H. R. R.

EASTERN STANDARD TIME	AM	AM	AM	PM	PM	PM	PM	PM
Lv Boston, Mass. (South Sta.)		*8.30	*11.00	*3.00	*6.00	*11.00		*11.50
Lv Providence, R. I.		9.25	11.48	3.48	6.48	12.05		12.45
Lv New Haven, Conn.	6.20	11.42	1.49	5.22	8.56	2.20		3.25
Ar New York, N. Y. (Penna. Sta.)	7.55	1.15	3.20	7.20	10.25	3.50		5.15
	AM					AM		AM

REFERENCE MARKS FOR TABLE 7

* Daily.
‡ Sundays only.
⊠ For Louisville service via Indianapolis, see page 18.
■ Taxicab service is available in both directions between Dennison and New Philadelphia-Dover when applied for locally by passenger.
▲ Additional train leaves Cincinnati 8.00 p. m., arrives New Orleans 3.10 p. m.

C.S.T. Central Standard Time.
c Stops only to receive passengers.
d Stops only to discharge passengers.
f Stops only on signal or notice to agent or conductor to receive or discharge passengers.
g Stops to discharge passengers from points east of Pittsburgh and to receive passengers.
h Stops only to receive passengers for Lewistown and points west of Pittsburgh.

o Stops only to receive passengers for Lancaster, Pittsburgh and points west.
p Regular stop daily except Sundays; signal stop Sundays.
q Stops only to receive passengers for Pittsburgh and points west.
r Stops to discharge passengers and to receive passengers for Pittsburgh and points west.
t Stops only to receive passengers for points west of Pittsburgh.
v Stops only to receive passengers for points west of Philadelphia.
z Passengers may use local sleeping car leaving Cincinnati 10.50 p. m., arriving Nashville 8.05 a. m.

COACHES ON ALL TRAINS EXCEPT No. 31

Table 8

For Sleeping, Parlor, Dining Cars and Coaches, see pages 6 and 7

Miles		The St. Louisan 202-32 Daily	The St. Louisan 32 Daily	The Allegheny 6-74 Daily	Iron City Express 204-16 Daily	The American 66 Daily	The Penn Texas 4 Daily	Cincinnati Limited 40 Daily	"Spirit of St. Louis" 30 Daily Except Dec.24,25, 26 & 31	The Jeffersonian All-Coach Streamliner 64 Daily
		PM	AM	PM	PM	PM	PM	PM	PM	PM
.0	Lv New Orleans, La. (L.&N.)	9.00			10.40					
415.8	Birmingham, Ala.	8.15			8.55			11.05		
621.2	Nashville, Tenn.	12.45			2.20			7.05		
694.1	Lv Bowling Green, Ky.	7.55								
807.7	Louisville, Ky.	2.30			8.15					
921.7	Ar Cincinnati, O. (Union Ter.)	6.05			4.15			9.01		
.0	Lv Cincinnati, O. (Union Ter.) (Pennsylvania Railroad)	6.10			7.30	12.05		4.50		
4.7	Winton Place, O.	11.20				1.10		5.15		
9.2	Norwood (Cincinnati), O.	11.30		6.53		1.10		5.26		
70.2	Xenia, O.	11.40		7.55		1.20	y 4.41	6.34		
124.9	Ar Columbus, O.	2.00	3.35	8.06		2.40	4.45		7.48	9.37
124.9	Lv Columbus, O.	2.00	4.20	8.48		3.05	4.50	6.53	7.55	10.15
158.0	Newark, O. (Granville)	3.15					5.25		8.25	
179.7	Trinway, O. (Zanesville)			9.26			f 5.46			
193.4	Coshocton, O.	4.35								
207.7	Newcomerstown, O.			10.07		6.15	7.15			
235.3	Dennison, O. (Uhrichsville) (*)	5.43	6.25	12.15		7.52	8.02			
272.6	Steubenville, O.		7.40			10.02				
315.8	Ar Pittsburgh, Pa.				10.15		d10.47	11.45		h11.02
315.8	Lv Pittsburgh, Pa.	8.00	8.00	2.00	11.59		d10.47	11.45	1.25	t12.31
392.5	Ar Johnstown, Pa.	9.30	9.30	3.40	1.05				1.25	1.40
429.1	Altoona, Pa.	10.37	10.37	4.45	3.49	12.45				1.40
560.5	Ar Harrisburg, Pa.	1.00	1.00	7.10		3.07	3.59			
560.5	Lv Harrisburg, Pa.	2.15	2.15	7.19		4.15	4.15	2.26	3.59	4.17
587.6	York, Pa.	2.57	2.57	7.52		4.52	4.52	2.50	5.20	6.39
643.8	Baltimore, Md. (Pennsylvania Station)	4.33	4.33	10.30		6.40	6.40	4.50		
683.9	Ar Washington, D. C.	5.20	5.20			7.35	7.35			
560.5	Lv Harrisburg, Pa.	1.10	1.10		3.49			4.50	6.20	6.39
593.8	Ar Lancaster, Pa.	1.44	1.44	7.20		3.07			6.59	7.24
643.7	Paoli, Pa.	2.30	2.30	7.53					7.45	8.07
669.2	Philadelphia, Pa.			8.40	5.17					
697.0	North Philadelphia Station							6.15		
745.1	Ar Newark, N. J.	d 3.59	d 3.59	9.06	5.45	d 5.06	d 5.55		d 8.11	d 8.31
	Lv Newark, N. J.	4.15	4.15	9.35	6.15		d 6.24	7.14	9.04	
	Ar Jersey City, N. J. (Exchange Pl.) (H. & M. R. R.)	4.18	4.18	10.30	7.06	6.41	d 7.10	8.03	d 9.20	9.50
	New York, N. Y. (Hudson Terminal)	4.38	4.38	10.57	6.56	6.58	7.38	8.30	9.42	9.54
755.1	Ar New York, N. Y. (Penna. Station)	4.41	4.41	10.50	7.31	7.01	7.41	8.33	9.45	10.11
		4.30	4.30	10.35	7.15	6.45	7.25	8.20	9.35	10.14
		PM	PM	AM	AM	AM	AM	AM	AM	AM

New York to Boston—N. Y., N. H. & H. R. R.

EASTERN STANDARD TIME	AM	AM	AM	PM	PM	PM	PM
Lv New York, N. Y. (Penna. Sta.)	*2.20		*3.10	*11.00	*2.00	*4.00	*7.00	*9.25
Ar New Haven, Conn.	3.55		4.40	12.53	3.40	5.30	8.28	9.59
Ar Providence, R. I.	5.32		7.05	2.30	5.25	7.28	10.35	
Ar Boston, Mass. (South Sta.)	7.45		8.10	3.45	6.45	8.25	11.25	
	AM		AM	PM	PM	PM	PM	

REFERENCE MARKS FOR TABLE 8

* Daily.
⊠ For Louisville service via Indianapolis, see page 19.
■ Taxicab service is available in both directions between Dennison and New Philadelphia-Dover when applied for locally by passenger.

C.S.T. Central Standard Time.
d Stops only to discharge passengers.
f Stops only on signal or notice to agent or conductor to receive or discharge passengers.
k Saturdays only.

q Stops only to discharge passengers from Pittsburgh and points west.
t Stops to discharge passengers or to receive passengers for points east of Pittsburgh.
v Stops only to discharge passengers from points west of Philadelphia.
y Stops only on signal or notice to agent to receive passengers for Pittsburgh and points beyond.

COACHES ON ALL TRAINS EXCEPT No. 30

Table 9 — New York, Philadelphia, Washington and Baltimore to Cleveland, Toledo and Detroit

Miles		The Metropolitan / Afternoon Steeler 25-361 Daily	The Duquesne 75-329 Daily	The St. Louisan 33-63-105 Except Sat., Dec. 25, 26, 31, Jan. 1 & 2	The St. Louisan 33-463-105 Dec. 26, Jan. 2	The Red Arrow 63 Daily	The Admiral / The Akronite 71-9 Daily	The Clevelander 39 Daily	The American 67 Ex. Sat. Nights & Dec. 26 & Jan. 1	Pittsburgh Night Express / The Statesman / Morning Steeler 35-363 Daily	Iron City Express / Morning Steeler 37-363 Daily
		AM	AM	PM	PM	PM	PM		PM	PM	PM
.0	Lv New York, N.Y. (Pa. Sta.)	8.05	v11.45	v12.55		v5.10	v8.00	o8.40	v10.25	----	v11.00
	Lv New York, N.Y. (Hudson Term.)	7.45	v11.24	v12.36	v12.36	v5.00	v7.42	o8.24	v10.12	----	v10.45
	Lv Jersey City, N.J. (Ex. Pl.)(H.&M.)	7.48	v11.27	v12.39	v12.39	v5.03	v7.45	o8.27	v10.15	----	v10.48
	Ar Newark, N.J.	8.05	v11.44	v12.56	v12.56	v5.20	v8.02	o8.44	v10.32	----	v11.05
10.0	Lv Newark, N.J.	8.20	v11.59	v1.10	v1.10	v5.25	v8.15	o8.55	v10.40	----	v11.15
58.1	" Trenton, N.J.	9.05	v12.43				v9.00	o9.39		11.20	v11.59
85.9	Philadelphia, Pa.: North Philadelphia Station	9.38	c1.13	c2.24	c2.24	c6.38	c9.31	o10.13	c11.54	12.20	c12.30
111.4	Penna. Station (30th Street)	10.07	1.41	2.53	2.53	7.06	9.58	o10.39	12.20	12.48	1.41
159.3	" Paoli, Pa.	10.59	1.27	3.37	3.37	7.29	11.16	r11.06	11.37	12.54	2.15
194.6	" Lancaster, Pa.	11.32	3.01	4.10	4.10	8.27		r11.59	11.27		
194.6	Ar Harrisburg, Pa.	8.10		1.10	1.10	5.20	7.45	8.50	10.30	10.30	5.20
.0	Lv Washington, D.C. (Penna. Sta.)	9.03		1.56	1.56	5.35	8.32	9.37	11.06	11.27	6.40
40.1	" Baltimore, Md. (Penna. Sta.)	10.37		4.22	4.22	8.27	10.01	11.06	11.50	11.58	7.35
96.3	" York, Pa.	11.20		4.40	4.40	10.56	10.45	r11.50			
123.4	Ar Harrisburg, Pa.	11.47	3.01			11.57	11.28	t12.12	1.47	1.55	2.25
194.6	Lv Harrisburg, Pa.	2.16	1.55	9.10	9.10	11.30	2.01	t2.33	4.06	4.20	4.43
325.4	" Altoona, Pa.	3.18	3.55				3.01	5.12	6.40	5.26	5.59
362.9	" Johnstown, Pa.	4.55	8.15				4.30			7.35	7.50
439.3	Ar Pittsburgh, Pa.								7.00		
439.3	Lv Pittsburgh, Pa.						5.00	5.30	9.20	8.20	8.20
505.1	Ar Wheeling, W. Va.	5 10	8 35				x6.02				
439.3	Lv Pittsburgh, Pa.		x9 47				e6.18				
486.9	Ar New Castle Junction, Pa.		e10 18				6.33			9.39	9.39
489.0	Ar New Castle, Pa.		10 14				6.54	f6.50		9.56	9.56
504.5	Ar Youngstown, O.	6 27	10 31					7.12			
514.0	" Salem, O.	6.43		11 01	11 01		7.26	7.35		10.26	10.26
509.9	" Salem, O.			11 16	11 16		7.48	7.49			
522.3	" Alliance, O.	7.13					7.48	a8.40		a10.30	a10.30
540.1	" Ravenna, O.						8.02	a9.00		a10.50	a10.50
552.0	Ar Hudson, O.	a7 30	a11.20				8.15	a9.15		a11.05	a11.05
552.0	Lv Hudson, O.	a7 50	a11 40								
550.8	Ar Cuyahoga Falls, O.	a8 05	a11 55								
	" Akron, O. (Greyhound Bus Term.)						8.20	d10.50		d10.50	d10.50
564.8	Ar Akron, O. (Union Station)						8.30	11.00		11.00	11.00
569.0	Ar Harvard Avenue, O. (Cleveland)	d7 40	11 35								
574.2	" Euclid Avenue, O. (Cleveland)	7.50	N 55								
577.4	Ar Cleveland, O. (Penna. Station)			11.00	11.00	1.30					
439.3	Lv Pittsburgh, Pa.			12.48	12.48						
522.3	Ar Alliance, O.			1.14	1.14						
541.0	" Canton, O.			2.47	2.40	5.51					
614.6	" Mansfield, O.			4.39	4.39	6.48					
657.9	" Tiffin, O.			6.10	6.10	7.19					
700.1	Toledo, O. (Summit St. Sta.)			6.40	6.40	8.05					
720.9	" Monroe, Mich.			7.40	7.40						
756.6	Ar Detroit, Mich. (Fort St. Un. Sta.)	PM				AM	AM	AM	AM	AM	AM

REFERENCE MARKS FOR TABLE 9

§ Sundays only.

▲ Central Greyhound Lines bus operating on public highway Hudson to Akron, hand baggage only carried. P. R. R. tickets honored.

c Stops only to receive passengers.

d Stops only to discharge passengers.

e Bus on public highway; hand baggage only carried.

f Stops only on signal or notice to agent or conductor to receive or discharge passengers.

o Stops only to receive passengers for [Pitts]burgh and points west.

r Stops to discharge passengers and [receive pas]sengers for Pittsburgh and points [west].

t Stops only to receive passengers for points west of Pittsburgh.

COACHES ON ALL T[RAINS]

Table 10 — Detroit, Toledo and Cleveland to Baltimore, Washington, Philadelphia and New York

Miles		Morning Steeler / The Juniata 360-72 Daily	Afternoon Steeler 362 Daily	The American 66 Ex. Sat. Nights & Dec. 25 & Jan. 1	Iron City Express 328-16 Daily	The Akronite 10-38 Daily	The Clevelander 38 Daily	38-36 Ex. Sat. Nights & Dec. 24 & 31	38-86 Sat. Nights & Dec. 24 & 31	The Red Arrow 68 Daily	Gotham Limited 106-462-54 Dec. 26, Jan. 2	Gotham Limited 106-62-54 Ex. Sat. Nights & Dec. 25, 26, 31, Jan. 1 & 2
		AM	PM	PM	PM	PM	PM	PM	PM	PM		
.0	Lv Detroit, Mich. (Ft. St. Un. Sta.)										11 40	11 40
35.7	" Monroe, Mich.									8 30	12.28	12.28
56.2	" Toledo, O. (Summit St. Sta.)									8.16	1.13	1.13
98.7	" Tiffin, O.									6.50	2.18	2.18
142.0	" Mansfield, O.									8.42	3.45	3.45
215.8	" Canton, O.									9.59	5.59	6.05
234.3	" Alliance, O.										6.11	6.31
317.3	Ar Pittsburgh, Pa.										8.00	6.20
.0	Lv Cleveland, O. (Pennsylvania Station)	8.00	4 00		5 50		8.25	8.25	8.25			
3.2	" Euclid Avenue, O. (Cleveland)	8.08	4 08		6 05		8.35	8.35	8.35	11.56		
7.5	" Harvard Avenue, O. (Cleveland)											
.0	Lv Akron, O. (Union Station)	▲7 50	▲3 50			8.00						
5.0	" Akron, O. (Greyhound Bus Terminal)	▲8 04	▲4 04		▲5 20							
12.8	" Cuyahoga Falls, O.	▲8 25	▲4 25		▲5 34	8.10						
	Ar Hudson, O.				▲5 55							
25.4	Lv Hudson, O.	8.34	4 34									
37.3	" Ravenna, O.				6 27		9.03	9.03	9.03			
55.4	" Alliance, O.				6 41	8.43	9.36	9.36	9.36			
68.8	" Salem, O.	9.05	5 05				9.52	9.52	9.52			
63.4	" Niles, O.	9.19	5 20									
72.9	" Youngstown, O.					7 10	9 13					
	Lv New Castle, O.					7 28	9 33					
90.5	Lv New Castle Junction, Pa.					9 7 35	9 27					
138.1	Ar Pittsburgh, Pa.	10.40	6.40			x 7 55	x10.02	11.20	11.20	11.20		
.0	Lv Wheeling, W. Va.			8.00		9 05	11.05					
65.8	Ar Pittsburgh, Pa.			10.02								
138.1	Lv Pittsburgh, Pa.	11.00		10.02	10 15	11.35	11.35	11.35	11.35	11.56	9.10	9.10
214.4	Ar Johnstown, Pa.	12.37			11 59						10.37	10.37
252.0	" Altoona, Pa.	1 40			1.05						11.40	11.40
382.8	Ar Harrisburg, Pa.	4 18		3.07	12.45	2.07	2.07	2.07	2.07		2.04	2.04
382.8	Lv Harrisburg, Pa.				3.49	4.30	4.30	4.30	4.30			
409.9	Ar York, Pa.			4.15		4.50	4.50			5.00	2.15	2.15
466.1	" Baltimore, Md. (Pennsylvania Station)			4.52		5.27	5.27				2.28	2.57
506.2	Ar Washington, D.C.			6.40		7.00	7.00				2.57	3.33
				7.35		7.50	7.50					
382.8	Lv Harrisburg, Pa.											
418.1	Ar Lancaster, Pa.	4 28		3.07		4.30	4.30	5.35	6.30	5.30	2.12	2.12
466.0	" Paoli, Pa.	5 01		3.49				6.12	7.12	6.04	2.45	2.45
	Philadelphia, Pa.: Pennsylvania Station (30th Street)	5 53		q4.38	d 5.17	6.02	6.02	7.05	8.22	6.55	5.34	5.34
	North Philadelphia Station											
491.5	" Trenton, N.J.	6 20										
519.3	Ar Newark, N.J.			d5.06	5.45	d6.29	d6.29	7.35	8.50	d7.20	4.00	4.00
567.4		7.40		6.28	6.15	7.00	7.00			7.50		
	Lv Newark, N.J.				7.00	7.54	7.54			8.40	d 5.17	d 5.17
	Ar Jersey City, N.J. (Ex. Pl.)(H. & M. R. R.)	7.49		6.41	7.06	8.05	8.05			8.45	5.29	5.29
	" New York, N.Y. (Hudson Terminal)	8.06		6.58	7.28	8.22	8.22			9.02	5.46	5.46
		8.09		7.01	7.31					9.05	5.49	5.49
577.4	Ar New York, N.Y. (Penna. Sta.)	7.55		6.45	7.15	8.10	8.10			8.55	5.50	5.50
		PM	PM	PM	PM	AM	AM			AM	PM	PM

REFERENCE MARKS FOR TABLE 10

q Bus on public highway; hand baggage only carried.

▲ Central Greyhound Lines bus operating on the public highway Akron to Hudson, hand baggage only carried. P. R. R. tickets honored.

d Stops only to discharge passengers.

f Stops only on signal or notice to agent or conductor to receive or discharge passengers.

q Stops only to discharge passengers from Pittsburgh and points west.

x No checked baggage handled at this station.

COACHES ON ALL TRAINS

Pittsburgh was the terminus for many Pennsylvania Railroad intermediate trains as well as a stop for all of the through trains. The beautiful Pennsylvania Railroad Station there was certainly busy when this photograph was taken in 1953. Most of the area has changed now, and many of the structures are gone. The tracks to the left lead over the bridge for Fort Wayne and Chicago while the tracks to the right are the line to St. Louis known as the Panhandle. As well as through trains, Pittsburgh also was the origin and terminus of many commuter trains which were still operating from the terminal in 1953. Today, the area to the right is a limited access road for buses and emergency vehicles and most of the buildings have been demolished. Most of the station's upper floors have been turned into luxury apartments, although Amtrak still maintains, of course, its facility in the building.

In this magnificent 1948 photo, eastbound train No. 30, *The St. Louisan*, is seen behind two E-7's rounding the famous Pennsylvania Railroad landmark in the summer of 1948. Behind the two E's are three headend cars, a modernized coach, two P85BR coaches, a dining car, a sleeper-lounge car, followed by five regular sleepers, including two still in the fleet of modernism paint scheme. *The St. Louisan* was still a popular train after World War II, as is evidenced by the ten passenger cars which trailed the three headend cars, making up the thirteen cars of No. 31.

Still in the Pennsylvania Railroad era, but with only months to live, observation lounge sleeper *Tower View*, with the drumhead prominently displayed on the rear, brings up the rear of Pennsylvania Railroad No. 28, *The Broadway Limited*, as it departs Englewood, Illinois on May 9, 1967. The observation section looks well populated with first class passengers on this day *The Broadway Limited* still an all Pullman train, one of the last in the United States. In fact, from this photograph, it might be hard to tell that this is 1967, and not the 1950s except for some of the paint schemes on the cars.

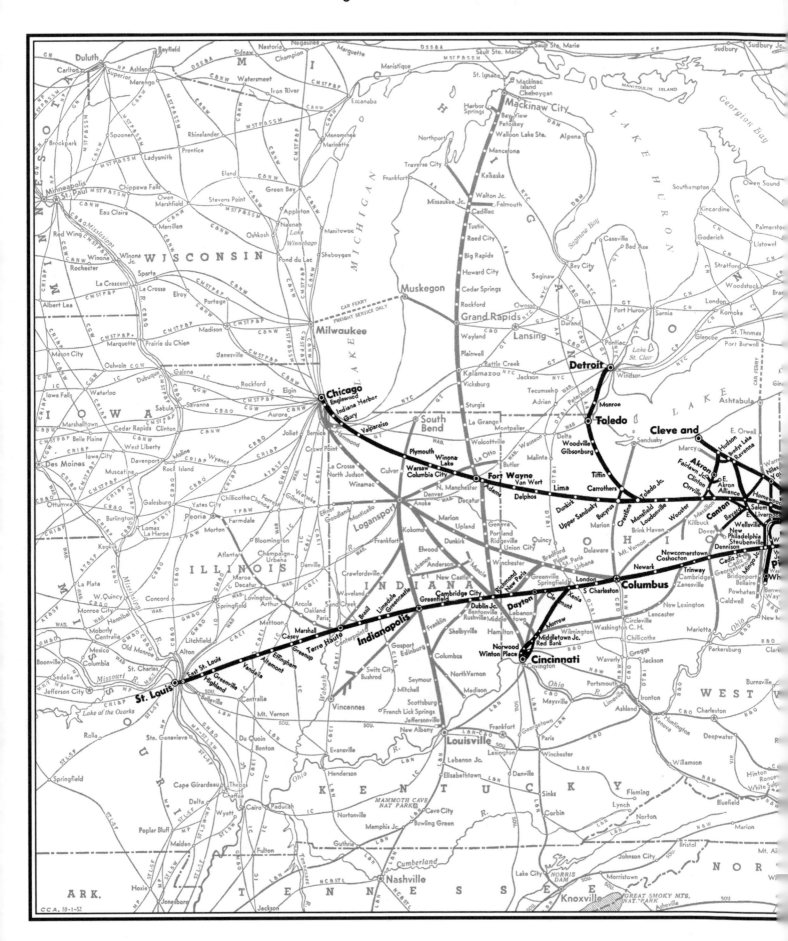